THE GREAT NORTHWEST NATURE FACTBOOK

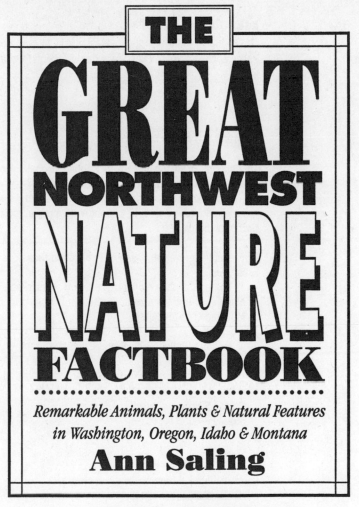

THE
GREAT
NORTHWEST
NATURE
FACTBOOK

Remarkable Animals, Plants & Natural Features
in Washington, Oregon, Idaho & Montana

Ann Saling

Illustrated by Mark A. Zingarelli

Alaska Northwest Books™
Anchorage • Seattle

ACKNOWLEDGMENTS
The author would like to give special thanks to Joan Gregory and Peggy Levin for their excellent editorial contributions to this book.

Library of Congress Cataloging-in-Publication Data
Saling, Ann.
    The great Northwest nature factbook : remarkable animals, plants & natural features in Washington, Oregon, Idaho & Montana / by Ann Saling.
        p. cm.
    Includes bibliographical references.
    ISBN 0-88240-407-5
    1. Natural history—Northwest, Pacific. 2. Natural monuments—Northwest, Pacific.
QH104.5.N6S25   1991
508.795—dc20   91-6381
                                                                  CIP

Edited by Joan Gregory and Peggy Levin
Cover and book design by Cameron Mason
Cover illustration and text illustrations by Mark A. Zingarelli

Alaska Northwest Books™
A division of GTE Discovery Publications, Inc.
22026 20th Avenue S.E.
Bothell, WA 98021

Printed in U.S.A. on recycled paper

CONTENTS

Preface
7

Animals
9

Plants
85

Natural Features
135

Suggested Reading
197

IGNORING NATURE WHEN YOU LIVE in the Northwest is almost impossible. Wild rivers, towering mountain peaks, roadless wildernesses and driftwood-strewn beaches, mossy rain forests, soaring sand dunes, and abundant wildlife—even in the elegantly austere deserts and lava beds—combine to make this region an exceptional part of the world. For the nature writer, Oregon, Washington, Idaho, and Montana are exciting places to live in and write about, not only because of the often-seen creatures, plants, and physical features, but also because of the seldom-if-ever-seen: the elusive lynx, the ocean-dwelling basket star, the rare phantom orchid. True Northwest nature lovers delight in every facet of nature for a simple reason: because it's there.

In selecting entries for this book, I tried to choose a wide variety of subjects, ones that would spark the interest of my readers as much as they sparked mine. Much of my information is gleaned from research I've done over the years while writing articles about the natural world. Or I may have stumbled across a fact—often a superlative about the largest, smallest, or deepest—and followed wherever the path led. Other times a natural happening or startling sight piqued my curiosity: a steamy hot spring streaming down a hillside near our Idaho campsite; an Oregon bog filled with carnivorous lilies, poised like cobras ready to strike; a ride in a pickup truck among grazing but potentially dangerous bison on Montana's National Bison Range; or the sight of two intertwined slugs, suspended by a strand of mucus from my brick garden wall, languidly mating.

I have included Idaho and Montana in the Northwest because those states formed part of the original western territories, and because they share many animals, plants, and natural features with Washington and Oregon. The four states have interacted physically in many ways. During the last Ice Age, floodwater that was backed up behind a glacial ice dam in Montana's giant Glacial Lake Missoula scoured Idaho's Panhandle and eastern Washington as many as forty times after the ice dam broke, released torrents of water, and then re-formed only to break again. Basalt lava pouring north from eastern Oregon covered eastern Washington's Columbia Plateau and spread into Idaho.

The earth's crust, 10 miles deep atop the Idaho Batholith, moved into Montana over a period of a million years, creating two mountain blocks.

For the convenience of readers, entries in this book have been grouped into three sections and alphabetized within those sections: animals, plants, and natural features. You can browse in alphabetical order if you like, taking pleasure in the joys of juxtaposition, the leaps from moles to moon snails, potatoes to rain forests, Dungeness Spit to earthquakes. Or you can zero in on a subject that particularly interests you, and then pursue related topics.

This book, neither field guide nor road guide, is designed to arouse your curiosity, and then to satisfy it, to answer not only questions about what, but how and why. If, as you read, you exclaim "I didn't know that!" I will be pleased.

But my purpose is far more serious. Every nature writer is an advocate for nature. Implicit in each factual description in this book is a subliminal message: Tread lightly upon this ancient and complex earth. Be a preserver, not a destroyer.

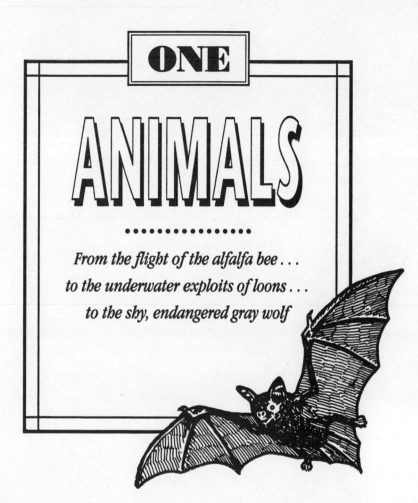

ONE

ANIMALS

· · · · · · · · · · · · · · · · ·

From the flight of the alfalfa bee . . .
to the underwater exploits of loons . . .
to the shy, endangered gray wolf

ALFALFA BEES Two wild bees, the alkali bee (*Nomia melanderi*) and the alfalfa leafcutter (*Megachile rotundata*), are the primary pollinators of Northwest alfalfa crops, which provide half of the nation's $100 million alfalfa seed crop each year. The alkali bee, known as a sweat bee for its attraction to human sweat, is native to western North America and common in eastern Washington; the alfalfa leafcutter bee was accidentally imported from Eurasia. Both bees are solitary, living alone rather than in hives.

The alkali bee and alfalfa leafcutter are the primary pollinators of the Northwest's alfalfa crop.

Both of the wild bee species, whose stings are very mild, are highly efficient alfalfa pollinators, visiting many blooms in succession to fulfill their heavy requirements of nectar and pollen for brood cells.

Although the honeybee also collects nectar from alfalfa flowers, it does so without pollinating the plants. By inserting its long tongue at the sides of the blossoms, the honeybee robs the nectar without activating the "trigger mechanism" on the flower that would dust it with pollen. The two wild bees, however, activate this trigger. As the bees collect nectar from alfalfa blossoms, the stamens shower pollen on them, which they collect on special leg or abdomen hairs and carry to the next blossoms.

◆ Northwest alfalfa growers encourage both of the wild bee species to nest nearby, preparing soil nesting beds for the alkali bee, whose larvae can be killed by pesticides or too much moisture in the soil, and drilling holes in wooden "bee boards" to encourage leafcutter bees to nest there. Young adult females by the thousands return to the same nesting area after mating.

◆ During their few weeks as adults, the wild alfalfa females work alone, day and night. In the mornings both species collect nectar and pollen for their brood cells. In the afternoon alkali bees excavate and, using a special secretion, waterproof their cells in the earth, polishing the walls carefully. Leafcutters snip out precise circles and ovals from alfalfa leaves, which they use to concoct thimblelike brood cells in either nest board holes or natural tubes such as hollow weed stems. They line up six or eight brood cells and neatly cap them with leaf circles. Both bees make a mound from the mixture of nectar and pollen to sustain the larva, lay an egg on it, and seal the cell. The next day they begin the process all over again. After several weeks, a larva is fully grown and enters a prepupal resting stage in the cell for nine months, emerging as an adult when the alfalfa blooms again.

ANGLERFISH In 1989 at Reedsport, Oregon, a shrimp fisherman caught a deep-sea anglerfish (*Cryptotsaras couesi*), also

A deep-sea anglerfish, which usually lives at depths of 6,000 feet, was caught at 636 feet in 1989 off Reedsport, Oregon.

known as the warted she-devil. Although caught at 636 feet, this rare fish usually lives 6,000 feet deep in the ocean. Permanently attached by the mouth to the head of a 12-inch female fish was a 2-inch male. These fish are among the largest male and female of the species ever caught; only a few females have ever been captured with a male attached.

Deep-sea anglerfish, lacking pelvic fins, float through the dark ocean depths. The female "fishes" with a long, slender filament, evidently adapted over eons from the first ray of her dorsal fin. This filament, which arches over her head and ends near her mouth, is tipped with several wormlike, luminescent lures. Small fish attracted by the glowing, wriggling lure fail to notice the dark-colored anglerfish.

The diminutive male attaches to the female with special teeth, becoming wholly dependent upon her, his flesh eventually fused to hers. Losing eyes, fins, and teeth, he soon turns into little more than a sperm-producing organ.

The unusual fish caught in Reedsport are now part of the Oregon State University collection.

Using all four feet, and even its jaws, a badger can dig 8 to 10 feet into the ground in seconds.

BADGER North America's densest concentration of badgers (*Taxidea taxus*) lives in Idaho's Snake River Birds of Prey Natural Area. Some ten to fifteen badgers for each square mile compete with raptors for the area's many rodents, rabbits, reptiles, beetles, amphibians, grasshoppers, and ground-nesting birds and eggs. The badger's voracious appetite extends to plants and fruit as well.

◆ The massive neck and shoulder muscles of these fierce, flat-bodied animals make them one of the most powerful of all animal excavators. Using strong, short legs, long, curved fore-claws, shorter, shovel-like hind claws, and sometimes even their strong jaws, badgers can disappear 8 to 10 feet into the ground in seconds, plugging the entrance hole behind them. They can dig even while holding onto a dog's snout. Slow above ground, they prefer to dig out rather than chase down their prey.

BADGERS

◆ Few animals, including dogs, can match the badger's fierceness. Opponents, who find its thick, loose skin difficult to grasp, are frequently outweighed by the badger, which weighs up to 25 pounds. Badgers will even tackle rattlesnakes and mountain lions. When two male badgers fight, they both may die, jaws locked together. Highly vocal when angry, they hiss, grunt, yap, and squeal. When in danger, the badger bristles, every hair standing on end, so that it appears to be twice its size.

◆ During the longest badger trek on record, in 1983 a tagged yearling female traveled some 60 miles from Idaho's Birds of Prey Natural Area over rugged mountains and badlands and across the Snake River to Oregon's Malheur County. When food is plentiful, most adult badgers stay within a home range of about 1,700 acres.

BARNACLES The world's largest acorn barnacle (*Balanus nubilus*) thrives in Pacific Northwest waters. It can grow 4 to 5 inches high with a base 5 to 6 inches in diameter. When crowded, especially in deep water, individuals may grow on top of one other in a foot-long tube. The Puget Sound giants prefer subtidal, deep water with strong, food-bearing currents. The acorn barnacle flexes some of the largest animal muscle fibers in the world, fourteen to twenty times thicker than those of humans.

The world's largest barnacle, which grows up to 5 inches high with a 5- to 6-inch base, lives in Pacific Northwest waters.

♦ Barnacles tolerate remarkable extremes in habitat. They rate as one of the very few marine animals generalized enough to live in fresh water, to withstand wave shock, and to endure high and low salinity, oxygen, and temperatures.

♦ The barnacle ranks as the most highly modified and the only sedentary crustacean. The free-swimming larva passes through seven stages before it anchors itself to a suitable spot, using a strong glue released from its antennae. During a dramatic, twelve-hour metamorphosis, the larva secretes the limy, interlocking plates of the shell house that will enclose it for the rest of its life, upside down and glued permanently by the back of the neck to its chosen site.

♦ A barnacle feeds by extending all six pairs of its hair-fringed legs (the cirri) into the sea through the top opening of its shell and sweeping them through the water, all in unison. It grasps tiny crustaceans, plankton, and organic fragments brought by the current, folding the cirri like a fist to trap the prey. It then sweeps the prey to its mouth, where appendages remove the food, rejecting inedible parts.

♦ The barnacle has the longest penis in the world relative to the animal's size. With a slender, extensible tube about 1½ inches long, a barnacle penetrates neighboring shells. Each barnacle, possessing both male and female organs, can give and receive sperm.

♦ The barnacle glue that the antennae secrete tops all other glues for strength. It congeals rapidly in a wet environment, sticks to almost any hard surface (even whale skin), cannot be dissolved with acid, alkali, or protein solvents, is impervious to bacteria, and resists pressure and temperature extremes. Barnacle shells are still attached to some Jurassic fossils after 150 million years. A strong glue found in mussels—which also attach to marine surfaces—is being studied as an anti-barnacle coating for ship hulls.

BATS Sixteen species of bats fill Northwest evening skies in pursuit of insects. Although the bat is, like a bird, capable of true and sustained flight, it suckles its young and is covered with fur, like the mammal it is. Bats are by far the most maneuverable of aerial animals, with a longer, stronger wing beat than that of birds, and much finer control of wing shape.

Bats can live twenty years, exceptionally long for so small a mammal. Their secret may lie in spending 80 percent of their lives resting, their metabolism almost at a standstill. During winter the majority of Northwest species hibernate after the insects they feed upon disappear. During that long winter nap, when they don't breathe for minutes at a time and their hearts barely beat, bats consume oxygen at only 1 percent of their normal rate. During summer days too, they rest almost in a torpor, with body functions drastically reduced.

One of the Northwest's sixteen species of bats, the western pipistrelle, is the smallest bat in the United States.

BAT

◆ Using its precise echolocation, a bat can identify different kinds of insects by body texture, wingbeat frequency, flight pattern, and speed.

◆ The smallest bat in the Northwest and the nation is the western pipistrelle (*Pipistrellus hesperus*), only 3 inches long, with a wingspan of less than 8½ inches. Although a slow, weak flyer, this desert bat can take off from almost any surface. Blackish feet, ears, face, and membranes accent the bat's smoke gray fur.

Unlike other Northwest bats that hibernate in caves, the western pipistrelle chooses the zone farthest from the cave opening in which to hang from the ceiling. Here the temperature is a bit warmer and more constant. With the humidity hovering around 99 percent, the bat's fur often beads with moisture as it hangs upside down, seldom rousing from its deep torpor. At its optimum temperature of 35.8°F, the pipistrelle expends only 20 calories a day. At that rate, if it never roused from complete dormancy, it could live on accumulated fat for six years.

◆ Largest bat in the Northwest, the hoary bat (*Lasiurus cinereus*) measures 5½ inches in length with a 16½-inch wingspan. The hoary bat's distinctive white-tipped fur covers the top surface of its tail membrane. Its brown wings have white or gray spots at the wrists and elbows. The hoary bat has powerful jaws and will bite humans if handled, often drawing blood. The hoary bat is one of only two Northwest bats that roost in trees. It does not hibernate; instead, it migrates south for the winter.

Even hibernators may fly several hundred miles to a cave with desirable conditions, returning year after year to the same hibernaculum. Since bat "sonar" operates effectively only at distances of 100 yards or less, migrating bats sometimes collide with lighthouses, television towers, and high buildings.

♦ Brown bats of the *Myotis* species and long-eared bats (*Corynorhinus rafinesqui*) have been seen hibernating in the dry sections of Ape Cave near Mount St. Helens.

BEAVERS The beaver (*Castor canadensus*) ranks as the Northern Hemisphere's largest rodent and the second largest rodent in the world, weighing up to 75 pounds. Some giant prehistoric beavers probably weighed 500 pounds.

Perhaps the most important animal in Northwest history, the beaver—"furred gold"—lured trappers into unexplored regions, opening the way for settlement.

♦ Beavers, the most intelligent of the rodents, impact their environment more than any other animal except humans. (In native American legends, the Creator asks beavers to help build the earth.) Beaver dams and ponds retard rapid summer runoff, keeping water tables high in pastures and hay meadows and providing habitat for trout, aquatic birds, and other fur-bearers. Snags that remain after beaver dams have flooded lowland forests provide perches and nests for fish-hunting hawks and eagles. In the northern Rocky Mountains, moose feed on aquatic plants growing in beaver ponds. As beavers cut down trees for their dams and for food, grassy meadows spring up in which elk and deer feed. Many of the flat valleys that early settlers valued so highly were silted-in beaver ponds, well watered and rich with grasses.

Only humans can match the beaver for technical skill in construction and for the size of their dwellings. With great skill, beavers engineer their cone-shaped lodges, which are often 20 feet in diameter. The central chamber, which must be above water for the air-breathing beaver, is built of sticks, limbs, and mud—which serves to strengthen and insulate the lodge—and has a ventilated vertical stack for temperature control and oxygen. One or two escape tunnels lead to underwater exits below. The lodge is so sturdy that even a bear cannot break through it. Beavers also may dig long canals to float large logs to the pond dam.

♦ Beavers are superbly adapted for aquatic life: their hind paws are webbed to the toe tips, their nose and ear valves shut out water, and a transparent eyelid allows underwater vision. In a unique adaptation, two folds of skin on either side of the beaver's teeth seal off the mouth, enabling the beaver to chew wood underwater without getting water or splinters inside its mouth. A large lung capacity, an oversized liver to filter out blood impurities, and a high tolerance for carbon dioxide help the beaver stay underwater for fifteen minutes at a time. The beaver's dense underfur and heavy guard furs insulate it against chilly Northwest waters. Two split claws on the hind feet help the beaver groom its fur, spreading waterproofing oil.

◆ The beaver possesses one of the most unusual tails of any mammal. In the water, this multipurpose, foot-long tail propels the beaver along, acting as a rudder when the animal is carrying something heavy. For a quick descent underwater, the beaver flips the heavy tail downward; to send a signal of alarm, it spanks the water noisily with its tail. On land the beaver uses its tail for balance when it stands erect to gnaw a tree, to carry with its agile front paws some mud or stones for building, or to tote, between chin and arms, one of its young. The heavy tail also stores fat for winter, when food is scarce. Fur trappers roasted and peeled the scaly tail, then roasted the porklike, gelatinous meat.

◆ Beavers rate as one of the most important animals in Northwest history. Their pelts contributed to the exploration and settlement of the Northwest by luring fur trappers into unknown country after "furred gold" and by bringing in fur-trading companies that built the Northwest's first permanent non-native settlements. In 1830, when fashionable British gentlemen yearned for very tall beaver hats, 8,000 thick, soft pelts collected in the Northwest were sent to London. By 1840 beaver hats were no longer in fashion, but the beaver population had been ravaged. Today, beavers are once again plentiful.

◆ Castoreum, a syrupy, territory-marking substance secreted by both female and male beavers from scent glands at the base of the tail, is one of the most ancient medicinal ingredients still used today. It contains salicylic acid, the main ingredient in aspirin. Small amounts of the acid also occur naturally in the roots, leaves, fruits, and blossoms of many plants.

Idaho's Snake River Birds of Prey Natural Area boasts North America's densest concentration of nesting birds of prey.

BIRDS OF PREY North America's densest concentration of nesting birds of prey, more than 700 pairs of 16 species of raptors, builds nests at Idaho's 600,000-acre Snake River Birds of Prey Natural Area, established in 1980 near Boise. Each year more raptors nest in the pinnacles and rocky ledges of this natural area than in any other place of similar size in North America. Basalt nesting cliffs, sometimes rising more than 500 feet above the Snake River, provide thermals on which the raptors soar.

Although rough-legged hawks and bald eagles use the area only during winter, American kestrels, golden eagles, red-tailed hawks, long-eared owls, great horned owls, and northern harriers stay in the Snake River natural area year-round. The area boasts an unusually dense population of nesting prairie falcons. A few species, such as the osprey and Cooper's hawk, only winter there. The birds feed upon the area's abundant snakes, lizards, jackrabbits, Townsend's ground squirrels, and kangaroo rats.

♦ One of the Northwest's greatest concentrations of resident and migrant birds of prey inhabits Washington's San Juan Island. The island has American rough-legged hawks, occasional golden eagles, goshawks, Cooper's hawks, dusky horned owls, and a large number of breeding bald eagles.

The island provides an ideal habitat for these hunters. It has a dry climate, a mix of open land for hunting and wooded land for nesting, a lack of large mammalian predators, a small human population, and a huge population of Belgian and Flemish giant hares, now wild, that provides a plentiful food supply. (See also Eagles; Falcons.)

BISON The largest, most massive land mammal in North America, the bison (*Bison bison*), can measure 6 feet high at the shoulders, 11½ feet from nose tip to tail tip, and weigh up to 3,000 pounds. For its size, the animal moves rapidly, walking at 5 miles an hour, galloping at 35. At one time, bison migrated north and south each year, some 100 to 200 miles, following the best grass pastures. Many western highways, especially across mountains, follow deeply rutted, former bison trails.

Montana's National Bison Range protects about 400 American bison, one of the country's most important remaining herds.

♦ Bison once roamed North American plains in numbers almost too vast to comprehend. Travelers in Montana in 1866 reported being surrounded at Milk River for six days by bison as far as they could see, perhaps 6 million shaggy beasts. In 1877 a Montana rancher had to wait three days and three nights in Yellowstone Valley while a Montana herd of bison passed by.

♦ The bison suffered one of the most deliberate attempts of all time to exterminate a large mammal. The United States federal government policy, which encouraged the slaughter of this animal on which the Plains Indians depended for food and hides, nearly resulted in the bison's total extinction. For some people, killing as many buffalo as possible, even shooting them from the windows of moving trains, became a sport. From an estimated 60 million in pre-Columbian times, the number fell to only 20 wild bison in 1900, plus a few small, private herds.

BISON

The American Bison Society was formed in 1905 to preserve the surviving bison. The National Bison Range in Moiese, Montana, established in 1908 by Theodore Roosevelt, now protects one of the most important remaining herds of American bison. Beginning with only 40 animals, the herd is now maintained at 400, the range capacity. The bison share their 18,540 acres of natural grassland with elk, pronghorns, bighorn sheep—about 75 of each—and several hundred deer. Another herd grazes on Montana's Crow Reservation, while a third, numbering about 2,000, thrives in Yellowstone Park.

◆ For centuries the native plains tribes centered their economy, and some of their religion, on the bison. They ate bison meat fresh or dried and used hides for clothing, bedding, tents, travois sleds, and canoes; they fueled their fires with bison dung and made weapons and tools from the bones, hides, and sinews. Although Indian tribes killed bison by running the easily stampeded animals off cliffs, they made little impact upon the huge herds.

The largest prehistoric Blackfoot Indian buffalo kill site in the nation is Ulm Pishkun, 10 miles south of Great Falls, Montana.

BLACK BEAR The Northwest has the largest black bear (*Ursus americanus*) population in the Lower 48. Of the probable 500,000 black bears in the United States, some 50,000 of the solitary, wide-ranging, and notably hard-to-census creatures may roam Northwest foothills, high meadows, and mountains below 5,500 feet. Resident in all Northwest national parks, black bears constantly move about in search of food, except during winter hibernation.

The largest population of black bear in the Lower 48 roams backcountry regions of the Northwest.

◆ The black bear, smallest of the three North American bears, measures only 3 feet high at the shoulder and 5 feet long, weighing 200 to 500 pounds. Often, however, this bear ranks as the largest mammal in areas it inhabits. More agile than the heavier, larger grizzly, black bears easily climb trees and grasp objects with their front paws. Like the grizzly, the black bear usually avoids humans but does venture out during the day, as berry pickers in the mountains can testify. Powerful and surprisingly fast at 30 miles an hour, the black bear, especially a female with cubs, can be dangerous.

Despite their common name, some black bears are the color of chocolate or cinnamon, others are grizzled or even blue black, with varying color phases in the same litter. They are almost silent as adults, only woofing when startled; cubs, however, howl when upset.

◆ A black bear cub captured on a hunt by President Theodore Roosevelt in 1902 was the model for the original Teddy Bear.

◆ Bears are the largest of North American omnivores; they are carnivorous when salmon, rodents, carrion, and fawns of elk and deer abound, but are content with berries, nuts, bulbs, grasses, and buds at other times. Twenty million years ago, bears split off from the dog family. The teeth of the two animals are similar except that, where the dog has cutting teeth, the bear has crushing teeth.

BRITTLE STARS AND BASKET STARS
Brittle stars, close relatives of starfish, are prolific in Pacific Northwest waters. Brittle stars are one of the most successful echinoderms. (Starfish, sea urchins, sea cucumbers, and sea lilies are also echinoderms.)

The five arms of the basket star branch and fork into thousands of white tendrils.

Also called serpent stars for the sinuous movement of their slim arms, brittle stars move ten times faster than starfish, rowing along with one pair of arms—almost swimming—as another arm leads and the two others trail. They do not extrude their stomach to digest food, as starfish do; their easily digested food does not require this strategy. Highly efficient scavengers, brittle stars feed on ocean detritus suspended in the water and on the ocean floor. The sensitive, suckerless tube feet on their arms are not used for locomotion but for burrowing, breathing, and feeding. The tube feet scrape off debris trapped on arms, spines, and mucus threads, molding it as they pass it along to the mouth, which tastes and then accepts or rejects the food. Five serrated jaws surrounding the mouth strain out indigestible bits.

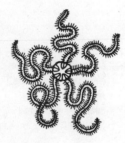

BASKET STAR

◆ The most startling member of the brittle stars in the Northwest, the basket star (*Gorgonocephalus eucnemis*) departs radically from the simple, five-armed brittle star anatomy. Large for a brittle star, the basket star may measure 10 or 12 inches across with arms spread out. Its arms branch and fork so extensively that the original five arms are barely discernible among thousands of white tendrils. Weirdly beautiful, often with salmon pink tinging the thick, whitish skin, this rococo deep-sea animal has no parallel among echinoderms.

Unlike other brittle stars, whose five slender, unbranched arms readily break off at vertebraelike joints when the animal is disturbed, the basket star seldom discards arms. Its flexible arms can move in all directions; other brittle star arms can move only laterally. To feed, the basket star often crawls up and clings to marine plants with two arms, its other arms forming a writhing openwork basket that captures food. The arms surround plankton, detritus, small copepods and shrimp, and bring the prey directly to the star-shaped mouth on the basket star's underside. Tiny hooks on the tips of the branches increase the effectiveness of this suspension feeder.

♦ When resting in groups, brittle stars often intertwine their arms with other members of their species. This togetherness pays off. Researchers have discovered that intertwined masses of brittle stars emit a protective substance, similar to a vaccine antibody, that renders individual brittle stars in the group more resistant to toxins. Basket stars, with their complexly branched arms, do not engage in this intertwining behavior.

♦ *Ophiopholis aculeata,* a delicate, rust-colored brittle star with five typically snakelike, spined arms, tolerates an unusual range of habitat in Northwest waters. It can withstand the wave shock of low intertidal zones as well as great water pressure at deep-sea bottom.

♦ Brittle stars are usually much smaller than starfish. The Northwest's smallest, *Amphipholis pugetana,* measures barely ¾ inch across, with arms fully spread. This black-and-white resident of upper tide pools does not readily shed its arms, nor does it intertwine them with others in its huge beds.

Nearly 200 species of butterflies live in the Northwest, including the rare and endangered Oregon Silverspot.

BUTTERFLIES Nearly 200 species of butterflies live in the Northwest, representing five major families. Some Northwest butterflies are found nowhere else in the world, clustered into small colonies that may be remnants from colder ages.

♦ Washington boasts one of the first successful butterfly preserves in the United States, established by The Nature Conservancy in 1966 on 14-acre Moxee Bog near Yakima. The preserve protects the endangered silver-bordered fritillaries (*Boloria selene*), which congregate in a few widely separated colonies near the wild violet they prefer. Other colonies are located elsewhere in eastern Washington, the northern Rockies, and central Oregon. Although the larvae of this butterfly can survive on the leaves of ordinary wood violets, the adults will lay eggs only on the leaves of the northern bog violet (*Viola nephrophylla*), which thrives in Moxee Bog. A dozen other butterfly species also live in Moxee Bog. (The bog is closed to visitors.)

♦ Another critically endangered Northwest butterfly is the coastal Oregon Silverspot (*Speyeria zerene hippolyta*), a reddish brown butterfly with a 2-inch wingspan that lives in salt-spray meadows, a scarce oceanside habitat. The salt spray slows the growth of some plants while encouraging others, including the western blue violet (*Viola adunca*), the only plant on which the Oregon Silverspot will lay its eggs.

Ocean erosion, human developments, and encroaching forest

growth have destroyed many salt-spray meadows along the Oregon coast. The two largest populations of the Oregon Silverspot live near the mouths of Rock Creek and Big Creek in the Siuslaw National Forest.

CHITON The world's largest chiton, the gumboot (*Cryptochiton stelleri*), lives in Pacific Northwest waters, also home to many smaller species of chitons. A reddish brown girdle—long, thick, and leathery—completely covers the giant chiton, which can grow as long as 18 inches and as wide as 6 inches.

Pacific Northwest waters are home to the world's largest chiton, up to 18 inches long and 6 inches wide.

The eight overlapping calcareous plates clearly visible on most chitons are enclosed within the mantle of the enormous gumboot. Those butterfly-shaped plates, which often wash up on beaches, allow the chiton to roll up into a "sea cradle," protecting its soft underparts when a predator or a rough sea tears it from the subtidal rock to which it clings during the day.
♦ Chitons rank as the most primitive of today's mollusks, similar to fossils 400 million years old, with very simple nervous systems and internal structures. The reduced head has no eyes, only light-receiving and tactile cells.

COUGAR The tawny-coated cougar (*Felis concolor*), also known as puma, panther, and mountain lion (in the Rockies), is the second largest New World cat and largest of three native Northwest cats. Males can measure 8 feet long with an additional 30 inches of tail. A cougar normally weighs around 150 pounds, although Theodore Roosevelt killed a 227-pound cougar in the early 1900s.
♦ The graceful, powerful cougar once enjoyed one of the widest distributions of any single species of mammal in the Western Hemisphere, partly because it adapts so well. At one time it lived in deserts, swamps, forests, and mountains in every one of the contiguous states. Now some 5,000 cougars live primarily in western wilderness. All four Northwest states provide ideal cougar country—rugged mountain terrain with sparsely wooded canyons inhabited by large game. Oregon and Washington each claim an estimated 2,000 cougars roaming their backcountry.
♦ Cougars, sometimes called "the ghosts of North America," are secretive and solitary, yet curious enough to stalk hunters and to spy on humans, often for hours. They reveal their presence mainly by the large tracks of their padded paws, 7 inches across, and by the prolonged, spine-tingling screams that may issue from females ready to mate, or from males signaling a mate or defying

Northwest states provide ideal habitat for cougars, "the ghosts of North America"; an estimated 4,000 roam the high country of Washington and Oregon.

another male. Cougars can leap as far as 30 feet on level ground and can run short distances faster than most other animals, a blur of speed. Also good climbers, they may jump from tree to tree when pursued by dogs, or leap from a tree onto large prey. Cougars have no predators except humans and hounds.

CRABS The largest and most valuable edible crab in the Northwest is the deepwater Dungeness crab (*Cancer magister*). Recent commercial catches for one year in Washington totaled nearly 20 million pounds, with 3 million of those pounds taken in Oregon waters. That adds up to revenue of more than $20 million a year. The most productive sites in Oregon are off Newport, and in Washington off Westport, Ilwaco, and the northern San Juan Islands.

When caught by its leg by predators, a crab can detach the leg and later regenerate it.

The Dungeness, which grows to a width of 10 to 12 inches across its outer shell, or carapace, is seldom seen side-stepping on beaches, although numerous empty and intact shells scattered on the beaches give the impression of a catastrophic kill. These are merely outgrown shells cast off during the crab's twice-a-year molting. The crabs, bluish brown on the carapace while alive but bright red after boiling, may come into shallow water during summer low tides to molt and mate, but they can burrow backward in the sand up to their stalked eyeballs in less than a minute. When not feeding, mating, or molting, Dungeness crabs spend much of their time buried to avoid predators such as octopus, squid, herons, stingrays, brittle stars, starfish, jellyfish, and large fish.

♦ Like most crabs, the Dungeness must molt in order to grow since its rigid exoskeleton will not expand. In the Dungeness lifespan of 5 or 6 years, it molts more than a dozen times, not counting several larval molts. The molt, which takes about 15 minutes, begins as old cuticle loosens from the underlying skin, aided by a fluid the crab secretes. New cuticle for the larger carapace begins to form under the old one before the crab slips out of its shell. To facilitate the withdrawal of legs and claws, the crab shrinks them. Fluid from them flows into the body, expanding it so that a special line of weakness across the rear of the upper shell breaks open. As limy material in its joints dissolves, the crab slips backward out of the old shell. Vulnerable to predators without its hard shell, the Dungeness crab hides for two days, not eating, waiting for its new carapace to stretch and harden. The crab takes in water to expand the still-soft shell for future space. Some crabs eat the old carapace, the lime salts from which help harden the new shell quickly.

When the female Dungeness is ready to molt and the male is ready to mate, an extraordinary courtship occurs. A non-molting male chooses a female ready to molt within a few days, and he holds her, belly to belly, for several days. Occasionally he strokes her with his pincers, evidently waiting for a sign that she is ready. When she nibbles at his eyestalks, he loosens his embrace just enough so that she can shed her outgrown shell. He pushes it away as he waits for her new carapace to harden slightly. Then he turns the female over and they mate. She extends her broad, rounded abdominal flap to receive sperm from his narrow flap. They continue their embrace for another two days before parting.

♦ Other edible Northwest crabs include the red crab (*Cancer productus*), almost as large as the Dungeness with a heavier brick red carapace. The red crab and the smaller red rock crab (*C. antennarius*), which has large claws, are more abundant intertidally and are as delicious as the favored Dungeness.

♦ Another group of edible crabs, the stone or lithode crabs, are more related to hermit crabs than to true crabs. The subtidal Puget Sound king crab (*Lopholithodes mandtii*), although not a giant like the Alaska king crab, is a respectable 12 inches across. Divers bring it up together with the box crab (*L. foraminatus*) from rocky bottoms 30 to 50 feet deep in the Strait of Juan de Fuca, Puget Sound, and around the San Juan Islands. Both crabs protect themselves when alarmed by folding their legs against their bodies to form a solid, sturdy box. *Cryptolithodes sitchensis* has a 2-inch-wide carapace, broad enough to cover its legs completely when it is at rest, displaying a turtlelike shell.

CRAB

♦ Since a leg is the easiest part of the crab's body for a predator to seize, crabs have developed a process called *autotomy* that enables them to break off a leg by a sharp contraction of the muscles at a fracture plane where the leg joins the body. The captive leg easily detaches, for no muscles pass through this joint, only blood vessels and nerves. A stub forms where the leg is gone, and after a few molts, the limb is fully regenerated.

♦ The Northwest is rich in species of decorator crabs, the popular name for the spider crabs that form the second largest family of crabs, the *Majidae*. They are often only an inch across the carapace, but they protect themselves well by masking their shells with material and organisms from their surroundings: seaweed, pieces of sponge, hydroids, bryozoans. Often the living organisms they attach to their shells continue to grow. Masking or decorator crabs common on Northwest beaches or in shallow waters include the sharp-nosed crab (*Scyra acutifrons*); the 1-inch-wide kelp crab (*Pugettia gracilis*) that inhabits seaweeds and impales bits of seaweed and other organisms on the sharp spines of its carapace; and a slightly larger kelp crab (*P. producta*), almost 4 inches across. This crab keeps its shell clean, but mimics the color and texture of the smooth, olive green seaweed in which it lives.

When moved into a new environment, decorator crabs change their shell coverings at once to mimic their new surroundings. They may actively hold plant and animal material against the carapace with their delicate pincers until it takes hold.

◆ The most visible and active crabs on Northwest beaches are hermit crabs (genus *Pagurus*). These distant cousins of true crabs, which lack protective armor on their soft abdomens, spend their lives moving to ever-larger empty shells they scavenge on the beach. Instead of molting as they grow larger, hermit crabs just choose a bigger shell. They carefully explore possible new homes, grasping a shell and rotating it so they can explore it with their antennae to make sure it is free of its occupant and of debris. Hermit crabs sometimes fight over shells, but the loser is always allowed to crawl back into an old shell. Since the soft-bellied crabs are very vulnerable while changing shells, they quickly wriggle out of the old shell and jump backward into the new larger shell. The crab can close the opening to its shell house with its claws.

The hermit's large soft abdomen flexes to the right to accommodate the spiraling of its adopted snail shell, and the appendages on the left side of its body have disappeared completely or been diminished. The hermit carries its shell along the beach, supported by its strong walking legs and claws. It holds the shell in place with a hook at the end of its body and with specially modified rear legs with a non-skid grip of tiny spines that press against the shell and help carry it. *Pagurus beringanus*, the largest intertidal hermit crab on the coast, chooses to live in Oregon triton shells, once occupied by the largest intertidal snails in the Northwest. Another hermit lugs around the heavy moon snail shell, further burdened with a load of barnacles.

◆ The most abundant crab on numerous Northwest seashores where waves break are 1-inch-long sand crabs (*Emerita analoga*), also called mole crabs for their habit of burrowing rapidly with rowing movements of their legs and the side appendages of the tail, which they also use for swimming. As waves break, the crabs may dig into the sand with only eyes and large feathery antennae extending from the sand. They feed by straining out organic bits as the water runs back down toward the ocean. Sometimes nearly half the population emerges and lets the water carry it up and down the beach to take advantage of food in the current. After the receding water slackens, the crabs dig in again, and the other half of the population migrates on the next wave.

CRANE Taller than any other Northwest bird, the greater sandhill crane (*Grus canadensis tabida*), one of the tallest cranes in the world, reaches 3 to 5 feet in height. This strong flyer, with a wingspan of 5 to 7 feet, can fly over mountains 14,000 feet high.
◆ Graceful and energetic, the dance of the sandhill crane is among the most unusual behavior of any Northwest bird. Cranes of any age—even 3 days old—perform this dance, although courting pairs dance most spectacularly.

The tall, shy cranes may dance alone or in couples, ignored by other cranes. Large groups sometimes pair off to dance. With wings partly spread, the dancers quickstep around one another, silent or calling noisily, bowing heads, leaping as high as 8 feet, spindly legs dangling, red-capped heads raised. They make sudden stops and may toss up vegetation or sticks, trying to catch them with their long, straight bills.
◆ The crane's deep, resonant call results from an unusual formation of the windpipe: half of its 5-foot length is coiled against the bird's breastbone. The trumpeter swan has a similar windpipe loop.
◆ The sandhill is the only crane that breeds in the western United States. North America's largest breeding population of the tall birds congregates at Grays Lake National Wildlife Refuge in southeastern Idaho, where some 250 nesting pairs and 600 nonbreeders gather in spring. In the fall, 2,500 cranes pause there before migrating south. Another important nesting area is the Klamath Forest National Wildlife Refuge in Oregon. Shy and unable to adapt well to change, the sandhill crane is becoming increasingly rare.

DEER The Columbian white-tailed deer (*Odocoileus virginianus leucurus*) occupies the most restricted habitat of any of North America's thirty-six white-tailed deer subspecies. One of only two endangered white-tails, it was believed extinct in the early 1930s. The deer now lives only in sloughs, floodplains, marshes, and meadows, mostly along the lower Columbia River near Cathlamet, Washington. Another small group lives near Roseburg, Oregon.

Once abundant west of the Cascades in Oregon's Umpqua and Willamette valleys, and along the lower Columbia north to Puget

The sandhill crane, one of the tallest cranes in the world, leaps as high as 8 feet during its spectacular "dance."

The endangered Columbian white-tailed deer, believed extinct in the 1930s, now finds limited but protected habitat along the lower Columbia River.

Sound, the deer lost their habitat as settlers cleared land. Considerably smaller than the more common white-tail, the Columbian white-tail flaunts a broad triangular tail, brown above and white below, which it flips up as a warning. The prongs of its unusual antlers extend from a single- rather than a two-forked beam.

The 4,800-acre Columbian White-tailed Deer National Wildlife Refuge, established in 1972 on three Columbia River islands and on part of the mainland, protects some 400 deer.

DRAGONFLIES One of the world's most primitive dragonflies, the *Tanypteryx hageni,* lives only in the Northwest. The black-and-yellow insect burrows into Washington bogs in the Olympics and Cascades. Unlike other dragonflies, the *T. hageni* lays its eggs in bogs, not in water, producing terrestrial instead of aquatic larvae.

One of the world's most primitive dragonflies lives only in the Northwest.

◆ Dragonflies are among the fastest flyers of all insects, too swift and active for most predators to catch. Airplane designers have studied the mechanics of dragonfly flight, to determine how an insect whose wings are restricted to up-and-down movement, with no coupling device joining front and back wings, can hover in midair and fly both forward and backward at speeds up to 60 miles an hour. Dragonfly wings have three times the lift, in proportion to weight, of the most advanced aircraft. Unable to fold their wings at rest, dragonflies must keep them extended on either side of the body.

◆ Constantly patrolling their watery territory, dragonflies watch for intruders with the most intricate compound eyes of any insect—more than 20,000 six-sided facets, or lenses, make up each eye. A ball-and-socketlike joint attaches the dragonfly's head to its body, allowing almost 360 degrees of lateral movement. Able to detect movement 40 feet away, dragonflies catch other insects in baskets formed by their hairy legs and crunch them with their strong jaws.

◆ Dragonflies, among the largest of modern flying insects, were also the largest prehistoric insect. Scientists in France have found fossil impressions of dragonfly wings 27½ inches long. Dragonfly fossils date back 300 million years.

◆ Dragonflies perform a curious, acrobatic tandem mating in the air. Once the male encounters a female of the same species, he flies ahead and grips her head with abdominal claspers. The female curls her abdomen forward so that its tip contacts the male accessory organ, which is filled with semen. She may even lay her eggs while still in tandem flight, embedding them in aquatic plants or submerging her abdomen to wash them off into the water.

♦ Dragonfly nymphs are among the most voracious of underwater invertebrate predators, with a unique enlarged lower lip set with hooks on the end. Folded when at rest, the lip shoots out to hook tadpoles and small fish and then retracts, bringing the food into the mouth.

EAGLE The Northwest's largest bird of prey, the bald eagle (*Haliaetus leucocephalus*) stands 3 feet tall, weighs 16 pounds, and possesses a wingspan of 6 to 7 feet. Its dark body, accented by a brilliant white head and tail in mature eagles, has become a common sight in the Northwest, soaring in large, graceful circles or perching in tall snags.

Bald eagles in increasing numbers are wintering and nesting in Northwest habitats; Washington is second only to Alaska in number of bald eagles.

♦ More than 300 bald eagles congregate annually at the Skagit River Bald Eagle Natural Area, only 60 miles north of Seattle, making that 10-mile stretch one of the five most significant bald eagle wintering spots in the Lower 48. Nowhere else in the world can people living in a metropolis the size of Seattle so easily observe such large numbers of eagles.

More scavenger than predator, the bald eagles are attracted to the Skagit River by numerous spawned-out chum salmon that die and wash up on gravel bars. Also attracting the large birds are the many suitable perching trees, often snags, where they rest, groom, and watch for prey.

♦ Washington is home to more bald eagles than any state other than Alaska—around 3,000, with more than 150 mating pairs. Oregon ranks a close second in mating pairs. Bald eagles have even nested within large cities such as Seattle.

BALD EAGLE

Oregon and California share the nation's largest group of wintering bald eagles—as many as 800—in the Klamath Basin complex of five national wildlife refuges. In one of them, Oregon's Bear Valley, as many as 300 eagles roost in a single night.

Most of Idaho's 600 bald eagles winter at Lake Coeur d'Alene, and many nest at the South Fork of the Snake River.

♦ Bald eagles display a variety of hunting techniques: harassing a flying osprey into dropping a newly caught fish, forcing a duck to dive until it is exhausted, diving underwater after a coot, and flying under a goose in the air, then rolling over and sinking talons into its breast. More often, however, the bald eagle goes for the easy meal—a dead fish on the shore.

ELK More than 5,000 Roosevelt elk (*Cervus elaphus*) reside within Olympic National Park, traveling in small bands of 10 to 100. These elk are the Lower 48's last large population of the

The country's largest population of Roosevelt elk resides in Washington's Olympic National Park, while North America's largest remaining herds of Rocky Mountain elk roam mountainsides in Idaho and Montana.

Northwest coastal form of *C. elaphus* that remains relatively undisturbed in its natural habitat. (These elk *are* hunted when they migrate out of the park and into the Olympic National Forest.) Roosevelt elk have roamed the Olympic Peninsula for some 3,000 years. The number of elk living outside the park is unknown, but is estimated to be a few thousand.

◆ The Roosevelt elk ranks as the largest land mammal of the Northwest coast, second in size within the deer family only to the moose. Larger than the more numerous Rocky Mountain elk, the bulls measure 5 to 5½ feet at the shoulder and weigh 600 to 900 pounds. Despite their size, they are agile and elusive, often racing through thick timber at a dead run. They have longer legs and a more graceful body than Rocky Mountain elk, with a richer, reddish brown coat. Both males and females often display a striking black mane and pale yellowish rump patches.

Roosevelt elk depend upon browse more than other elk; the unmistakable sign of their presence is neatly pruned, 4-foot-high shrubs that normally grow 15 feet high.

◆ The Northwest's largest remaining herds of Rocky Mountain elk roam mountainous areas of Idaho, with the large herds in Montana's Glacier National Park running a close second. Rocky Mountain elk grow huge antlers, among the most impressive in the world and much prized by trophy hunters.

◆ Scientists were surprised by how quickly Roosevelt elk returned to the devastated Mount St. Helens area. Soon after the eruption, large herds of elk were feasting on thousands of newly planted conifer seedlings.

◆ One of the most unforgettable sounds made by any animal, and unique among mammals on this continent, is the bugle of the male elk during the fall rutting season. No other mammal uses this kind of call to attract a mate or intimidate a foe. It begins with a low chesty growl or bellow, rises to a clear yodeling bugle, and ends with a series of coughing grunts.

The peregrine falcon, the fastest and most skilled flyer of all birds, dives at speeds of more than 200 miles an hour.

FALCON The World Center for Birds of Prey, established south of Boise, Idaho, by the National Peregrine Fund in 1984, supports the world's largest scientific complex for research and breeding of the peregrine falcon (*Falco peregrinus*). The program to restore the species to its natural range began with 119 peregrine falcons, the nation's entire captive breeding population of the endangered bird. Using incubators and foster parent nests, scientists at the center preside over the hatching of 250 eggs a year. The center has released some 2,000 peregrines into the wild.

Still endangered, the peregrine falcon is slowly returning to the Northwest, but falcon lovers often keep sightings secret for fear that the rare bird may be illegally captured. It is no secret, though, that where thousands of shorebirds gather, so do peregrine falcons: Washington's Grays Harbor, San Juan Islands, Skagit mud flats, Oregon's Coos Bay, and assorted bird-nesting rocks.

◆ Peregrine falcons rank as the most highly skilled flyers of all birds, performing spectacular aerial acrobatics. They are also the fastest; a peregrine falcon diving at a bird may reach speeds of more than 200 miles an hour. While in flight, it can kill a bird that is twice its weight. A large peregrine can reach 20 inches in height, with a wingspread of 25 to 40 inches.

◆ The peregrine possesses the keenest eyesight of any bird of prey. Flying at 3,500 feet, it can spot a pigeon more than 5 miles away. Its eyes are more than twice as sharp as those of the golden eagle.

FISH Rare fish that survived the Ice Age in isolated pockets now live in several extremely restricted habitats in the Northwest. Many are found nowhere else in the world. A number exist only in lakes in Oregon's desert basin.

◆ The endangered Borax Lake chub lives only in Oregon's Borax Lake, a protected preserve. The 10-acre lake, isolated in arid country, is fed by thermal springs that warm the water.

◆ The Wood River sculpin, found in only one other U.S. stream system, is protected in Idaho's Stapp-Soldier Creek Preserve, a Nature Conservancy acquisition in 1983. The sculpin inhabits highly alkaline Silver Creek, whose water filters through subterranean sedimentary limestone to rise from an arid valley floor in south-central Idaho.

◆ Four prehistoric native fish, found nowhere else in the world, have been isolated for millions of years in high, cold Bear Lake on the Idaho-Utah border: the Bonneville cisco, the Bear Lake whitefish, the Bonneville whitefish, and the Bear Lake sculpin. Bear Lake, 21 miles long, 8 miles wide, and 200 feet deep, is the largest freshwater remnant of ancient Lake Bonneville, which once covered most of southeastern Idaho and northern Utah. Some of the rare fish may have evolved in Lake Bonneville and moved into Bear Lake after the larger lake disappeared.

◆ The Olympic mudminnow (*Novumbra hubbsi* Schultz) was probably once widespread—its fossils are found in Oregon—but now it lives only in quiet waters in coastal Olympic Peninsula bogs, swamps, and marshy streams. The male, only 2 to 3 inches

Remote Northwest lakes provide restricted habitat for rare fish that survived the Ice Age in isolated pockets.

long, stalks prey and warns intruders by a threat display—swimming very slowly toward the intruder, stiffening its body, expanding and vibrating its fins. It then strikes quickly and repeatedly with its head or body. When meeting other males at territory boundaries, the mudminnow expands membranes that double its head size.

The largest flea on record was found in 1913 in a mountain beaver nest near Puyallup, Washington.

FLEA The largest flea in the world (*Hystrichopsylla schefferi*) was found in 1913 near Puyallup, Washington, in the nest of its preferred host, a mountain beaver. Most adult fleas are about 0.03 inch long; this one was 0.31.

◆ A number of fleas are highly host-specific. Fleas parasitic on subterranean hosts such as moles, shrews, and mountain beavers usually have very reduced eyes. Fleas carry their own parasitic mites in the spaces between their external cuticle plates.

◆ Of all animals, the flea can jump farthest in relation to its size, from 130 to 150 times its body length, both vertically and horizontally. It can jump hundreds of times an hour without tiring.

Four of the eight Tyrannosaurus rex skeletons ever discovered were unearthed in Montana.

FOSSILS The largest and most complete fossilized skeleton of *Tyrannosaurus rex* ever found was discovered in 1988 in Montana. Located in the badlands of northeastern Montana near Fort Peck Reservoir on the Missouri River, the skeleton was finally disinterred in 1990. The 40-foot-long skeleton, believed to be 90 percent complete, includes a 5-foot-long skull and banana-sized teeth. Only eight nearly complete *T. rex* skeletons have ever been discovered; four were found in Montana, the first in 1902. The latest includes some fossil parts, especially the lower part of the arms, which have never before been found, giving a clearer picture of the huge reptile's anatomy. The arm bones may provide clues to how the dinosaur used its stubby limbs when fighting and eating. The skeleton will be displayed in Dinosaur Hall at the Museum of the Rockies, Montana State University.

More dinosaur fossils have been unearthed in Montana than in any other Northwest state. Montana abounds in fossils partly because erosion and uplift have exposed rock more than 80 million years old. Dinosaur finds near Glendive, Montana, include a nearly complete skeleton of a *Triceratops*, which bears a 3-foot-long horn over each eye and another on its nose. A rare 15-foot-tall *Hoplitosaurus*, a relative of the horned toad, was discovered near Billings.

◆ Washington's Blue Lake Rhinoceros Cave, actually a fossil mold that formed about 10 million years ago around an 8-foot-long rhinoceros, was discovered in 1935, high in a wall of

Jasper Canyon south of Dry Falls. No other mammal fossil has ever been found in a lava flow.

Millions of years ago, one of the many Columbia Plateau flows of very fluid basalt evidently invaded a shallow pond in which the rhinoceros was floating, perhaps killed by heat or fumes. Normally the intense heat and pressure of the 100-foot-high lava flow would have crushed and burned the body. But this lava cooled rapidly upon contact with the water, forming protective, 2-foot-high basalt pillows around the animal. The body decomposed within the lava, and later lava flows buried the mold. Flood erosion eventually cut away the lava across the rump and left hind leg, creating an opening.

A jawbone with teeth and bone fragments found inside the rhino-shaped cave provided positive identification.

The rhinoceros is one of a number of animals no longer found in North America who lived in the Northwest between 1 and 25 million years ago: elephants, small six-toed horses, giant ground sloths, and camels. Remains of many such animals have been preserved in Oregon, but always in volcanic ash or sedimentary rock layers. In Washington such fossils are rarely found because the deep lava of the Columbia Plateau covers any large ash deposits that may exist. (See Natural Features, Columbia Plateau Basalt.)

♦ One of the most unusual fossils ever found from the age of the dinosaurs is a three-in-one Montana fossil that includes the world's oldest paddlefish fossil. The skeletal remains of a paddlefish and a sturgeon were found trapped inside the rib cage of a large, 65-million-year-old duck-billed dinosaur fossil unearthed in 1938 in McCone County. The dinosaur was probably dead in the water when the paddlefish and a sturgeon swam inside it, perhaps to feed on the flesh, and became trapped in the rib cage. The three were preserved together under layers of silt. (See also Paddlefish.)

♦ Oregon's John Day Fossil Beds National Monument contains the nation's richest concentration of prehistoric mammalian fossils. Since the discovery of the fossil beds in 1861, more than 120 species of animals have been identified there. The formations attract students and paleontologists from many countries, studying evolution in certain species over millions of years. Although most of the major finds were made in the nineteenth century and are displayed in museums worldwide, heavy rains continue to wash out new vertebrate material.

The beds comprise five major rock formations and evidence of eight past geological epochs. Embedded there are fossils ranging from more than 50 million to less than 5 million years old, constituting the longest, nearly continuous mammalian fossil record found anywhere on earth.

Several different layers have yielded animal fossils, but the greatest number were preserved in the John Day Formation. This formation contains some of the most beautifully colored volcanic ash in the Northwest—brown, green, and yellowish brown— deposited in a continuous sequence over a period of 7 million years. New volcanoes in the western Cascades violently erupted that ash 30 million years ago, sending huge clouds of ash swirling over central Oregon. The ash, deposited more than 1,000 feet deep in the John Day Formation, smothered animals such as flamingos, camels, rhinoceroses, giant sloths, tapirs, and saber-toothed cats. A thick cap of Columbia Plateau lava protected the ash from erosion. (See Natural Features, John Day Fossil Beds National Monument.)

FROG The nation's only tailed frog (*Ascaphus truei*) lives in all four states of the Northwest. This frog belongs to one of only two families of tailed frogs in the world. The boneless tail-like appendage, more prominent in the male, is really an extension of skin, not a true tail. The frogs use the tail for excretion and for internal fertilization, essential in the fast water where the frogs live. (External fertilization of eggs is normal for other frogs.) The eggs of the 2-inch-long female rank as the largest of any native frog in the United States—¼ inch. She uses her tail to deposit her string of eggs under river rocks.

◆ Tailed frogs prefer life in swift, icy, boulder-strewn mountain streams or cold coastal streams, with water barely above freezing in winter and from 48°F to 52°F in summer. They are highly adapted for life in these small, noisy streams, spending most of the day under river rocks and emerging at night to feed on flying insects. Both male and female lack eardrums, and the male lacks a vocal sac, present in most other frogs. The toes show partial webbing, but the flexible fingers, which cling to boulders in the rushing water, are unwebbed. Tailed frog tadpoles cling to rocks in the swift current with a unique sucker mouth. Equipped with a small larval tail fin, the muscular larvae swim well. At higher elevations they may remain larvae for two years.

◆ These tailed frogs, only 1 to 2 inches long, have the oldest lineage of any frogs in the world. Rocks 135 to 190 million years old hold their fossils. The skeleton of the very primitive frog bears a strong resemblance to that of a salamander.

◆ Among the frogs, only the tailed frog has ribs, which allow it

The nation's only tailed frog lives in swift, icy streams in all four Northwest states.

TAILED FROG

to pump air in and out, a most unfroglike manner of breathing.

GEODUCK The Northwest's geoduck (*Panopea generosa*) is the largest clam in North America and one of the world's largest intertidal burrowing bivalves. Its nearly rectangular shell, up to 10 inches long, cannot contain the tough, wrinkled siphon, which protrudes nearly a foot and can stretch another 2 or 3 feet. The biggest geoducks on record have weighed in at as high as 35 pounds in the shell. Age is measured by rings or lines in a polished, etched cross section of shell. The oldest Northwest geoduck on record lived for 115 years near Washington's Protection Island at the head of Discovery Bay. (A geoduck over 130 years old was found in Canada.) Geoducks stop growing at about 20 years. A 3-pounder has lived for 10 to 13 years.

The world's densest population of geoduck, the largest clam in North America, lives in southern Puget Sound.

After floating freely for a month after hatching, the geoduck digs itself a burrow 3 to 4 feet deep, and then the digging foot atrophies. The geoduck remains sedentary for the rest of its life. Only the siphon can move, extending or pulling back into the sand. As it withdraws, it often forcibly expels a jet of water an inch in diameter for several feet. Its two-hole siphon ranks as one of the largest of all marine animals.

♦ Puget Sound has the only geoduck fishery in the nation, begun in 1970 after U.S. Navy divers accidentally discovered huge beds of the giant clam. Southern Puget Sound boasts the world's densest geoduck population, estimated roughly at 165 million. Major beds cover more than 20,000 acres between 18 and 50 feet deep, with more millions of geoducks probably living deeper. Known harvests have totaled 8 million pounds a year. Divers in helmets and dry suits that protect against frigid Sound waters harvest the giant clams year-round, using water jets to expose the geoducks, then pulling them out of the sand by the neck.

GRIZZLY BEAR The grizzly bear (*Ursus horribilis*) ranks as the largest terrestrial omnivore in the Lower 48. At 800 to 1,000 pounds, it outweighs black bears (200 to 500 pounds) but not Alaska brown bears (1,175 pounds) or polar bears (2,000 pounds). A male grizzly killed in 1894 weighed 1,656 pounds. Preparing for its winter sleep, a grizzly eats for more than 18 hours a day.

An estimated 450 to 700 grizzlies survive in isolated ecosystems in Montana, Idaho, Washington, and Wyoming.

Agile and fast despite its tremendous size, the grizzly can charge at 30 miles an hour. With a blow of its paw, it can fell a bison that outweighs it and then drag off the carcass. Rather than climb a tree after its prey, it will knock the tree down if possible. Not only massive and powerful, grizzlies are also aggressive,

GRIZZLY BEAR

intelligent, wary of humans, and methodical—yet unpredictable. Clark wrote with awe in his journals of "the farocity of those tremendious animals." A grizzly's tolerance for pain is extraordinary; it keeps moving even with gaping wounds.

◆ The grizzly is the only bear with a marked hump on the shoulder, revealing powerful shoulder muscles that it uses, along with very long, strong fore claws, for digging out everything from glacier lily bulbs to a plump marmot.

◆ An estimated 450 to 700 grizzlies may survive in six isolated areas in Montana, Idaho, Washington, and Wyoming. Two of the few remaining refuges for the grizzly in the Lower 48 are Montana's Flathead National Forest and Glacier National Park. Park policy seeks to preserve natural ecosystems such as those of grizzlies and gray wolves.

Some grizzlies may wander down from Canada into the Selkirk Mountains of Idaho and Washington. In Washington, where grizzlies lived originally as part of the Cascade ecosystem, a grizzly was last sighted—and shot—in the North Cascades in 1968. In 1987 a grizzly skull was found at Cascade Pass; grizzly tracks have been seen near Cle Elum, in the North Cascades, and near Baker Lake. Oregon's last known grizzly killing occurred in 1937 in Wallowa County.

◆ The grizzly's skeleton bears a startling resemblance to a human skeleton.

◆ Grizzlies have one of the lowest reproductive rates of any mammal and a natural cub mortality rate as high as 50 percent—reasons enough for the fierce protectiveness of the mother grizzly, who also has to drive off cannibalistic male grizzlies.

◆ Although the grizzly's eyesight is poor, its sense of smell is many times keener than that of bloodhounds.

◆ Grizzlies make one of the most deeply rutted of all animal trails, always stepping in the footsteps of their predecessors. The large, oval depressions, 6 to 12 inches deep and 3 feet apart, may be used for thousands of years and become nearly permanent parts of the countryside.

During growth, the left eye of the very young halibut drifts over the snout to the right side of its head.

HALIBUT The halibut, a member of the flounder family, ranks among the largest species of fish in the sea. This biggest of the flatfish has the plumpest, most elongated body of any flatfish. The largest undocumented specimen was an Atlantic halibut 12 feet long, weighing 700 pounds, live weight. One record Pacific halibut female measured 8 feet long and weighed 450 pounds, dressed weight. The Washington state record for a halibut caught by rod and reel, achieved in 1984, is 240 pounds. Although halibut don't leap from the water like game fish, their weight and strength test a sport fisherman's endurance. The average halibut caught today off the Northwest coast averages about 30 to 40 pounds, dressed weight. Females run much larger than males, who seldom exceed 80 pounds. Halibut are long-lived. The oldest female on record lived to be 42 years; the oldest male, 27.

Most flatfish are sedentary bottom dwellers, which swim by undulating their fins. By contrast, the halibut swims by moving its entire body and strong tail as it actively pursues squid, octopus, and crabs as large as 7 inches across, and such fish as cod, herring, skate, and flounder. Sharp teeth arm the powerful jaws of its rather large mouth.

◆ Female halibut reproduce at 12 years of age. A large one can lay nearly 3 million eggs. The eyes of a newly hatched halibut are normally placed, and its body is uniformly colored. But when the fish grows to 1 inch in length, the left eye begins to drift over the snout and ends up above the right eye. The left side then fades to a pearly white. Halibut resemble other flatfish in being able to change color on their right side—the upper side—to match the substrate. If the head rests on sand and the body on mud, the head will be pale and the body dark brown or black. The halibut's eyes control the color change; a blind halibut cannot change color. The eyes, which move independently, can see the area around the head very well.

Young halibut live inshore while small, swimming as any fish does. But when they are 6 months old and still less than 1 foot long, they come to rest in shallow waters on the ocean bottom, preferably on sand and always on the left side. After 1 to 3 years, they move to deeper waters. Mature halibut migrate seasonally from shallow water in the summer to deeper water in winter. They have been caught as deep as 3,600 feet on the continental shelf, although in summer most are hooked at 90 to 900 feet. Smaller halibut also migrate along the coast, traveling some 60 miles from summer to summer. A few swim great distances over a period of 3 to 5 years. One tagged halibut traveled 2,500 miles from the Aleutian Islands to Coos Bay, Oregon.

◆ Northwesterners have been catching Pacific halibut (*Hippoglossus stenolepsis*) for at least 2,750 years. Wooden halibut hooks of that age have been found at the ancient Makah fishing camp east of Neah Bay at the mouth of the Hoko River on Washington's Olympic Peninsula. Contemporary members of the Makah tribe recognized the hooks upon discovery, so similar are they to "circle hooks" long used by tribal fishermen and by commercial and sports fishermen today. The ancient hooks, perfectly preserved in riverbank mud, were made of steamed and bent wood, with the bone point still lashed on with wild cherry bark. Similar 500-year-old wooden hooks, equally well preserved, were among the first artifacts to wash out of the Ozette archeological site at Washington's Cape Alava. The catch of Makah Indians at Neah Bay in the late 1880s was 600,000 pounds annually.

Native halibut fishermen paddled long fishing canoes 20 miles out from the Olympic Peninsula, equipped with stone weights, a club for killing the fish, fishing line made of long, thin stipes of giant kelp or of twisted cedar bark, and springy wooden hooks. The hooks were sometimes as simple as crooked branches of red or yellow cedar or as elaborate as the V-shaped hardwood hooks whose shanks northern tribes carved with figures that had magical powers.

Stylized halibut, easily recognized by the two eyes on one side of the head, appeared on coastal Indian totem poles and paintings on the front of community houses. In some Indian myths, halibut swallow tribal fishermen along with their canoes and are cut open to release them alive. Undoubtedly some halibut canoes and their crews were lost. Even modern halibut fishermen who bring live halibut aboard small boats are sometimes maimed or killed by the thrashing of their powerful bodies. The cautious fisherman ties the fish to the boat.

♦ Commercial fishing off Washington's Cape Flattery began in 1888 with New England fishing vessels. At first large sailing vessels, and later, steam-powered vessels, carried as many as twelve dories, each manned by two men who fished by hand. By the 1920s hand fishing was replaced by longline gear from the decks of larger vessels, which could go farther to sea.

The Pacific halibut fishery is one of the more valuable commercial fisheries in North America, netting about $102 million annually. Oregon's most productive halibut fishing area is off Newport; Washington's is off the northernmost coast and in the Strait of Juan de Fuca. Each year the International Halibut Commission allocates 650,000 pounds, dressed weight, to the California-Oregon-Washington area, divided among tribal, sports, and commercial fishermen. The catch of British Columbia and Alaska fishermen accounts for most of the 67 million pounds of halibut legally caught along the Pacific Coast each year.

HERON The beautiful breeding plumage of the male coastal great blue heron (*Ardes herodius fannini*) is striking in both color and texture. A black crest of plumes sweeps back over the head, contrasting with longer white plumes accenting the lower throat and breast. Slate blue plumage on the back further enhances the dazzling display. During courtship the male holds the plumes erect and stretches out his neck.

Protests over the slaughter of herons and egrets for their breeding plumes, used on women's hats, resulted in the nation's first large conservation movement, which led to the 1918 federal Migratory Bird Treaty Act.

♦ The long-billed, long-necked, and long-legged heron, 52 inches tall, is the second tallest wading bird of the Northwest, second only to the greater sandhill crane, yet it weighs only 6 to 8 pounds. Unlike cranes, herons in flight double the neck back against the shoulders in an S-shaped curve.

♦ The heron, which lacks oil glands, has an unusual way of keeping its feathers water-repellent and free of slime. When the bird preens with its bill, it crumbles thick patches of special down located under breast and flank feathers. Then, using its flattened, serrated middle claw, the heron combs the powder through its feathers.

♦ The rather timid herons are solitary except when breeding and nesting. They often nest near urban areas in river basins and wetland areas. Spokane, Washington, boasts a heronry with nineteen breeding pairs along the Little Spokane River. All of the nests are in two large cottonwoods. At the south end of Lake Washington near Renton, some sixty-five breeding herons have built more than twenty nests in the cottonwoods on a 4-square-mile island that was once wetland but now has an artificial pond and a number of buildings. Portland, with two nesting areas near its downtown area, has named the great blue heron its official bird.

Portland, with two great blue heron nesting areas near its downtown section, has named the heron its official bird.

GREAT BLUE HERON

ICE WORM Ice worms (*Mesenchytraeus solifuga*) are true, segmented annelids that live in glacial ice or permanent snow. They live in coastal glaciers from Alaska in the north to Mount Rainier in the south. In Washington, just fifteen glaciers maintain the year-round internal temperature ice worms require. The worms, ⅖ to 1⅕ inches long and possibly Ice Age relics, were discovered in 1887 on Alaska's Muir Glacier.

♦ Ice worms can move through ice so hard an ice ax is needed to cut it. Lubricated by a film of water, the worms may slither along irregularities caused by melting at the boundaries of the large glacial ice crystals. The worm's optimum temperature, 32°F, is several degrees below the biological zero of most animals—the point at which body functions cease. Its entire life is spent in temperatures close to the freezing point of water. Even

The ice worm, which lives only in coastal Northwest glaciers as far south as Mount Rainier, can move through ice so hard an ice axe is needed to cut it.

the warmth of a human hand can disintegrate an ice worm, making research on them difficult.

♦ The worms avoid not only sunlight but bright moonlight, descending into the ice or its snow cover during the day and on moonlit nights. On cloudy nights they ascend to the surface to feed, crowding together in groups as large as 500 to each square meter, often in meltwater furrows containing much of their food—snow fleas, bacteria, diatoms, pollen grains, red algae, and fern spores. Ravens and rosy finches often feed on the worms. They pass winters deep in the snow-insulated ice, avoiding surface subzero weather.

LOON North America's highest concentration of wintering loons touches down in the San Juan Islands each fall and stays through spring. This group includes members of the two largest species, the 35-inch-long yellow-billed loon (*Gavia adamsii*) and the 32-inch-long common loon or great Northern diver (*G. immer*).

North America's highest concentration of wintering loons spends fall through spring in Washington's San Juan Islands.

Despite their abundance in saltwater areas during the winter, few loons now breed in coastal Washington lakes. More plentiful in inland lakes during the summer, especially in Idaho and Montana, loons may soon be listed as a threatened species in Washington. Loons often winter off the Oregon coast at Yaquina Head and at other favorite seabird haunts.

♦ The loon is one of the few birds that divide their time between salt water and freshwater, normally nesting on northern lakes but wintering or pausing during migration on salt water. Their winter plumage is drab, very unlike their spectacular white-on-black breeding plumage.

♦ Anatomically, loons rate as the most primitive of all birds, belonging to an ancient family of divers that evolved 50 million years ago. Loon fossils found from the last Ice Age are almost identical to today's loons.

♦ The heavy loon, with a body up to 3 feet long weighing some 15 pounds, is very poorly adapted to land and air. In contrast with the light, hollow bones of most flying birds, the loon's bones are solid. Moreover, body skin almost completely encases the loon's legs, nearly down to the ankles, and its webbed feet and legs, set very far back on the body, make moving on water easy but moving on land an ordeal. Walking is almost impossible for the loon; achieving the running start necessary for a takeoff on land is totally impossible. Loons rarely fly or go ashore, except to their nests, which are built so near the edge of the water that the loon can slide back in the water on its belly. If disturbed on the nest, the loon slips into the water and submerges, surfacing far from the nest to hide its location.

Even when taking off on water, most loon species must taxi for perhaps 100 yards before becoming airborne. A loon landing is a true spectacle. Wings beating rapidly, it comes in at a steep angle, dragging its lowered feet in the water as a brake, often skidding a long distance on its breast, throwing up spray on both sides. Once in the air, however, the loon is a strong and fast, though graceless, flyer, which can reach speeds of 60 miles an hour. Hovering and flying at slow speeds are impossible for the heavy bird.

◆ Loons rank as one of the best underwater swimmers of all birds. They are unique in being able to submerge only partially, leaving just the head and neck above water, thus decreasing their visibility when danger threatens. Loons dive effortlessly and smoothly, expelling air quickly from body and plumage, sometimes descending to 200 feet in pursuit of fish. They can submerge so quietly that not a ripple stirs the water. Underwater, they swim only with their legs, using their wings as stabilizers.

◆ The cries of the common and yellow-billed loon, heard only in breeding season, are often considered the most complex, prolonged, and haunting of any bird. The special cry of the male warning against potential aggressors is even longer, more complex, and has a wider frequency range than any of the other calls.

LYNX The Canada lynx (*Lynx canadensis*), a solitary, nocturnal relative of the bobcat, lives in high, remote lodgepole forest areas of the Northwest. The largest population of lynx in the Lower 48 resides in the Okanogan National Forest in northeastern Washington. Lynx also find suitable habitat in Montana's Glacier National Park.

The Canada lynx, which lives primarily in northeastern Washington, is the only North American cat adapted to hunting in snow.

◆ The lynx, the North American cat best adapted to hunting prey in snow, ranks as the most efficient predator on snow. In the winter heavy pads of fur grow on its outsized paws, which are twice as large as those of the bobcat. These heavy pads insulate and support the paws in soft snow, allowing the lynx to move quickly. Just 2 feet high at the shoulder and weighing only 20 pounds, the lynx looks larger because of its dense fur, huge feet, and fairly long legs—which also aid its movement in deep snow. Huge tracks separated by long strides give away the presence of this seldom-glimpsed cat. The lynx has distinctive pointed tufts of hair at the ear tips and a ruff of hair around the face.

◆ Canada lynx have evolved into predators largely dependent on a single prey species, the snowshoe hare. As a result, population cycles of lynx and hare correspond closely. When snowshoe hares are plentiful, they make up more than 80 percent of the lynx diet, and the lynx population soars. When hares are scarce, the lynx reproduction rate and population plummet. During such periods of scarcity, the lynx may travel up to 400 miles hunting for hares or may even kill snowbound deer, birds, and small mammals.

CANADA LYNX

On both snow and bare ground, the lynx hunts the snowshoe hare by alternately freezing and waiting for the hare to make a dash for safety, then rushing after it with bounds of 6 to 10 feet. Since lynx and hare are equally fast, the lynx often fails to make the kill and at times will give up the pursuit after 50 yards. (See Snowshoe Hare.)

◆ The only lynx predator, the human, hunts them for their soft, dense fur with long, silky hairs. Very curious, like all cats, lynx can be caught in traps baited with bright cloth, aluminum, or even Christmas tree ornaments.

◆ Northwesterners who have heard the loud yowling of the male lynx during breeding season describe it as one of the eeriest sounds in the wilderness. Despite the horrible screams accompanying male quarrels, Canada lynx, to judge from their generally scar-free pelts, are more aggressive verbally than physically.

MARINE LIFE Pacific Northwest waters—especially the Strait of Juan de Fuca, the water surrounding the San Juan Islands, parts of Puget Sound, and the outer coast—closely rival the richest waters in the world in diversity of marine animal genera, large size of individuals, and numbers of organisms. Northwest waters contain as many genera as do tropical waters.

Pacific Northwest waters support some of the world's largest and most diverse populations of marine life.

The diversity of species results from the diversity of Pacific Northwest shoreline habitat. Washington's long, irregular saltwater coastline, including that of Puget Sound and the Strait of Juan de Fuca, provides a great variety of habitat for marine organisms: rocky shores, tide pools, quiet bays, estuaries, sandy beaches, and muddy inlets. Rocky tideflats of the protected coast host the greatest variety of animals, which hide in crevices, cling to and under rocks, and blanket every suitable square inch. Organisms attach to rocks, seaweeds, and each other. Mussel beds seethe with the activity of thousands of tiny animals living in spaces between the mussels or upon the mussel shells.

Even Northwest sand is densely populated by bivalves, crustaceans, amphipods, egg cases of marine animals, insects, and worms. Mud flats, especially those flourishing with sea grasses, host dozens of species of marine animals.

♦ Puget Sound is one of the world's most fertile saltwater areas for plankton—the microscopic animals and plants that produce 90 percent of all marine plant and animal tissue in the world's oceans. Runoff from a number of large rivers brings copious amounts of nutrients into the Sound, and the action of tidal currents stirs up sediments from the ocean bottom in a strong upwelling that brings deep, cold water rich in decaying plant and animal matter toward the surface.

Tidal currents in Puget Sound, where tides can reach 15 feet, sweep nutrients past filter feeders such as clams, mussels, and oysters, which strain food from the water, trapping particles on mucus-covered gills. Those same currents disperse vast numbers of marine larvae over large areas, providing food for larger animals. As a result of this tidal action, Northwest marine animal species often grow much larger than their tropical counterparts.

Puget Sound marine life ranks so high among marine biologists that researchers have been coming to the Northwest since at least 1859, when naturalist Louis Agassiz studied local jellyfish. A complex of marine laboratories located near Friday Harbor on San Juan Island, established by the University of Washington in 1904, draws more than 100 researchers from all over the world each year to study marine animals in their natural habitats.

♦ Neah Bay, at the most westerly point on the Strait of Juan de Fuca, abounds in diverse underwater life: huge red sea urchins, fish-eating sea anemones, pink coralline algae, white plumose anemones more than 2 feet high, and giant kelp.

♦ Washington and Oregon display some of the richest tide pools on the Pacific Coast, with those in Oregon usually more accessible. At minus tides on the outer coast, these natural aquariums display sponges, nudibranchs, starfish, sea cucumbers, tube worms, sea anemones, shrimps, sea urchins, periwinkles, small rock crabs, hydroids, an occasional jellyfish, and such clingers as limpets, chitons, barnacles, and snails. Oregon's Yaquina Head boasts a tide pool area so rich in marine animals that it has been designated a state marine garden.

MARMOT The Olympic marmot (*Marmota olympus*) lives in the high country of Olympic National Park and is the only marmot species in the Olympic Mountains. Believed to have been isolated by Ice Age glaciers, this marmot species may be an offshoot of an earlier North American alpine form of hoary marmot (*M. caligata*). The hoary marmot, largest of North American marmots, lives in the Cascades and Rockies at

During the marmot's hibernation, its heart rate slows from four beats a second to only four beats a minute.

elevations below 8,000 feet.

◆ Olympic and hoary marmots are the most sociable and playful of all marmot species. Each morning the marmots go from burrow to burrow, greeting other colony members. Their highly developed greeting system involves rubbing noses and cheeks (where there are scent glands), touching mouths, and nibbling on neck and ears.

◆ Marmots, the largest members of the squirrel family, can weigh as much as 18 pounds. Plump with fat stored for winter hibernation, a marmot offers a tempting meal for bears and golden eagles as it browses in an alpine meadow for food or sunbathes on a rock. Marmots protect themselves by building extensive burrow systems that may cover 5 acres with tunnels, many of them interconnected. They also dig many short escape burrows with single entrances.

◆ Olympic and hoary marmots have one of the lowest reproduction rates of all rodents—only six to eighteen young in seven years.

◆ The marmot undergoes the most complete hibernation of any animal. Lying curled in the burrow, its body temperature drops nearly as low as the ambient temperature, its blood pressure falls, its brain partly closes down, and its heart slows from the usual four beats a second to only four beats a minute. This state lasts for eight or nine months. However, during some winters unseasonable warmth melts the snow insulating the burrows, and the cold kills the young marmots, which lack adequate stored fat to survive.

In the spring, recovery from hibernation takes only two hours. Then the marmots begin digging for food, sometimes through snow several feet deep, eating any shoots they can find. They will also eat grubs and even other hibernating rodents.

MOLE The world's smallest mole, the shrew-mole (*Neurotrichus gibbsi*), lives only in the Northwest. A mere 2¼ to 4½ inches long, including its short tail, the adult shrew-mole may weigh no more than ⅔ of an ounce. The shrew-mole and the mountain beaver are the two Northwest specimens most frequently sought by museums in other parts of the country.

A mere 2¼ to 4½ inches long, the tiny shrew-mole—unique to the Northwest—is the world's smallest mole.

This insectivore, although it resembles a small shrew, is a true mole. However, it is less specialized for subterranean life than are larger moles and spends more time above ground than they do. It prefers cloudy days and moist, shaded ravines with soft soil. The shrew-mole forages for earthworms in leaf litter and mold, and nests in rotting stumps and wood. The shrew-mole's front paws resemble, in miniature, the digging hands of the huge Townsend's mole, but the shrew-mole, unlike the larger mole, swims, climbs, and moves around on the surface with ease.

The shrew-mole, like the shrew, has one of the highest metabolism rates of all animals. Day and night, seldom resting, the shrew-mole searches for food, doomed to die if it fails to find food after more than 12 hours.

TOWNSEND'S MOLE

◆ Townsend's mole (*Scapanus townsendi*), North America's largest mole, lives only in the Northwest and northwestern California. The mole population is especially abundant in moist coastal areas of Washington and in Oregon's fertile Willamette Valley. The giant can grow as long as 9 inches, plus a 2-inch tail.

Although few Townsend's moles are found in home lawns and gardens in the Northwest, the huge mole is a serious pest in farm-lands, especially in the Willamette Valley. During the rainy season a single mole can create as many as 500 mounds that are 1 foot across and spaced every 3 feet. In spring, a male searching for a mate can bulldoze soft dirt at the rate of 50 yards an hour.

◆ Moles are some of the animal world's most talented engineers. They easily repair collapsed roofs and outwit trappers by digging detours around traps. Their tunnels, especially those dug in clay soil, can last for many generations of moles.

◆ Equipped with powerful muscles and huge, shovel-like forepaws armed with long claws, moles almost breaststroke their way through soft dirt. The mole's streamlined body, which lacks hips and external ears, is covered with velvety fur without a "set," a characteristic that allows the animal to reverse direction easily in its tunnels.

◆ Moles are among the most ferocious of small mammals, fiercely independent except for a brief mating season. Viciously antisocial, they will, if caged together, try to kill each other.

◆ Moles are unusual among mammals in maintaining living caches of food. They catch and store huge numbers of earthworms over the winter, disabling each with a nip so that it cannot escape. Actively hunting food all year long, moles work their burrow feeding grounds at roughly four-hour intervals, requiring rest between each food search even when they have found no food. Seldom above ground, the nearly blind mole, whose barely visible eyes are overhung with skin and fur, may poke its head out in the spring to hunt for nearby nesting material.

MOON SNAIL The world's largest species of moon snail (*Polinices lewisii*) commonly inhabits protected sandy mud flats and beaches in the Northwest wherever there are clams.

Moon snails kill their favorite prey, clams, by drilling a hole in the shell and sucking out the tissue.

Voracious feeders, the snails are seldom seen because they spend most of their time 1 to 12 inches under the surface searching for clams. The snail moves easily through muddy sand. Its strong, rounded shell, 4 to 6 inches long, has one main whorl and several small ones. Its huge fleshy foot, filled with water, extends far beyond the shell to stir up the sand. When the snail must retract its foot to close the shell opening, it quickly drains that water, shrinking the foot.

This most efficient burrower of all Northwest gastropods has a keen sense of smell. It kills clams, mussels, and other snails by drilling a hole in their shells with its rasping tongue and sucking out the tissue, or it may enfold the clam with its foot, blocking the siphon to suffocate the clam. Then it can easily open the shell.

◆ Pacific Northwest beach visitors often see the moon snail's durable egg case, or sand collar, stranded at low tide without knowing what it is. The circular egg case, described as resembling a doll's shoulder cape or a rubber plunger, may measure 6 inches across and 3½ inches high. Between two folds of its foot, the snail secretes a gelatinous sheet embedded with eggs the size of sand grains. Mucus and sand cement the eggs into a rubbery mass with sandpapery texture. Left on the sand, the egg case withstands wave action until the larvae hatch, at which point it disintegrates and the larvae wash into the sea.

MOUNTAIN BEAVER Lewis and Clark were the first to describe the mountain beaver (*Aplodontia rufa*), which lives only in the Northwest and northern California. The mountain beaver is the only survivor of an ancient family (known from its fossil record to have consisted of at least thirty species) that evolved before the families of modern rodents such as squirrels and mice. The mountain beaver has changed little during 60 million years on earth.

The mountain beaver, the most primitive of living rodents, digs tunnel complexes up to 5 feet deep, often destablilizing the ground above.

The shy, nocturnal animals reside in Oregon and Washington on moist, brushy Cascade slopes at elevations as high as 9,000 feet and in moist, lowland valleys and ravines with easy-to-dig soil and a source of water. Their primitive kidneys require them to drink a great deal of water.

◆ Despite its name, the mountain beaver is neither beaver nor exclusively a mountain dweller; in appearance it resembles a tailless muskrat. It displays some beaverlike habits, however, such as diverting streams into its tunnels, gnawing bark from trees, and nipping off small trees.

◆ The mountain beaver is one of the worst garden pests in the moist uplands of the Northwest. In addition to fern sprouts, seedlings, skunk cabbage, and devil's club, it relishes delicacies such as roses, rhododendrons, and domesticated vegetables, standing upright to nip them off or climbing to feed on trees.

◆ Slow moving and thus an easy prey, mountain beavers spend most of their time underground, often tunneling to their food. They seldom stray farther than 100 feet from their extensive burrows. Rather than eating in the open, where a weasel or skunk might surprise them, mountain beavers often pull plants, roots and all, into their tunnels.

Mountain beavers burrow year-round. A tunnel is about 6 inches in diameter, but an entire complex can be 5 feet deep, with special rooms for nesting, winter food storage, feces, and garbage. Farmers dislike the animals because their tunnels often undermine the soil so that it collapses.

MOUNT ST. HELENS ANIMAL LIFE A surprising number of animals survived or quickly returned to the area surrounding Washington's Mount St. Helens after the volcano's 1980 eruption. More than three-fourths of all the small mammal species and most of the reptiles and amphibians known to have lived there before the eruption soon reestablished themselves.

Many of the animals, such as hibernating colonies of ants, termites, weasels, and pocket gophers, were protected underground. The gophers aided the regrowth of vegetation by pushing mounds of rich soil from their burrows onto the sterile ash. Some frogs and salamanders bred a few months after the eruption. Flying insects and spiders returned quickly, often becoming prey for the surviving animals. Birds with varied diets, such as dark-eyed juncos, were soon back, but woodpeckers, with their specialized needs, have not yet returned.

Plant-eating animals fed on islands of surviving vegetation. Despite the lack of forest cover, Roosevelt elk and deer returned, browsing on thousands of newly planted tree seedlings. Salmon, which again spawned in the area's rivers and streams, proved unexpectedly tolerant of suspended sediment.

◆ Bacteria found on the lava dome in Mount St. Helen's crater, where temperatures reached 212°F, have strengthened the theory that submarine volcanic hot springs reacting with minerals and metals in the ocean produced the earth's first living microorganisms.

MOUSE The red tree mouse (*Phenacomys longicaudus*) has the most unusual habitat and diet of any Northwest mouse. It lives high in fir trees in coastal Oregon and extreme southwestern

More than three-fourths of the small mammal species and most of the reptiles and amphibians that originally lived around Mount St. Helens reestablished themselves soon after the 1980 eruption.

The red tree mouse lives high in fir trees, existing on a diet of conifer needles and seldom descending to the ground.

Washington, seldom descending to the ground. The small, sure-footed rodent moves slowly along branches, balancing with a 3-inch-long tail that makes up more than half its total length.

This arboreal mouse eats only conifer needles, saving the resin ducts and midribs for the nest in which it gives birth. Compared to other mice, the red mouse has a longer gestation period, much smaller litters (one to three), and slower development of its young—perhaps as a result of poor diet.

NESTS Bald eagles, one of the glories of the Northwest, build the largest nests of any bird. A world record eagle's nest measured almost 9½ feet across and 20 feet deep. Eagles have occupied some nests for more than forty years; however, in some cases a pair may use more than one nest in a season. Since young eagles continue to return to the nest even after they can fly—the parents chase them away at the end of summer—the nests eventually are trampled flat, requiring the addition the following year of another wall 1 foot high. With eagles adding to their already huge stick nests each year—at times using such novelties as a stalk of corn with ears still on it—a nest can weigh as much as a ton, heavy enough to break down a tree. (See Eagle.)

Bald eagles build the largest nests of any bird in the world, the great blue heron builds perhaps the sloppiest, and the water ouzel builds one of the neatest.

♦ Great blue herons build some of the sloppiest nests of all Northwest birds. Their often-reused nests, built 40 to 100 feet high in trees or snags, are crude stick platforms. A single tree may hold 100 nests, each more than 2 feet deep and 3 feet in diameter. Added to year after year, the poorly built nests become so heavy they can topple during a storm. (See Heron.)

♦ The bulky, 2-foot-deep stick nest of the osprey, often built in dead trees near good fishing lakes and reservoirs in the Northwest, can grow to be 5 feet across. Each year the male repairs the nest with long sticks of driftwood or dead branches from small trees, lugging the material to the nest, wings pumping hard, and then interweaving it into the nest. Some of their nests are nicely symmetrical. (See Osprey.)

♦ John Muir described the water ouzel's nest as one of the most extraordinary pieces of bird architecture he had ever seen. The small bird so often seen bobbing on rocks in Northwest mountain streams plucks mosses from streamside rocks and logs and weaves them together into a domed nest about a foot in diameter, with an arched entrance near the bottom. Because water ouzel nests are always built very near water, even within misting distance of waterfalls, spray helps keep the outer moss fresh and green. As Muir wrote, the nest "appears to be a moss cushion growing naturally." (See Water Ouzel.)

◆ More than a dozen 6-foot-wide nests of *hadrosaurs*, duck-billed dinosaurs that lived 80 million years ago, were discovered in 1978 on Montana's Egg Mountain near Choteau. This discovery altered the once-accepted view that dinosaurs did not take care of their young. The nests contained fossilized skeletons of baby dinosaurs and eggs, mixed with bones of grown dinosaurs. Later, near the same area, fossils of hundreds of eggs, rare embryos, babies, and juveniles were found at the nesting grounds of a newly discovered dinosaur, *Maiasaura,* which lived in herds of thousands. The teeth of some of the juveniles showed wear, suggesting that the parents brought food to the nest for months after the babies hatched.

NUDIBRANCH Northwest waters are awash in nudibranchs, also known as sea slugs. Nearly fifty different species live in area waters. Most are small and delicate, with elongated bodies that flatten into a broad foot. Branched or plumed projections called *cerata* protrude from the sides and back, possibly acting as gills for breathing.

Two of the world's largest nudibranchs, each measuring a foot or more in length, live in Northwest waters.

◆ The nudibranch's beauty of form, with dorsal outgrowths shaped like wings, frills, plumes, and ruffles, is enhanced by brilliant color. The often-translucent nudibranch may be colored lemon yellow, pale blue, red, gold, or violet, and its *cerata* are often edged or tipped with color. The pure white body of Oregon's *Triopha carpenteri* is adorned with brilliant orange *cerata.* The sea lemon (*Anisodoris nobilis*) is yellow with white gill plumes and two thick tentacles which it withdraws when touched. Its rough body, textured like lemon peel, erupts with warty tubercles.

The opalescent nudibranch (*Hermissenda crassicornis*), one of the most common Northwest nudibranchs, is also one of the most beautiful. Highly variable in color of body and plumes, the tiny nudibranch, 1 to 2 inches long and ½ inch wide, often has bright orange *cerata* springing lushly from its back. Pale blue lines edge its body. When courting, these tiny inhabitants of tide pools, eelgrass, and rocks mouth and bite each other, and sometimes the larger one eats the smaller.

ORANGE PEEL
NUDIBRANCH

◆ Two of the world's largest nudibranchs inhabit Northwest waters. One of the giants, the broad, foot-long orange peel nudibranch (*Tochuina tetraquestra*), has short, white gills fringing an oblong, orange-colored body covered with knobby growths. The other, the spectacular rainbow nudibranch (*Dendronotus iris*), measures 1 foot long and 3 inches wide. Along its back are two rows of pointed gills, tipped with white or purple. One of a few nudibranchs able to swim, it moves by folding the edges of its foot together lengthwise and gracefully flexing its body. Other nudibranchs crawl on their muscular foot, moving up eelgrass and seaweeds, and across tide pool rocks. Most can suspend themselves in the water, using mucus threads secreted by the foot.

◆ Although lacking a shell, nudibranchs are not defenseless. Predators often find brightly colored ones unpalatable because of unsavory secretions. The almost nauseating fruity odor of some nudibranchs deters predators. Others, like the opalescent nudibranch, are believed to convert into weapons the stinging cells of corals, hydroids, and jellyfishes on which they feed, ejecting into a predator the undigested, untriggered stinging cells they have stored in the *cerata.* Some nudibranchs live on specific hosts and camouflage themselves accordingly. For example, the *Rostanga pulchra,* which lives on a red sponge, exactly matches the color of its host; even its egg coils are red.

The world's largest octopus, weighing as much as 100 pounds with an arm spread of 16 feet, lives in Northwest waters, especially in Puget Sound.

OCTOPUS The world's largest octopus (*Octopus dofleini*) thrives in frigid Pacific Northwest waters, particularly in Puget Sound, where it feeds on the abundant crabs. Commercial fishermen sometimes catch giants weighing more than 100 pounds, with an arm spread of 16 feet. In 1973 an octopus weighing 118 pounds, 10 ounces, with a relaxed radial spread of 23 feet, was caught in lower Hood Canal. Another giant, estimated to weigh 300 pounds, was pulled to a boat by a fisherman using a set-line after the octopus had eaten three dogfish from the line. Since the octopus was too large to hoist aboard without damage, the fisherman let it go. In contrast, one Puget Sound octopus is small enough to hide in a beer bottle.

◆ The octopus and the squid are the most active mollusks and have the most highly developed brains, eyes, and nervous systems of any of the mollusks. Nocturnal, shy, intelligent, and curious, the octopus is seldom seen in open water. It holes up in dark caves or rocky crannies, covering the opening with stones or debris. (See Squid.)

With its strong, sensitive, suckered arms, it feels for food, perhaps inserting an arm into a cranny. Or it may dart out to seize a fish or passing crab. It kills by first injecting a paralyzing toxin and then biting the prey with its horny beak. Although the octopus can travel by jet propulsion when necessary, shooting backward with arms streamlined in front, it tires quickly, preferring to move along the bottom using its arms. Occasionally an octopus crawls onto a beach in search of crabs.

◆ The Puget Sound octopus (*O. dofleini*) is a master at changing body color rapidly and at will, producing endless patterns: stripes, blotches, or one solid color. Red expresses agitation.

◆ The female octopus spends more time caring for her eggs than does any other mollusk. She lays eggs only once, when she is about 3 years old. The male dies soon after fertilizing the eggs. The female attaches her 50,000 rice-sized eggs to the ceiling of an aquatic cave and spends the next 6 months caring for them, scarcely eating even when she is offered food. Using nozzlelike funnels on the sides of her head, she blows debris away from the eggs and sprays clean water over them, also cleaning them with her tentacle tips. Soon after they hatch, she dies.

ORCA The Northwest's popular orca, or killer whale (*Orcinus orca*), rates as the largest of the true dolphins; they can grow to be 25 feet long and weigh as much as 6 tons. Orcas are among the fastest mammals in the sea, capable of brief spurts at more than 34.5 miles an hour.

Three pods of orcas, perhaps the most intensively studied killer whale population in the world, inhabit the waters of Puget Sound and the San Juan Islands.

◆ Three pods of orcas totaling eighty-three individuals reside in Puget Sound; four calves were born during 1989 and 1990. In winter and spring, the three pods remain separate. In their search for food during that time, they cover about 100 miles a day, extending their feeding range to the tidal area near Vancouver Island and out into the Pacific. In summer and fall, the pods unite to follow the nation's largest sockeye salmon run, working together to herd the salmon. Often they synchronize their movements, all coming up for air at the same time. Members of the three pods hunt and travel together; they also interbreed. Each pod uses calls shared with other pods as well as distinctive calls restricted to pod members. Transient orcas, which travel in smaller pods of three to five animals, are far less vocal than the resident orcas when inside Puget Sound, perhaps so they do not alert the marine mammals on which they feed.

Puget Sound's resident orcas make up the most intensively studied killer whale population in the world. The nation's only park for whale watching and study, Lime Kiln Whale Watch Park, was established in 1984 at Lime Kiln Point on San Juan Island. It is located along the regular route these resident orcas swim in summer while following salmon along the southwest coast of the island. The park is one of the few places in the nation where scientists can study the same group of orcas year-round, and where Northwest viewers can see them with predictable regularity.

◆ Although usually gentle with humans, compassionate with its own kind, highly social, intelligent, playful, and articulate, the killer whale—which has no natural enemies—is one of the most formidable of all marine predators. The voracious, sharp-toothed orcas differ from other cetaceans in having teeth in both upper and lower jaws. Killer whales are the only cetaceans that eat other cetaceans and marine mammals. Although the three resident pods of orcas in Puget Sound feed primarily on salmon, transient orcas passing through Puget Sound eat seals and other marine mammals. In the open ocean, orcas, unlike whales, travel side by side in precisely ordered packs, attacking whales many times their size.

A photographer once filmed a pack of thirty orcas attacking a young 60-foot blue whale. The orcas efficiently divided up the labor: some tried to cover the blue whale's blowhole, while others prevented its escape by herding on both sides, above, and below. After crippling the whale by chewing off its dorsal fin and shredding its tail flukes, the orcas stripped away chunks of flesh and blubber. Orcas will also chew a whale's lips, force open its snout, and tear out the tongue.

♦ The orca birthrate is extremely low for a social animal. Because a mature female may give birth only once every ten years, the four births in two years among the Puget Sound pods were rare events. Mortality is low, except during the first year of life. A slight increase in the birthrate has been observed after the capture of a pod member. Pods are believed to stay together permanently, each a close family group. The orca female can live to be about 100 years old; the male lives to around 50.

OSPREY The osprey (*Pandion haliaetus*), the only raptor in North America that dives into the water after live fish, is one of the most efficient of all Northwest birds of prey. The sharp-eyed bird, a powerful flyer with a 6-foot wingspan, flies and glides high above rivers, lakes, and reservoirs, watching for a shadow or movement in the water that might indicate a fish. The osprey may hover briefly before beginning a high-speed but controlled dive, often from heights of 80 to 100 feet. Near the water, the bird makes last-minute wing adjustments so that its flared legs and talons enter the water first, often with a great splash. The osprey may even submerge briefly, a maneuver for which its wings are specially adapted. Useful in securing its slippery catch are the bird's long, sharp talons, reversible toes, and spiny knobs on the bottoms of the feet. More than half of the time, it emerges with a fish in its talons, shaking off water as it flies away. Occasionally a bald eagle, the osprey's only natural enemy, harasses the osprey into dropping its catch, which the eagle then snatches in midair.

Diving from heights of 80 to 100 feet, the osprey can capture live fish in a single, high-speed swoop.

♦ Oregon has one of the largest nesting populations of ospreys in the Northwest. Birds nest in Deschutes National Forest, especially at Crane Prairie Reservoir Osprey Management Area; along the Deschutes River (more than 100 pairs); and near high country lakes. In Idaho, annual flooding where the St. Joe River flows into Lake Coeur d'Alene killed many large trees, now used by nesting ospreys. Baker Lakes Recreation Area hosts Washington's largest flock—twenty-two adults. Ospreys will build nests on artificial nesting platforms; installation of eleven of the high platforms along Oregon's Umpqua River increased the osprey nesting population there by 50 percent in five years. (See also Nests.)

OWLS The importance of the northern spotted owl (*Strix occidentalis caurina*) as an environmental symbol overshadows its intrinsic interest as a creature with 60 million years of lineage.

Modestly sized—16 to 19 inches high with a wingspan of 12 to 13 inches—the northern spotted owl is one of the "earless" owls, with a rounded head that lacks ear tufts. Its common name refers to the spots of white on its dark brown upperparts, as well as its whitish underparts, which are spotted with brown.

The hoot of the northern spotted owl can sound like the bark of a small dog.

The spotted owl's distinctive, high-pitched hoot, a series of three or four "hoos," resembles the sound of a small dog barking. Owl language is complex, with a dot-dash quality as monosyllabic hoots combine with drawn-out "phrases." Sometimes the owl voice is almost human, its sounds resembling coughs or wild laughter. Owls, such as the spotted owl, that hunt in the darkness of dense forests are much more vocal than those that live in open habitats. They call out frequently to keep in touch with mates, especially when danger threatens. Owl mating rituals are more vocal than visual.

The spotted owl's eyes are unusual in being dark. All other owls have yellow eyes except for the barn owl. Although an owl's eyes are fixed in their sockets, the owl can swivel its head with remarkable speed to extend its field of vision. Owl vision is 35 to 100 times more sensitive to light than that of humans, an obvious advantage for a nocturnal hunter in dark forests.

Owls also possess keen hearing, with an unusually large number of nerve cells in the brain area dedicated to hearing. The spotted owl is believed to hunt almost entirely by sound. The slightest rustling enables it to pinpoint the position of a mouse, young rabbit, or chipmunk. Its soft feathers and a loose fringe at the leading edge of its wings silence an owl's flight, enabling it to pounce unannounced on prey. Aeronautical engineers have reduced the noise of jet engines by studying the special construction of owl flight feathers with their extremely narrow outer vanes and adapting their designs accordingly.

♦ Each pair of spotted owls requires several thousand acres of habitat for hunting, much more than is provided by the fragmented islands of forest left in clear cuts as token but inadequate refuges. As owl groups become more and more isolated from each other by clear cuts in private and state-owned old-growth forests, their breeding opportunities decrease. The spotted owl reproductive rate, never high, is also linked to the availability of small rodents and mammals, whose populations can fluctuate sharply.

Owls breed less frequently when food is scarce, not at all in some lean years. Owl eggs hatch over a period of as much as two weeks, so that less food is needed for voracious owlets at one time. But when food is scarce, the older owlets are fed first; the younger birds often die. Even juvenile spotted owls surviving the first weeks can starve to death for lack of hunting habitat.

It is estimated that there are only 3,000 northern spotted owls in the old-growth forests that range from Washington to northern California. The spotted owl population problem of low reproductive rate combined with steady loss of habitat was worsened by the practice of designating as spotted owl nesting sites some areas that totally lacked spotted owls.

♦ The Northwest's burrowing owl (*Speotyto cunicularia*) behaves in a most unowllike manner. The small bird, 9 inches long, nests and raises its young in burrows in Northwest prairies, deserts, and farms, often taking over an abandoned burrow. Digging with its talons, it enlarges its recycled home, creating a sharp bend to protect the nest at the end.

BURROWING OWL

So terrestrial has this owl become that it is almost flightless. When disturbed, it flattens itself against the ground rather than flying. Unlike most owls, it is active during the day, although it may also hunt at night. It is agile and at ease walking on the ground; when perching on the ground or on fence posts, it often bobs like the water ouzel. The burrowing owl catches large beetles and grasshoppers in the air with its talons. It pounces upon larger prey, such as mice, ground squirrels, or newly fledged birds, gripping them in the back with its talons and pecking the neck.

OYSTER The world's smallest edible oyster—and one of the world's rarest bivalves—is the native Northwest Olympia oyster (*Ostrea lurida*), only 2 inches long, 2 inches wide, and ¾ of an inch thick. Many gourmets consider the thin-shelled oysters, brought back from near-extinction in 1983, the world's best in flavor.

Once naturally plentiful all along the Pacific Coast, these small oysters are now grown commercially, primarily in southern Puget Sound. Oysters were long harvested and dried by native Americans and were a valued trading item. Native people told two pioneers about the oysters in Willapa Bay in 1850 and soon bitter oyster wars were under way, with the oysters exploited for San Francisco's gold rush trade. In 1853 sailing ships carried 21,000 bushels of Olympia oysters to San Francisco.

The world's smallest edible oyster—and one of the most delectable—is the native Northwest Olympia oyster, harvested primarily in southern Puget Sound.

Overharvesting ended the Northwest oyster boom around 1875. The nearly fatal blow came with the opening of a pulp mill in Shelton in the 1920s. By the time the mill closed, sulfite wastes had so polluted the bay that nearly twenty-five years passed before the tiny oysters began to reproduce well again. Today they are once again threatened by pollution.

◆ Washington produces more than 90 percent of the total West Coast harvest of the large Pacific oyster (*O. gigas*). Shallow Willapa Bay contains the nation's largest oyster beds.

◆ Coast Oyster Company's hatchery in Quilcene, Washington, is the largest in the world, growing oysters to maturity in Quilcene Bay and shipping oyster seed all over the United States. The company ships oyster seed to the Chesapeake Bay area in the Northeast, where pollution has almost destroyed the once-prolific oyster industry.

PADDLEFISH Montana's most ancient and bizarre fish, the paddlefish (*Polyodon spathula*), is even more archaic than the sturgeon. Fossils show that this contemporary of the dinosaurs has changed very little in 65 million years. The only other paddlefish species lives in the Yangtze River in China.

Fossil records show that Montana's ancient paddlefish, whose 2-foot-long snout is shaped like a paddle, has changed little in 65 million years.

In front of the paddlefish's mouth extends a 2-foot-long snout shaped like a paddle. Despite its apparent suitability for digging in the mud for food, the very sensitive paddle is not used for this purpose. Rather, the fish feeds by swimming with its toothless mouth open, sucking in water containing small crustaceans and tiny planktonic organisms, which are filtered out by its comblike gill-rakers.

Like the shark and sturgeon, Montana's paddlefish has a cartilage skeleton and notochord, a structure replaced by a backbone in higher animals. Its rough-skinned body retains only traces of primitive scales on the upper tail lobe. Slow growing, paddlefish may live for fifty years, growing to 6 feet and averaging 40 or 50 pounds. (See also Fossils.)

Phalaropes, members of the sandpiper family, may spend months at sea, sometimes perching on whales and feeding off their parasites.

PHALAROPE Many phalarope species, members of the sandpiper family, spend more time at sea over the northern Pacific than any other Northwest wading bird. Phalaropes fly inland in the Northwest mainly to breed in freshwater, but also to follow schools of fish, or to avoid persistent westerly gales. The red phalarope (*Phalaropus fulicaria*) may spend months over the Pacific, sometimes perching on whales to feed off parasites. Special adaptations, such as broadened, lobed toes slightly webbed at the base, and breasts, bellies, and underparts that are densely feathered for buoyancy and insulation, aid their ability to swim and feed on water.

♦ The red-necked phalarope (*P. lobatus*) and Wilson's phalarope (*P. tricolor*) display an unusual sex role reversal. The females flaunt larger and more colorful plumage than the male, with bright, rusty markings during breeding season. The female chooses her mate, courts him, and defends the territory, driving off other females. She does not develop brood patches and she secretes a high concentration of testosterone.

The female leaves the breeding ground before her eggs hatch, and the male takes over, incubating the eggs and feeding the young. Males, which do not fight with each other, lure away predators with typically female distraction displays. Their drab plumage is an advantage for nest-tending.

Wilson's phalarope, often seen at brackish lagoons and even at farm ponds in the San Juan Islands, displays unusual behavior in another area. It sometimes traps aquatic insect larvae by creating a vortex in the water with its rapidly moving feet, spinning around some sixty times a minute.

The pronghorn antelope, which lives primarily in the Northwest, can outrun a cheetah for distances over 1,000 yards.

PRONGHORN ANTELOPE A true native of North America, and living nowhere else, the graceful pronghorn antelope (*Antilocapra americana*) ranks as the Northwest's fastest land animal. Over a sustained distance, it is the fastest in the world, outrunning the cheetah when racing more than 1,000 yards. Aided by large heart and lungs and padded hoofs that protect against rocky ground, the pronghorn can accelerate almost instantly, cruise at more than 35 miles an hour, maintain 60 miles an hour for half a mile, and reach 70 miles an hour in short bursts.

♦ Once totaling perhaps 40 million, the pronghorns were almost exterminated by the early 1900s. Protected now, they may number several million in all the West. Two of the largest Northwest herds browse in Oregon's Hart Mountain Antelope Refuge and four valleys in Idaho's Lemhi Mountains. Some

75 roam with the bison on Montana's National Bison Range at Moiese.

♦ The pronghorn, which is not a true antelope, is a handsome animal with an orangish brown coat, two white bands on the neck and a black strip up the snout. It sheds an outer sheath of black, fused, hairlike keratin from the bony core of its horn, the only true horned animal in the world to do so. The horns are heavy, 20 inches long, and—unlike other horns—they branch, curving backward with the prong projecting forward.

♦ Only 3 feet high at the shoulders, the pronghorn depends upon speed, hearing, and eyesight to protect itself from wolves, golden eagles, and coyotes in its open habitat. Its large, heavily lashed eyes are eight times keener than human eyes.

Muscles in the skin move hollow, insulated hairs of the coarse coat up for cooling, down for minus-zero protection. To warn of danger, each pronghorn raises 3-inch-long hairs on a brilliantly white rump rosette, visible for miles.

RAZOR CLAMS The razor clam (*Siliqua patula*), which grows in abundance on beaches in southern Washington and northern Oregon, can move faster than any other clam in the Pacific Northwest. With eight or nine movements of its foot, the razor clam can bury itself in very wet sand at the rate of 1 inch a second. The pointed muscular foot, extended half the length of the narrow, 6-inch-long shell, digs into the sand, then swells up with the saltwater body fluid that circulates throughout the mantle and is stored in the mantle cavity. Once securely anchored, the foot muscle contracts by expelling some of the fluid, creating a hole in the sand into which the body is drawn. This procedure is repeated until the clam is buried 12 to 18 inches deep. The extended foot clings so firmly to sand that the fragile shell may be pulled off before the muscle lets go.

Found in abundance only in the Pacific Northwest, the razor clam can bury itself in wet sand at the rate of 1 inch a second.

RAZOR CLAM

♦ The razor clam does not dig a permanent burrow, for it must feed near the surface on suspended organisms that the waves wash in and out, its siphon protruding beyond the shell an inch or more. The razor clam lives in one of the least hospitable beach habitats of any marine animal. Sandy beaches, constantly built and undercut by waves, provide little food and security; they offer a much harsher environment than rocky shores, and homes for far fewer species of animals than do tide pools. The wet sand allows the clam to burrow quickly and deeply, which it must do to survive on the wave-scoured beach.

♦ During the winter of 1984, a parasite killed 19 million razor clams in Washington, producing within a very short time an

unprecedented and disastrous drop in population—a drop estimated to be as high as 95 percent. Similar in effect to the AIDS
virus in humans, the parasite breaks down the clam's immune
system and attacks the gills, causing breathing difficulties and
often suffocation. The slow growth of the long-lived razor clam—
4½ inches in 3½ years—means slow recovery from disasters.
Although some razor clam populations have increased, the dis-
ease remains, and harvesting has been limited.

RHINOCEROS AUKLET

Washington's Protection Island provides sanctuary for nearly half the breeding population of the rhinoceros auklet in the Lower 48.

RHINOCEROS AUKLET Nearly half the breeding population of the rhinoceros auklet (*Cerorhinca monocerata*) in the
Lower 48—as well as many nesting colonies—find sanctuary on
Washington's Protection Island. In all, 17,000 noisy pairs of
rhinoceros auklets raise their young on the island.

The dark, chunky, crow-sized auklet excavates burrows, using
its clawed feet and a short horn atop its yellowish beak. After fishing all day, the auklets, male and female alike, work noisily and
constantly on their nesting burrows, which are used year after
year. They dig them 3 to 10 feet back into the sides of sandy cliffs
300 feet high. Protection Island is ideal for the auklets because of
its easily dug soil and high, unobstructed slopes, which assist the
bird's clumsy takeoff. The stubby-winged auklet drops many feet
before becoming airborne; on its return it often crash-lands. Far
more at home underwater, auklets enter the water headfirst, tip-
ping over like ducks but with wings open. They swim rapidly not
far under the surface, webbed feet steering. At dusk the sky over
the island is filled with returning auklets, with small fish such as
herring dangling in a neat row from their beaks. When catching
new fish, the birds press their exceptionally stiff tongues against
the fish already in their beaks to avoid losing them. (See also
Seabird Sanctuaries.)

RUBBER BOA The rubber boa (*Charina bottae*) is the
Northwest's most primitive snake, as well as its only boa. Shy and
gentle, the drab, slow-moving, nocturnal snake, which can be up
to 30 inches long, slithers along on a rubbery body covered with
small, smooth scales. Rubber boas prefer partly forested areas
and mountain meadows, often hiding in rotten logs or wet sand.

The Northwest's only boa, the 30-inch-long rubber boa, suffocates its prey within its coils and then swallows the prey whole.

The boa can swim, burrow in forest debris, and climb trees,
using its prehensile tail to grasp branches. Harmless to humans,
boas kill such prey as birds, reptiles, and small mammals by
tightening their coils around the prey to suffocate them. They
then swallow them whole.

◆ The rubber boa, whose blunt tail looks much like its head, defends itself uniquely. When attacked, it may coil as if to strike, but the "head" that it waves is really its tail. The true head is hidden under its body. The subterfuge must be effective; rubber boa tails often bear scars made by predators.

SALAMANDERS The Northwest is home to the Pacific giant salamander (*Dicamptodon ensatus*), largest terrestrial salamander in the world. Most abundant and reaching its maximum size on Washington's moist Olympic Peninsula, the Pacific giant also lives in Oregon and Idaho. It is the only salamander that produces a variety of sounds: rattles, yelps, and even screams.

The largest terrestrial salamander in the world, and the only one to produce a variety of sounds, lives in the Northwest.

The Pacific giant, which can grow longer than 12 inches, has a rounded snout, thick tapering tail, large mouth, and a heavyset dark brown or purplish gray body, splotched with black in crumpled rings. The giant salamander seeks out coastal forests near cold streams, hiding during the day under logs, rocks, or riverbank overhangs. Its skin is permeable to water in both directions, making loss of internal body fluids a constant danger. This salamander relishes banana slugs.

♦ Despite its size, the Pacific giant can climb as high as about 8 feet up trees and shrubs in search of food or to escape predators. The slender clouded salamander (*Aneides ferreus*), which lives west of the Cascades, is the only Northwest salamander that climbs trees well. It often settles in hollows high above the ground.

♦ Some Pacific giant salamanders never leave the water after their larval stage. Displaying a unique salamander trait, neoteny, these individuals retain such larval characteristics as small legs, a flat tail, and external gills. Yet they are sexually mature.

♦ Salamanders engage in spectacular mating orgies in ponds and pools, rubbing snouts and performing aquatic ballets with their bodies intertwined. They have developed a unique form of internal fertilization of eggs. The male deposits sperm capsules on the ground, and then arouses the female so that she will pass over them, pick one up with the lips of her vent, and bring the sperm capsule inside her body for later fertilization of her eggs.

♦ Of all Northwestern salamanders, only the northern rough-skinned newts (*Taricha granulosa*) have rough skin, and only they stay active during the day, making well-publicized mass migrations to water during breeding season.

♦ Salamanders have the greatest regenerative capability of any vertebrate, and are able to regrow tails, digits, limbs, snouts, eye lenses, some internal organs, and even entire embryos. Salamanders share with lizards the ability to detach their tails in a defensive maneuver (autotomy). The self-amputated tail writhes, distracting the predator while the salamander escapes.

SALMON Of the six species of Pacific salmon, five live in Northwest waters: pink or humpback (*Oncorhynchus gorbuscha*), sockeye or red (*O. nerka*), coho or silver (*O. kisutch*), king or chinook (*O. Tshawytscha*), and chum or dog salmon (*O. keta*). Chinook are the largest, with some fish weighing more than 100 pounds; pinks from 7 to 10 pounds are the smallest. The size and habits of the different species vary, but all are born in freshwater, spend varying lengths of time there before migrating to the ocean, return as reproducing adults to the same streams in which they were born, and die within days after spawning. A few go no farther than Puget Sound, and landlocked sockeyes, called *kokanee*, remain in lakes, spawning in tributary streams. Many Northwest lakes yield kokanee of several pounds.

Native Americans in the Northwest have been fishing for salmon for more than 9,000 years.

The migration of salmon to the sea as young fish evidently is related to the far greater supply of food in the ocean. No river is rich enough in food to sustain a huge year-round population of such large fish, which do not eat when they return to spawn. The rivers and streams they return to are much safer spawning areas than the ocean. While in the ocean for one or two years, or even longer for chinook salmon, Northwest salmon may travel as far north as the Gulf of Alaska and as far south as northern California. Some lie off river mouths for another year before ascending to spawn.

◆ Atlantic salmon (and seagoing steelhead trout) differ from Pacific salmon primarily in that they survive to spawn again. The two salmon species are believed to have evolved from a common ancestor that lived 2 million years ago when a passage was open in the north between the two oceans. After Arctic ice blocked that passage, distinct Atlantic and Pacific species evolved. The most highly prized salmon, because of its size and flavor, has always been the huge chinook or king, which spends more time at sea than other species of Pacific salmon. Its young may go to sea soon after they hatch, or they may stay in freshwater for more than a year. The smaller coho young remain in the freshwater streams where they were born for about a year before migrating, feeding on floating insects.

◆ When the first European explorers and settlers arrived in the Northwest, the major Columbia River salmon runs ranked among the largest in the world, despite steady harvesting by native people for more than 9,000 years.

The winter food supply of most Northwest Indian tribes

depended heavily upon the abundance of salmon. Dried, salmon provided a valued trading item for native Americans who lived near the rivers or could travel to them during the runs of different species of salmon and steelhead. Catching, cleaning, and preparing the salmon for winter was a cooperative affair for native people. Fish were dried or smoked, roasted on special sticks standing upright over open fires, and sometimes cooked in watertight baskets by the addition of fireheated stones to the water inside the basket.

In those days before salmon canneries and dams, salmon fought their way some 1,200 miles up the Columbia and 900 miles up the Snake, into many tributary streams and lakes. In the 1800s, native Americans caught and processed an estimated 18 million salmon, steelhead, and cutthroat trout a year, more than 120 million pounds, without diminishing the runs.

◆ Native fishermen on the rivers used a variety of nets, hook and line, and spears, including the ingeniously designed three-pronged *leister,* whose stone or antler points, directed inward and downward toward the lower, larger point, were lashed with wild cherry bark to the shaft. The native people constructed woven openwork fences called *weirs* to direct fish into traps or toward waiting fishermen. Occasionally cedar root and bark stakes nearly 1,000 years old from abandoned weirs are found still upright in Northwest streams and river mouths.

Coastal fishermen and those fishing in the Strait of Juan de Fuca and North Puget Sound used long reef nets anchored at parallel canoes and built various devices to direct salmon toward harpooners in canoes. At the 2,750-year-old Hoko River fishing camp on the Olympic Peninsula, fishing gear, knives with stone cutting blades, and fish baskets have been unearthed, presumably once used for the fall chum salmon runs.

◆ Small-scale commerce in salmon by non-natives began with the Hudson's Bay Company, which bought salmon from the Indians or bartered for it, and sent barrels of salted salmon to London. Boston fishing ships arrived by 1829 and carried salted salmon back to Boston. The exploitation of salmon and the diminishment of a once-prolific natural resource began in 1866 with the first salmon cannery on the Columbia. Soon, more canneries appeared along the Columbia and along many coastal rivers in Oregon: the Tillamook, Rogue, Umpqua, Coos. In 1867 4,000 cases of salmon were shipped out; in 1883, when 43 million pounds of salmon were caught, 630,000 cases were sent to the eastern United States.

Of the different methods of commercial fishing practiced, one

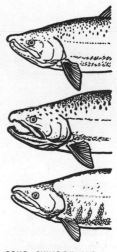

COHO, CHINOOK, AND SOCKEYE SALMON, RESPECTIVELY

of the more picturesque involved using horses to pull drag seines in shallow water. One of the most devastating employed the current-powered fish wheel. The device harvested enormous quantities of salmon and steelhead effortlessly, scooping them up in wire baskets that dumped them into boxes or troughs. By 1879 three major canneries were using fish wheels on the Columbia River, some with wheels 30 feet in diameter. Salmon runs were drastically reduced decades before Oregon outlawed the fish wheels in 1927 and Washington in 1934.

♦ Dams on the main stem Columbia and Snake rivers caused the most damage of all (Grand Coulee, Chief Joseph, Hells Canyon dams). The dams either blocked the fish from passing upriver or back to sea, or created a host of problems for successful migrators: nitrogen supersaturation, unscreened turbines that chopped up juveniles as they passed through, and predators waiting at dam pools for young fish in shock after being trucked around dams. The latest dam problem is the competition for water among salmon fishermen, electric power generation interests, and farmers who withdraw huge amounts of water for irrigation.

Aquaculture, the farming of young salmon, was once seen as a major answer to declining salmon runs. However, such farming concentrates wastes from so many salmon in so small an area that it has already caused increased pollution in Puget Sound.

Even the last natural spawning area for steelhead and chinook salmon on the lower Columbia, Hanford Reach, is not secure. The Army Corps of Engineers has proposed dredging it, which would disturb salmon spawning beds thousands of years old.

The sand dollar, one of the Pacific Northwest's most familiar "sea shells," feeds in a vertical position with its body partially buried in sand.

SAND DOLLAR One of the most familiar of all "sea shells" in the Northwest, the sand dollar (*Dendrastus excentricus*) has strayed far from the spiny aspect of echinoderm anatomy, yet this flattened sea urchin displays in its familiar flower design the typical radial, five-rayed echinoderm organization. The petal design of *D. excentricus* is lopsided, not quite on the apex of the skeleton. The design of a species more common from Puget Sound to the north, *Echinarachnius parma*, is more perfectly centered.

On the inside of the sand dollar's shell, calcareous pillars support the flat circular skeleton; on the outside, thousands of dark, fine spines, 1/16th of an inch long, bristle on both upper and lower surfaces of the live animal. The spines provide both protection to the skin and a manner of locomotion. The longer spines on the underside, so dense they feel like velvet, ripple in coordinated waves, moving the sand dollar vertically up and down in the soft sand where it lives.

◆ Most sand dollars live in sandy-bottomed lagoons and in relatively shallow water, burrowing a few feet deep and surfacing mainly for feeding and breeding. When it feeds, the sand dollar keeps two-thirds of its body buried in the sand. Its body remains vertical but angled to the current in order to feed on minute bits of organic material, detritus, and diatoms in both water and sand. When in feeding position, all sand dollars orient themselves at precisely the same angle to the current. They do not swallow sand, as sea cucumbers often do.

As in all echinoderms but the sea cucumber, the sand dollar stomach opens on its underside. Food travels toward the mouth down five visible grooves radiating out from the mouth, moved along by tube feet or the currents created by hairlike cilia that cover its surface. At the mouth, several jaws sift and divide the particles.

◆ Whenever a predator starfish appears, every sand dollar within a few feet begins to burrow in a panic. Soon, a cleared path 4 or 5 feet wide appears in the bed of sand dollars. They remain safely buried for about half an hour, long enough to allow the starfish to pass by.

Northwesterners seldom see these animals alive. When the tide occasionally strands them, they lie flat, partly or completely buried, protected by their dark color. Once turned over, a sand dollar cannot right itself, as a starfish can. To change direction, a sand dollar must stop and pivot on its axis, whereas a starfish can move in any direction without first reorienting itself.

SANDPIPERS Sandpipers make up 85 percent of the migratory shorebird population that flies each spring and fall along the Pacific flyway. They are the most numerous and diverse of all Northwest shorebirds, noted for their quick running movements and gregariousness. They demonstrate a variety of feeding strategies and many lengths and shapes of bills, which allow many species to feed in the same area at the same time without competing.

Almost the entire world population of western sandpipers— 1.5 million—touch down in Grays Harbor, Washington, and in Canada's Fraser River area during their migrations. Others cluster in sand and mud flats, lake shores, and marshes of such places as Washington's San Juan Islands and Oregon's Coos Bay.

The sandpipers form huge, noisy flocks, both when feeding and flying. They feed by probing with their bills into moist sand, soil, or mud for small invertebrates. The birds fly in perfect

No other Northwest shorebirds are as numerous or as diverse as sandpipers, which make up 85 percent of the shorebird population that migrates along the Pacific flyway.

unison, with extraordinary precision and nimbleness. The aerial maneuvers of these great flocks tend to discourage such predators as peregrine falcons from singling out individuals to attack.

Among the sandpipers are many bearing the sandpiper name (western, semi-palmated, sharp-tailed, buff-breasted), and also whimbrels, turnstones, sanderlings, short- and long-billed dowitchers, greater and lesser yellowlegs, dunlins, snipe, and phalaropes (which prefer the open sea but come inland to nest and feed). (See Phalarope.)

SCALLOPS The largest free-swimming scallop in the world, the weathervane (*Pecten caurinus*), thrives in Northwest waters. The thin, fan-shaped shells (valves) are distinctly ribbed and measure 8 to 10 inches across. Unlike most bivalves, which rest erect on the shell edge, scallops generally lie on one side in beds in offshore waters with gravelly or sandy bottoms. The lower valve of the weathervane lies on its right, which becomes flattened as a result. The scallop normally keeps the valves slightly open in order to bring in water bearing oxygen and microscopic organisms.

The upper valve of most Northwest scallops usually is covered with yellow sponges that grow only in the Northwest—*Mycale adherens* and *Ectyodoryx parasitica.*

◆ All scallops differ from clams and mussels in having only one large muscle for closing the shell, instead of two. Among the most active of the bivalves, scallops are alerted to danger by the numerous shining, beadlike eyes that are spaced along the upper and lower mantle fringe. Each eye has a cornea, lens, and retina and can see shadows and movement of nearby large objects. Scallops quickly swim away from slower predators such as starfish, although an octopus can easily catch them.

◆ Although large scallops do not swim as often or as rapidly as smaller scallops do, the weathervane will swim when large starfish appear. During routine movement, scallops move with their shell openings forward. But when fleeing, all scallops, including the weathervane, reverse direction and move hinge-first. The valves open to take in water, which they then expel forcefully by closing the shell with a rapid muscular contraction and spurting water out in jets on either side of the hinge. The water jets can be directed by pressure of the mantle, so that the scallop can turn and flee. A swimming scallop has been likened to a pair of swimming dentures opening and closing. Since scallops lie unprotected in large beds on the surface of mud flats or sea bottom, unable to burrow like clams or to cling like mussels,

The Northwest's weathervane scallop, which measures 8 to 10 inches across, is the world's largest free-swimming scallop.

SCALLOP

their ability to move rapidly assures survival against slower-moving predators.

◆ A commercial scallop industry exists in the deep salt water of the Pacific Northwest, where nets scoop up scallops by the hundreds. Although usually only the muscle is eaten, the entire animal is delicious. Northwestern beachcombers occasionally find scallops in the intertidal zone and below low-tide mark.

SEA ANEMONE
The quiet waters of Puget Sound encourage the growth of a host of sea anemone species, which thrive on protected rocky shores. One of the most beautiful, the white plumose sea anemone (*Metridium senile*), also lives in deep Northwest waters. It grows to be one of the largest sea anemones in the world—up to 20 inches tall and 6 inches across when fully extended and supported by the sea. Smaller plumose anemones, which can crawl slowly, inhabit pilings in the lowest intertidal zones and, occasionally, Puget Sound tide pools. Voracious eaters, they swallow almost anything offered, later regurgitating indigestible parts.

The plumose sea anemone, which thrives in the waters of Puget Sound, grows up to 20 inches tall and 6 inches across, making it one of the world's largest.

◆ Plumose anemones are not always white; some reveal rich brown and reddish yellow variations, often in clusters with all individuals colored alike—the result of asexual division into many clones. Time-lapse photography reveals that the plumose sea anemone, which appears to be motionless, in fact moves its tentacles and column constantly, moving more rapidly in reaction to food.

◆ The white plumose anemone aggressively defends its territory. Each anemone is equipped with fighting tentacles that inflate and stretch above the feeding tentacles in response to intruders. Upon contact, the fighting tentacles release a tip that sticks to the intruder, injecting tissue-damaging toxins. The anemone, differentiating between an anemone of its own genetic makeup and sex, and an outsider, attacks only intruders.

◆ Sea anemones, which resemble "flower animals" when the hundreds of tentacles are extended in the water to feed, are among the most primitive of multicelled animals, barely above the sponge on the evolutionary ladder. When food is scarce, anemones decrease in size and grow more slowly; they may live for several hundred years by adapting their size to food supply.

When feeding, the normally slow-moving anemone is a voracious carnivore. After a small fish or crustacean touches the tentacles, it is seized, paralyzed by stinging darts, carried into the mouth, and devoured—all within a minute. Larger animals that blunder into the tentacles are held outside the body with special sticky cells, slowly turned, and gradually eaten.

◆ Giant green sea anemones (*Anthopleura xanthogrammica*) are common to Oregon and Washington seacoasts and are often seen in tide pools. These solitary anemones, which can measure 10 inches across, also thrive in the lowest tidal zones, where fresh water continually washes in, and in bright sunlight, which most anemones avoid. Their green color derives from one-celled, photosynthesizing algae that live symbiotically within them. (See Plants, Algae.)

◆ Primitive as anemones are, one species, the small aggregating anemone (*A. elegantissima*)—probably a color and size phase of the giant green anemone—has developed a surprisingly sophisticated social order. Every year each anemone divides in half, producing two individuals that remain near each other. As the colony grows, a division of labor develops. Anemones on the outer rim become "soldiers," developing more and larger *acrorhagi*—large, white, inflatable saclike weapons—to fend off intruders. The anemones in the center concentrate their energy on growing and reproducing.

These hardy anemones form extensive beds on boulders, often camouflaged with bits of gravel or shell, expanding in sunshine and contracting at night into 1½-inch lumps. Pink and lavender bands adorn tentacles and parts around the mouth.

◆ Although sea anemones have no central nervous system or brain, they are capable of rather complicated muscular behavior and rapid reactions. They spread their tentacles to catch food and then, in response to an outgoing tide, bright light, or mechanical danger, pull the mouth disk with its tentacles inside the central column and shorten it into a less vulnerable lump. They can glide on their basal disk 3 to 4 inches an hour or attach it so firmly to floats and intertidal rocks that they cannot be removed without damage. Some flagella within the central column are reversible, beating upward to carry out waste but quickly reversing direction to bring in prey that touch the tentacles.

SEABIRD SANCTUARIES Washington supports the largest concentrations of seabird nesting sites in the contiguous United States. One of them, boomerang-shaped Protection Island at the northeast corner of the Olympic Peninsula, is the most important seabird nesting area in that state's inland waters, and perhaps in the entire Northwest. With no ground predators to molest eggs and chicks, this rugged 365-acre island provides nesting habitat for nearly 60 percent of seabirds that nest in Puget Sound. That includes 60,000 seabirds of more than thirty species,

Sixty thousand seabirds of more than thirty different species nest on Washington's Protection Island.

such as pigeon guillemots, long-necked cormorants, black oystercatchers, the state's largest glacous-winged gull colony (4,300 pairs), 64 percent of its tufted puffins, and nearly half the breeding population of the rhinoceros auklet outside Alaska. (See Rhinoceros Auklet.)

Protection Island was designated a national wildlife refuge in 1982 after a long battle with developers. Although no drinkable water exists on the island and the wind blows strongly enough to overturn a tractor, developers had subdivided the island into 1,100 small lots and bulldozed an airfield and marina.

♦ Many of the seabird species that nest on Protection Island also find protection on Destruction Island off the Washington coast, another important seabird sanctuary. As many as a million seabirds at peak nesting season use the 870 rocks, reefs, and islands in the 100-mile-long stretch, designated in 1970 as the Washington Islands Wilderness Area.

An estimated 100,000 pairs of alcids, including the common murre, nest in the Washington Islands Wilderness Area and on Destruction Island. Like puffins and auklets, the murre spends most of its life at sea and is a superb swimmer and diver. Trawling nets sometimes bring up murres from a depth of 200 feet.

♦ In July 1990 Northwest biologists solved the longtime avian mystery of where the marbled murrelet (*Brachyramphus marmoratus*) nests. An intensive search for the nests began after Forest Service employees found a dead marbled murrelet chick in 1989 in the Darrington (Washington) District. From May to September 1990, wildlife researchers found five nests in old-growth forests 20 to 26 miles inland in Oregon and Washington. Most nests were located 100 feet high in western hemlock and Douglas fir trees.

All of the nests contained fledglings. Each day parent murrelets flew from the sea to bring food to the chicks. The chicks gain weight and fledge quickly in order to reach the safety of the sea as soon as possible.

At 9½ inches, the marbled murrelet is one of the two smallest common alcids. It is known for rocking back and forth during its rapid flight. The birds are believed to mate for life.

♦ Three Arch Rocks National Wildlife Refuge, created in 1907 by President Theodore Roosevelt, protects Oregon's largest seabird colonies. Common murre nests cling to every available ledge of the three 300-foot-high main rocks and six adjacent smaller rocks of the refuge. Some 75,000 murres breed there, out of the total Oregon Coast population of 250,000, as do many of the same species that nest in Washington.

Although an old-growth forest of Sitka spruce and western hemlock covers most of Oregon's Cape Meares National Wildlife Refuge on the mainland, vertical sea cliffs several hundred feet high provide nesting habitat for thousands of tufted puffins, pelagic cormorants, and pigeon guillemots.

The California sea cucumber distracts its predators by ejecting its internal organs into the water; another type of sea cucumber breaks apart into several pieces when threatened.

SEA CUCUMBER Sea cucumbers, common in Northwest waters in a variety of species, colors, and shapes, have developed a unique method of defense against predators. One of the most common and most edible sea cucumbers in Northwest waters is the reddish California sea cucumber (*Parastichopus californicus*). When startled or threatened, this warty sea cucumber, like many others, contracts its body muscles so forcefully and rapidly that internal body fluids compress and rupture the wall of the anus. The fluid rushes out, carrying with it the sea cucumber's two distinctive internal lungs—respiratory trees that run the length of each side of the body. These multibranched organs, provided with oxygen-bearing water pumped into the anus, are unique to sea cucumbers among all echinoderms, most of which breathe through appendages on the skin. The predator, distracted by the appearance of the organs, soon begins to feed on them, allowing the sea cucumber to escape. The sea cucumber, while waiting for its branched lungs to regrow, can still breathe by pumping water into its body cavity and absorbing oxygen through the cavity walls.

Some species of cucumbers have developed an alternative to expelling their respiratory trees. They grow specialized tubules at the base of the trees and expel them instead. The tubules swell into a sticky tangle of threads several feet long, entangling even large crustacean predators. The sea cucumber can quickly regrow the accessory organs.

The 2-inch-long *Leptosynapta albicans,* a very common cucumber in Northwest waters, can, when annoyed, break its fragile, wormlike body into several pieces by contracting its muscles. It breaks easily because of its delicate skin and its lack of respiratory trees. The head later grows a new body.

This tiny sea cucumber digs anchor-shaped spicules loosely embedded in its skin into the sand to provide traction as it moves along with muscular contractions. All sea cucumbers lack conspicuous spines, bearing instead within the skin intricately shaped calcareous bits that stiffen it: rods, anchors, wheels, perforated plates.

♦ The sea cucumber's large body, measuring 3 inches in diameter and up to 18 inches in length, provides five lean strips of muscle running the length of the tough body wall. Early coastal Indians, who regarded sea cucumbers as a delicacy, dried the meaty muscles for later use. The warty California cucumbers are netted by contemporary Northwesterners as well, but no commercial sea cucumber fishery exists in the Northwest.

◆ The saclike bodies of all sea cucumbers are unique among echinoderms, with the mouth at one end (instead of on the underside) and anus at the other. They move with the mouth end leading, unlike other echinoderms. Sometimes sea cucumbers are limp bags of water, but the water vascular system common to all echinoderms allows the cucumber to stiffen its body.

◆ A few sea cucumbers provide surprisingly advanced egg care. Some keep fertilized eggs safe in pockets on the parental skin, perhaps pushed in by the mother's tentacles or tube feet. Others have developed pouches that hold several eggs and the developing embryos. Some even retain eggs in their body cavities.

SEA LIONS The only northern (Steller's) sea lions (*Eumetopias jubata*) that now breed on the Northwest mainland belong to a herd of some 200 living in a huge natural sea cave on the Oregon coast near Florence. Normally, these largest of the eared seals (a separate group from true seals, which lack external ears) and largest of American sea lions breed offshore, many on Oregon's islands and rocks. This herd, however, mates and rears its pups on the mainland in the sheltered Sea Lion Caves. (See Natural Features, Sea Caves.)

A herd of about 200 northern sea lions mates and rears its pups in Oregon's protected Sea Lion Caves.

Although these sea lions do not breed in Washington, several hundred winter in Puget Sound. They are twice the size of the California sea lions (*Zalophus californianus*) that have gained notoriety in recent years by devouring steelhead and salmon near the Ballard locks and fish ladder in Seattle. Male northern sea lions, which develop a heavy mane, reach 13 feet in length and weigh a ton or more, with massive forequarters and muscular neck. Much of the weight consists of body fat, which provides water and food during the two-month breeding season when the bull keeps so busy defending his twenty to thirty cows and his rock ledge territory outside the caves that he seldom eats.

◆ Better swimmers than true seals, northern sea lions also move faster on land and are able to rotate their long hind limbs forward and raise their bodies, enabling them to lope rather rapidly for a short distance. Noted for their belligerent roar, these marine mammals spend considerable time ashore. Broad flippers on supple forelimbs help them walk and keep their body

STELLER'S SEA LION

partially erect while ashore.

♦ Northern sea lions were designated a threatened species in April 1990 because their population in Alaska's Aleutian Islands had dropped sharply. This decrease may have been the result of overfishing of pollock, their primary food, or entanglement of the sea lions in trawl and gill nets.

SHOREBIRD REFUGES North America's densest and often most spectacular concentrations of shorebirds migrating along the Pacific flyway touch down to feed and rest in the Northwest each spring and fall. They include almost the entire U.S. population of western sandpipers, numbering 1.5 million. The Northwest's many national wildlife refuges, created primarily to protect these migrating birds, offer some of the nation's best bird-watching. Shorebirds that find temporary haven in Northwest protected areas include avocets, oystercatchers, plovers, stilts, and the highly diverse sandpipers. (See Sandpipers.)

Shorebirds, which strongly prefer marine habitats, feed in many specialized ways. Different species arrive at different times and often feed differently, lessening competition. Shorter-billed birds feed on organisms close to the top of mud, longer-billed birds feed deeper.

♦ Washington, with the three largest coastal estuaries between San Francisco and British Columbia, attracts a particularly large number of migrating shorebirds, which stop at refuges that include Grays Harbor, Willapa Bay, Padilla Bay, Dungeness Spit, the San Juan Islands, and the Skagit Flats.

♦ Washington's Willapa Bay, which exposes nearly a mile of mud at low tide, is the nation's last large, unspoiled estuary. Its 10,000 acres of salt marshes and lagoons attract more than a million migrating shorebirds. In its southwest corner, Long Island provides a particularly protected habitat, since it is accessible only by private boat.

♦ Grays Harbor, which includes Bowerman Basin, ranks as one of the five most vital shorebird resting and feeding areas in the Western Hemisphere, because of the numbers of birds that stop there. It became a national wildlife refuge in 1988 after fourteen years of efforts by environmental groups. It is one of only four major estuaries in North America that support more than a million shorebirds.

Most of the twenty-four species of shorebirds that visit Grays Harbor congregate in Bowerman Basin, in the harbor's northeast corner. The spring gathering of birds there ranks as one of the largest anywhere in North America south of Alaska. More than a

Each spring and fall, more than a million migrating avocets, stilts, plovers, and sandpipers touch down in Northwest shorebird refuges to feed and rest.

million birds make the basin their last major feeding and resting stop before they begin the 1,500-mile, nonstop flight to Alaskan breeding grounds. Although the 500-acre basin comprises only 2 percent of the intertidal land in Grays Harbor estuary, it supports half of the shorebirds, which cluster at the edge of tidewater. Bowerman Basin is the last area in the refuge to be swamped by the incoming tide, and the first to emerge as the tide ebbs.

The magnitude of the migration and the ecological significance of Bowerman Basin were not fully realized until 1981, when Evergreen University students making a daily census realized that peak counts totaled up to half a million shorebirds. Of the large areas critical to shorebirds on the West Coast south of Alaska, Bowerman Basin was the last to be protected. More than 4,000 acres of it had already been lost, filled with dredge spoil from the sediment-laden Chehalis River, and more was scheduled for development.

The birds especially relish a small, shrimplike amphipod concentrated as densely as 55,000 for every square meter in the thousands of acres of rich mud flats exposed at low tide. Deeply buried when the tide is out, amphipods and other organisms such as mud-dwelling worms become more active as water moves up the mud flats.

Thousands of bird watchers gather in the basin each year to view the acrobatic flights and incessant probing of bills into mud, and to listen to bird chatter and the rush of wings as large flocks take flight. Thousands of birds will whirl up and maneuver in unison through the air along the water's edge, as precisely as if choreographed. The abundance of shorebirds makes Bowerman Basin one of the best places in the Northwest to see birds of prey in action, especially peregrine falcons, which follow the migrating birds. (See Falcon.)

SHREW The pygmy shrew (*Microsorex hoyi Washingtoni*), living only in northeastern Washington and northern Idaho, is North America's smallest mammal and smallest of all twelve Northwest shrew species. The 3-inch-long shrew, weighing less than 4 grams, is one of the three shrews in the greatest danger of extinction.

Weighing only 4 grams, the Northwest's pygmy shrew is North America's smallest mammal.

The reddish brown, thickly furred pygmy, with a hairless, two-toned tail, lives in grassy meadows in open, semiarid pine woods and sometimes at the edges of marshes. It pokes around with its long snout in forest debris, uttering high-pitched squeaks, moving with sudden starts and stops, disappearing down burrows a scant half-inch across.

Endowed with sharp teeth and the characteristic voracious-
ness of all shrews, which each day must eat food equal to 150
percent of their body weight, the tiny shrew eats insects, berries
and seeds, and even other animals its own size, biting them in the
neck to kill them. All shrews are active day and night, seldom
resting, feeding at least every three hours in order to maintain
their high body temperature. Although many predators find
shrews unpalatable because of disagreeable skin secretions from
a musk gland, owl pellets often contain their remains.

SLUGS High rainfall and calcium-poor soil, both ideal for
slugs, have given the Northwest one of the world's densest slug
populations. The only gastropods that have left the sea, slugs and
snails may have been among the first animals to make the transi-
tion to land; however, they have not outgrown their need for
moisture. Because their permeable skin quickly dries out, they
prefer humidity near 100 percent, a condition often present in
the Northwest. When the air becomes dry and hot, slugs hole up
in damp places to conserve moisture, emerging only at dusk
and dawn.

*Although the
Northwest has one of
the world's densest
populations of slugs,
only the banana slug
is native to the
region.*

◆ The banana slug (*Ariolimax columbianus*), the only native
slug of the Northwest, may be the world's second-largest land
mollusk. During its life of perhaps six years, it can reach 8 to
10 inches in length and up to 4 ounces in weight. This mush-
room-loving slug of coastal forests, often olive green or yellowish
with black spots and a keeled hump, dines on fungi, lichen, and
native shrubs. The spores of some mushroom species must pass
through the digestive system of a slug before they will germinate.
Slug droppings are rich in nitrogen.

◆ Although slugs are hermaphroditic and solitary creatures,
they seem to enjoy the mating game, for the courtship ritual of
the banana slug can last for more than twelve hours. The two
slugs circle each other, eat each other's slime trail, lick mucus
off each other with their sharp-toothed radulas, and, even bite
before they intertwine and copulate. Afterwards, one or both
slugs may gnaw off the inch-long penises, perhaps because withdrawal is so difficult. The organ is believed to regenerate.

◆ The *Limax maximus,* a ravenous garden slug, engages in
equally remarkable sexual behavior. The two slugs suspend
themselves from a tree branch on a string of mucus extruded
from a tail pit and dangle in space, intertwined, turning gently,
extruding a white flowerlike mass as they mate. In a less amiable
mood, this slug may raise the front of its body and slash another

slug with its sharp-toothed radula.

♦ *Prophysaon* is the only North American slug genus with the ability to detach one-third of its tail when roughly handled or under attack by predators such as shrew-moles and beetles. It can regenerate its tail end within five weeks. This species, up to 1½ inches long, can tolerate even less heat or drought than most slugs and therefore hibernates for nearly half the year within decaying logs. A distinctive sulphur-yellow margin borders its mantle and foot.

BANANA SLUG

♦ Another unusual Northwest slug genus, *Hemphillia*, is one of only three mollusks in the world that display a startle reaction when handled. To escape predators, it may twitch and writhe, lash its tail, and even jump an inch or two. These cold-adapted slugs, more than 1 inch long and almost entirely nocturnal, have been found near glaciers on the Olympic Peninsula and on Mount Hood at elevations up to 4,250 feet, and in ravines of the Columbia River Gorge. Most slugs retain an interior vestige of a shell; this slug bears a horny, yellowish exterior plate on its hump.

♦ A more common Northwest slug, *Arion ater rufus*, is black or reddish with a ridged body. It displays the unusual behavior of curling into a ball when in danger and rolling back and forth. When swallowed by a bird, it can block the bird's throat and suffocate it, later crawling out alive.

♦ Ultraefficient eating machines, slugs consume each day the equivalent of their body weight, aided by 27,000 sharp, renewable teeth in the tonguelike radula.

Slug mucus is such an efficient lubricant that slugs can crawl over broken glass or an upended razor blade without harm. When slugs are in danger, they exude especially thick mucus.

SNAIL The largest subtidal rock snail of the Pacific Coast is the Oregon triton (*Fusitriton oregonensis*). Often found in water as deep as 300 feet, the snail sometimes ventures closer to shore on rocky coasts. The handsome shell, spiraled and spindleshaped, grows up to 6 inches long. The seven or eight ribbed whorls are completely covered with coarse, brown bristles. Hydroids and tube worms often adhere to it. The snail's short proboscis marks it as a carnivore that eats the soft body parts inside other shelled animals. Its very unusual eggs resemble corn kernels in size and shape. The firstborn in each capsule eats the others.

The Oregon triton, often found in water as deep as 300 feet, is the largest subtidal rock snail on the Pacific Coast.

SNOWSHOE HARE The only adult hare to have mastered several calls, the snowshoe hare (*Lepus americanus*) normally

The snowshoe hare can reach speeds of 30 miles an hour and can leap distances of 12 feet.

lives in brushy forested areas of the Northwest, including all Northwest national parks. Although other rabbits and hares are nonvocal as adults, both young and adult snowshoe hares grunt or growl when angry or afraid, and utter a piercing scream when injured or captured. They also make a clicking sound the significance of which is unknown, and they thump their hind feet while hopping to warn other hares of danger. They may also thump during mating season, when the hares chase one another in circles and leap over each other.

◆ The snowshoe hare shares many traits with its main predator, the lynx. Both animals, active during the winter, have wide, furry hind feet that spread over the snow, enabling them to move more easily. Dense winter hair on the soles form insulating "snowshoes." Both animals are nocturnal, both are fast runners and excellent leapers. When running in a huge circle, the adult hare, which is about 18 inches long, reaches speeds of 30 miles an hour; it can leap a distance of 12 feet. Newly born snowshoe hares can run within minutes of birth, an obvious survival aid.

Like the lynx, the hare often uses dash-and-freeze tactics. Although it maintains an intricate escape network of runways in brushy thickets, the hare also relies on "freezing" in open country, blending into the snowy landscape. Camouflage helps it escape detection; brown in spring and summer, the hare turns white in fall and winter where snow piles up. On Mount Rainier, snowshoe hares living above 3,000 feet turn white; those below, where snow is scarcer, stay brown, as do Olympic Peninsula snowshoe hares.

Few other predator-prey populations are as closely correlated as those of the lynx and snowshoe hare. (See Lynx.)

In 1978 a squid weighing 225 pounds and measuring 24 feet from arm tip to arm tip was caught off the Oregon coast.

SQUID   The first giant squid (*Architeuthis*) caught off the Oregon coast (in 1978) was the only whole squid of this type ever caught off the Pacific coast north of Chile. *Architeuthis*, the largest squid genus and the world's largest invertebrate animal, was believed not to inhabit Northwest waters.

This *Architeuthis*, caught by a commercial fisherman trawling for bottomfish off Oregon's Mack Arch, was small, weighing 225 pounds. Its body was 5 feet long, and it measured 24 feet, arm tip to arm tip. Bruised flesh of the arms proved that the squid was alive when trawled at 800 feet, but nothing survives the rapid pressure change as trawling nets are hauled up. After weighing, measuring, and photographing the squid, the fisherman gave it to a restaurant owner, who dumped the iodine-tasting carcass into the sea before biologists could examine it.

Identification was positive because of the photographs and some parts that were saved: a large, horny, parrotlike beak, and thumb-sized suckers.

◆ Although the opalescent squid (*Loligo opalescens*) is commercially fished farther south on the Pacific Coast, this squid, which ranges in length from 8 inches to 2 feet, appears in Pacific Northwest waters in highly varying cycles. More live in Oregon waters than in Washington, which is the northern part of its range. On cold winter nights, however, sport fishermen on Puget Sound fishing piers jig for opalescent squid, which are attracted by lights and can be caught on bare hooks, often in large numbers. The squid, whose bodies are an opalescent white, come close to shore to spawn, often at Port Angeles, Washington.

Wherever these smaller squid are found, they appear in large numbers. Although schools of smaller squid are often so immense that they give false bottom readings to ships, thousands of drift nets caused a significant drop in the squid catch in the late 1980s.

◆ In August 1989 a jumbo Northwest squid, *Moroteuthis robusta,* washed ashore on a beach in Redondo, Washington, still alive but dying, its heaving body orangish pink. Individuals of this squid species, which inhabit Northwest waters about a mile deep, are occasionally caught by fishermen, who throw them back because the flesh tastes too strongly of iodine and ammonia to be palatable to humans, although whales gorge on them. One or two a year wash ashore, perhaps having followed the sockeye salmon run. This one, with a 4-foot-long body, measured 11 feet in total length, but dogfish or seals had eaten off the tips of its arms. Other *Moroteuthis* caught in Northwest waters have measured more than 20 feet.

M. robusta has two rows of hooks at the end of its longest pair of tentacles. These flexible tentacles shoot out to seize prey and then retract, bringing the captured animal within reach of the other arms. These short, stronger arms convey the victim to the parrotlike peak, which tears it to pieces. One of the jumbo squid caught by a trawler had a 2-foot-long mackerel inside it.

◆ The squid and the octopus are the most highly developed of all mollusks and invertebrates and have the largest invertebrate brains, which are protected within cartilage.

The fastest of all invertebrates over a short distance, the squid moves by jet propulsion, backward as well as forward. It has to be fast to survive in the open water in which it lives. As vicious as it is voracious, the squid kills even when not hungry.

The high-pressure blood system of the squid and octopus is unique among invertebrates. It is fully enclosed, with veins, arteries, and capillaries and has two auxiliary hearts, which provide the extra oxygen cephalopod speed requires. (See Octopus.)

STARFISH Pacific Northwest waters host the world's largest number and diversity of starfish species. Area waters contain more than seventy species of starfish, many of them deepwater species; Puget Sound alone has forty species. Starfish, which prefer cold water, thrive in chilly Northwest waters, where the food supply of bottom-dwelling sea creatures is abundant. Starfish are more heavily concentrated in Washington than in Oregon waters because Washington's often rocky, irregular coastline provides more solid places for their tube feet suckers to attach to, and a more varied and abundant food supply: mussels, clams, sea cucumbers, scallops, barnacles, and sea urchins.

Pacific Northwest waters support the world's largest and most diverse number of starfish species, including the 3-foot sunflower, the world's biggest and most active starfish.

♦ The world's largest and most active starfish, the sunflower (*Pycnopodia helianthoides*), lives only on the Pacific Coast. As large as 3 feet across, the broad-disked, soft-bodied sunflower displays striking colors, often salmon pink with mottled gray and touches of violet. Since the huge, soft body needs water support, sunflower adults are always subtidal. Despite its size, it can squeeze through the 2½-inch openings of shrimp pots.

Born with five rays, or arms, the sunflower adds additional rays in pairs. Although twenty-four rays are usual, the giant starfish has been seen with as many as forty-four. It can readily regenerate the soft rays, which are easily torn off. Severed arms retaining a bit of the central disk can form a new animal.

♦ The voracious sunflower occasionally digs for clams, ending up after a few days in a deep pit, its arms sticking up around the edges. It feeds by sucking up into its ventral mouth whole prey such as scallops and clams, later discarding the shells. Moving along on 40,000 tube feet at speeds of 8 to 10 feet a minute, the sunflower star inspires a strong escape response in its prey: sea cucumbers crawl away, sand dollars bury themselves in the sand, scallops swim off. Fortunately, it prefers to dine on sea urchins, pests that can destroy entire seaweed beds. It engulfs urchins with its extruded stomach, later discarding the neatly cleaned spines and skeleton.

♦ The heavy-bodied purple starfish (*Pisaster ochraceus*) is the most common Pacific Northwest starfish. Although it has three color phases—brownish black, orange, and purple—the Northwest species displays more purple, with lighter colored spines forming a network on its arms and disk. This thick, rigid starfish with stubby arms can exert such a strong grip with its tube feet that it can scarcely be pried off rocks without the tube feet being detached.

The purple starfish specializes in stomach feeding, an odd method of eating that is unique to starfish. It humps over a clam or mussel, attaching several tube feet to opposite sides of the shells and pulling until the bivalve's muscle weakens. The starfish uses different tube feet as they tire. Once the shell opens a tiny gap, the purple starfish extrudes its stomach through the mouth on its underside and forces it into the shell. Digestive juices then dissolve the soft parts of the animal, and the stomach absorbs the liquid. Starfish in aquariums sometimes extrude their stomachs against the glass walls of their tank to dissolve organisms growing there.

The purple starfish occasionally uses a faster method of eating, extruding the stomach in a billowy mass over a clam, mussel, or barnacle, smothering it until it gapes open. This starfish controls the population of the common California mussel, which dominates long expanses of rocky ocean shore and prevents other species of mussels from attaching.

In twenty years the long-lived purple starfish can reach up to 16 inches across, its size directly related to the amount of food available. This starfish can live for months without eating; it slows its growth or even decreases in size, like the sea anemone. Many starfish are predators of other starfish species, but when food is scarce, the purple starfish will cannibalize smaller members of its own species.

◆ Because starfish breathe through pouchings of their thin skin, they have developed complicated structures to help clear their skin of debris. Hairlike cilia on the animal's upper surface create currents that wash away finer sediment settling on the skin. Tiny jawlike pincers on ball-and-socket joints (pedicellariae) seize heavier debris on the skin and discard it into the water or grind it into powder, which is then washed away by currents created by the cilia. Drop a piece of chalk on a purple starfish and the chalk becomes powder at once. Hold the starfish upside down against your hair or skin, and then jerk it away; the grip of the many tiny pincers is noticeable.

◆ One of the most beautiful and graceful of intertidal starfish in the Northwest, the sunstar (*Solaster stimpsoni*), combines orange or rose hues with streaks of gray, and a wide blue band bordered with pink that often runs from the center of the disk up each slender arm to the tip. This 8-inch-wide starfish, which lives no farther south than Oregon, feeds primarily on four species of small sea cucumbers.

◆ Among several starfish with rays webbed near the base, the leather starfish (*Dermasterias imbricata*) grows particularly large, up to 10 inches, in sheltered bays of Puget Sound. Smaller leather stars often live in tide pools. The common name of this star, which is mottled with reds, browns, greens, and purples, derives from its smooth feel, almost like wet leather. Its spines are small and deeply embedded in its thick skin.

◆ The blood starfish (*Henricia leviuscula*), which lives on the protected outer Northwest coast, glows blood red from disk to stiff, tapering arms. Only 2 to 5 inches across, it lacks pincers to clean its skin, and it has no spines, one of only a few starfish without them. It is among the least predacious of starfish, browsing from mucus threads that trap food particles in the water.

The largest white sturgeon on record in the Northwest— 20 feet long and weighing 1,500 pounds— was hooked in 1898 in Idaho's Snake River; a jackrabbit was used as bait.

STURGEON The lower Columbia River contains the world's largest and healthiest wild population of white sturgeon (*Acipenser transmontanus*). The white sturgeon, North America's largest sturgeon species, also ranks as one of the world's three largest, and the biggest freshwater stream-ascending fish of North American coastal waters. In the Northwest, white sturgeon have been found in the Umpqua, Rogue, Willamette, Snake, and Kootenai rivers, and in Puget Sound, Lake Washington, Willapa Bay, and Grays Harbor.

◆ The largest white sturgeon recorded in the Northwest— 20 feet long and weighing 1,500 pounds—was hooked in 1898 in Idaho's Snake River near the Weiser River, on a hook baited with a jackrabbit. After hooking the sturgeon, the fisherman tied the line to a tree, allowing the fish to exhaust itself.

The largest recorded Columbia River white sturgeon was 12½ feet long and weighed 1,285 pounds, including 125 pounds of eggs. Record fish are always females; a 50-year-old female may carry four million eggs weighing several hundred pounds.

◆ The primitive sturgeon, more ancient than dinosaurs, is a survivor of prehistoric armored fish. Today's sturgeon grow larger than any prehistoric fossils found, but structurally they have changed little since originating 1 to 2 million years ago.

◆ Northwest sturgeon were once so plentiful and so little valued that they were sometimes burned, used for fertilizer, or killed with an ax when taken from salmon nets and then thrown back. When the completion of the transcontinental railroad in the 1880s made iced railroad cars available, fresh sturgeon were sent to the East Coast. The suddenly valuable fish were caught on devastatingly efficient lines studded with 200 to 400 hooks.

At the peak of the Columbia River sturgeon fishery, from 1885 to 1895, more than 25 million pounds of sturgeon were harvested each year. But by 1896 the catch had fallen to 100,000 pounds, partly because so many large females had been taken for their eggs. The slow-growing, slow-maturing fish were very near extinction. By 1900 the boom had collapsed; too few sturgeon had survived. Now fishing regulations protect the giant fish in the Columbia, with a minimum catch size of 40 inches and a 6-foot maximum, to protect the females with their huge supply of eggs.

♦ Some very strange foods have been found in sturgeon stomachs, which resemble gizzards, highly muscular with a tough inner lining. One large sturgeon had eaten a bushel of onions, another a house cat. The toothless bottom-browsers suck up food using their lips, which they can extend into a tube.

♦ In 1989 an 11-foot-long female sturgeon weighing more than 600 pounds, with 100 pounds of eggs, was found dead and floating in Lake Washington. The fish, which probably died of old age at about 100 years, may have entered the lake by way of the ship canal at the turn of the century before the Ballard locks were built. This may have been one of the sturgeon released in 1909 after the Alaska-Yukon-Pacific Exposition in Seattle.

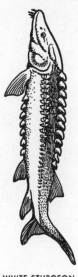

WHITE STURGEON

TROUT The Northwest is famous for its two native trout, the rainbow (*Salmo gairdneri*) and the coastal cutthroat (*S. clarki clarki*). The fighting rainbow, which repeatedly breaks water when hooked and played, is named for a bright pink streak on its side from gills to tail. It has been successfully transplanted to many places in the world.

Trout and salmon are members of the same family and very much alike, not only in appearance and fighting spirit but also in behavior. Both are predacious on smaller fish and have strong teeth for seizing and holding prey. Both spawn in a similar way. Although most trout remain in freshwater, some species go to sea like salmon.

Trout show a great variation in size and color, depending upon their environments, and as a result are difficult to classify. Trout that spend their entire life in lower lakes and streams may reach 1 to 2 pounds. Lake rainbow, sometimes called Kamloops trout, migrate from their birth streams into large lakes instead of going to sea and spawn in lake tributaries. Depending on the food available, they may grow as large as seagoing steelhead, 30 pounds or more.

♦ All three races of rainbow trout—the seagoing steelhead, the stream or river trout, and the landlocked lake trout—

Three races of native rainbow trout thrive in different Northwest habitats: streams and rivers, lakes, and the Pacific Ocean.

spawn in freshwater. Stream and river trout are smallest, especially in the high mountains where cold water slows growth rate and food is scarce.

While the fast-growing rainbow has an unusual tolerance for variations in water temperature, it prefers cold water that is unpolluted and rich in oxygen. In order to spawn, the rainbow needs a gravel bottom through which water circulates. Although native to the Northwest, sport fishing pressure is too great for rainbow populations to self-sustain. Most streams and lakes are planted with hatchery rainbow each year.

◆ The steelhead, once believed to be a distinct species, is a rainbow that migrates to the sea and spends two or three years there, feeding and growing much larger than freshwater rainbow. It can grow to be more than 40 pounds. Strong and active after its period of ocean feeding, larger and darker than stay-at-home rainbows, the steelhead leaps like a salmon as it fights its way back upstream to spawn. Unlike the Pacific salmon, it usually survives spawning, returns to the sea, and then comes back to its birth stream the next year to spawn again, sometimes repeating the cycle several times.

◆ The cutthroat, named for a scarlet slash on either side of the jaw that often is lacking in sea-run cutthroat, is native to the inland waters of the western United States and abundant in all four Northwest states. Plentiful in the lower Columbia, cutthroats go to sea wherever access is available, but their timetable is notoriously variable. They spawn in small headwater streams and tributaries of coastal rivers, staying in freshwater for a year or two, then sometimes moving to a larger body of water and staying another 3 years or longer before migrating to the sea. Often traveling in schools, they seem to stay fairly close to their home streams while in salt water. In inland waters such as Priest Lake, cutthroat can reach 41 pounds.

◆ Lake Crescent on Washington's Olympic Peninsula produces large trout of a species claimed to be unique to the lake: the Beardslee trout. This landlocked trout, full of fight, is found only in the mountain-surrounded lake, 8½ miles long and 624 feet deep. But because rainbow and other trout species have been planted in Lake Crescent, and trout interbreed readily, the Beardslee's ancestry is impossible to trace. In 1989 the largest Beardslee trout whose size was verified by the state wildlife department was caught in 100 feet of water: 16 pounds, 5 ounces. Unverified reports boast of 30-pound Beardslee trout.

◆ The Dolly Varden, brook trout (introduced to the Northwest from the eastern United States), and Mackinaw (often called lake trout) are all chars, members of the salmon family but a different genus from trout—*Salvelinus*. They differ from trout in lacking teeth on the back part of the roof of the mouth. Their scales are smaller and they have red, blue, or pale spots instead of the dark spots that cover many trout and salmon.

TRUMPETER SWAN   The Northwest provides winter homes for North America's largest aquatic bird, the trumpeter swan (*Olor buccinator*). This rare bird with white plumage and black bill and feet is the larger of two swans native to North America. The other is the whistling swan, now called the tundra swan.

The Northwest attracts the continent's largest wintering group of wild trumpeter swans.

One of the world's largest flying birds, the trumpeter swan measures 4½ to 5 feet tall and can weigh 30 to 35 pounds, near the upper weight limit for flying birds. Although the swans fly strongly, with a wingspan of 7 to 8 feet, the heavy birds have trouble taking off and maneuvering in the air. They land on water to cushion the shock. Using a slow, undulating wingbeat, trumpeter swans easily fly 50 miles an hour and can reach 80 miles an hour with a tail wind.

♦ The Northwest attracts the continent's largest wild (not fed by humans) wintering groups of trumpeter swans. Washington provides major wintering grounds. As many as 500 swans gather each season on Skagit County's Barney, Clear, and Beaver lakes, dining on crustaceans, insect larvae, roots, and stems, which they capture by stirring the muddy lake bottoms with their long beaks. In Idaho, 350 to 500 of the swans gather at Henry's Fork.

TRUMPETER SWAN

Red Rock Lakes National Wildlife Reserve, a 43,166-acre refuge in Montana, was established in 1935 to protect trumpeter swans. It provides their most important nesting area in the Lower 48, where nesting trumpeters are rare. Some 225 trumpeters live there year-round in an area of snowfed lakes and marshes. Most years, about 450 swans winter at the refuge, but occasionally as many as 800 may stop there. Red Rock Lakes deserves much of the credit for having brought the trumpeters back from near extinction.

♦ The swan's memorably beautiful two-note call, a low-pitched, hornlike trumpeting, can be heard a mile away. The source of its resonance is a loop in the long windpipe that rests in a cavity about 2½ inches deep in the breastbone. (The sandhill crane has a similar windpipe.)

♦ Early settlers hunted trumpeter swans almost to extinction for their skins and meat. The large, low-flying swans made an easy target. They once flew by the thousands over central and western North America, but as they lost their isolated habitat, they migrated west and to Canada. By 1932 only 69 were known to survive south of Canada. Today, the trumpeter swan population totals more than 11,000, still protected but no longer endangered.

WATER OUZEL Of all the perching birds, the water ouzel (*Cinclus mexicanus*) is the most exclusively aquatic. Also called a dipper, this bird lives along streams and rivers in all four Northwest states. Although a terrestrial bird, the water ouzel seldom leaves the water. Even seabirds spend more time ashore, nesting and feeding, than the dipper, which acquired that name because it bobs constantly when perched on rocks and logs in the middle of rivers. Northwesterners can see water ouzels even in winter; they are one of very few birds that remain all winter in the high mountains. Dippers even dive through skim ice. Surprisingly, the small, plump bird appears to lack predators. It builds its enclosed nest of moss close enough to water to be misted by its spray. (See Nests.)

Although a perching bird, the water ouzel lives near rushing mountain streams, where it walks and swims under the surface in search of food.

◆ This songbird displays some unique adaptations to its aquatic lifestyle. Its third eyelid, a blinking transparent membrane, protects the eye during underwater stays that last as long as half a minute. This eyelid allows the bird to see as it swims underwater and walks along the bottom of rushing streams, turning over pebbles in its search for insect larvae, small mollusks, crustaceans, minnows, and newts. Movable flaps cover the dipper's nostrils. A dense undercoat of down, unusual for a perching bird, protects the dipper in frigid weather. The dipper waterproofs its feathers with the help of an unusually large preen gland near the base of the tail. Despite these adaptations, however, when on the surface, the water-oriented dipper paddles laboriously and seldom gets very far, for it lacks webbed feet.

◆ The dipper is one of the few birds that dare to enter rushing water. It plunges into torrents and down and through waterfalls. If the current carries it away, it returns to its original location. The water ouzel has light bones, but even without the solid bones that loons and other divers have, the ouzel is able to dive and remain underwater without waterlogging its feathers.

Although it can dive as deep as 15 to 20 feet, the bird's usual depth is 1 to 2 feet. Underwater, the dipper "flies" with its wings open, stroking gracefully and powerfully, guiding itself with water-repellent tail feathers. When it emerges from the water, it can be airborne at once. So wedded to water is the dipper that even when flying, it often skims the water, following a stream's curves instead of taking shortcuts over land.

♦ The water ouzel possesses one of the most remarkable repertoires of all songbirds. Unlike other birds, it sings all year long, not just during breeding season.

WEASEL   North America's smallest true carnivore, a Northwest subspecies of the short-tailed weasel (*Mustela erminea Olympicus*), measures only 6 to 7½ inches in length and weighs 1.5 to 2 ounces. Living only on the Olympic Peninsula, this densely furred weasel, reddish brown above and white below, is unusual among weasels in not turning white during winter.

Weasels—good swimmers and climbers—can slip through mouse holes and knotholes in search of prey.

Sharp-eyed, active both day and night, the short-tailed weasel can kill prey larger and heavier than itself, biting them repeatedly in the neck. It relishes mice, fish, frogs, moles, and birds. A good swimmer and climber, the weasel can slip its slim, short-limbed body through mouse holes or knotholes as it pursues its prey tirelessly through water, up trees, over logs, and onto rock piles.

WHALES   Gray whales (*Eschrichtius robustus*) make one of the longest and largest annual migrations of any animal on earth, more than 6,000 miles from summer feeding grounds in Arctic seas to winter breeding lagoons in Baja California. Twice a year, the huge animals, 35 to 50 feet long and weighing 20 to 40 tons, swim along the Pacific coast, staying within 2 miles of land on their journey of six to eight weeks.

Twice a year, some 20,000 gray whales pass within 2 miles of the Pacific Northwest coastline during their 6,000-mile migration.

Some 20,000 whales are involved in the mass migration, with groups of as many as 30 whales an hour often visible from many points on the Washington and Oregon coastlines. Seldom pausing to rest or feed, the whales cover about 100 miles a day at a steady 10 knots. The whales are believed to navigate by following sea bottom contours, and by using sun, ocean currents, and the taste of sediments flowing from river bays and lagoons. They find their way in darkness or murky water by vocalizing in very low tones.

♦ The gray whale, a midsized baleen whale, is unique among all marine mammals in being a bottom grazer. Although it also eats swarming crustaceans and schooling fish, the bulk of its diet is small, shrimplike amphipods. One whale was found with more than ten wheelbarrow loads of the tiny creatures in its three-chambered stomach. During feeding dives, it rolls over on its right side to suck up bottom sediment into its huge mouth. With the tongue it squeezes water and silt back through the baleen filter, retaining its meal.

♦ During the migration, juveniles often stray to feed or explore.

An unusually large number of young gray whales entered Puget Sound in late spring of 1990. A number of them died, one after ten weeks in Puget Sound. The whales, which left deep depressions on the bottom of the Sound from their feeding, may have picked up pollutants from contaminated bottom sediments. Scientists, however, did not find that these pollutants killed the whales.

♦ Because their migration route brings the gray whales so close to the coastlines of three countries—the United States, Canada, and Mexico—they have become one of the most observed and studied of the great whales. Their coast-hugging habit made them easy prey for whalers, who brought the Atlantic gray whale to extinction, and the Pacific gray perilously close to it.

The recovery of the Pacific gray whale population, after it was declared a depleted, endangered species in 1946, marks one of the most remarkable comebacks in animal history. The whales now may exceed their former numbers.

♦ Even though a gray whale carries barnacles weighing several hundred pounds imbedded in its hide, it often breaches, sometimes more than a dozen times in succession. In breaching, the whale bursts from the water, lifts more than half its body clear of the water, pivots onto its side or back, and lands with an enormous splash. The activity may be playful, a courtship display, or a stress-relieving movement. Gray whales also spyhop, heads rising 8 to 10 feet above the surface and turning slowly to scan the horizon for thirty seconds or more. When they sound, their flukes thrust the body into a steeply angled dive to about 120 feet.

WHALE STRANDING   In the only recorded mass stranding of sperm whales (*Physeter macrocephalus*) in the western United States, forty-one of the world's largest toothed whale and largest marine carnivore were stranded on a beach at Florence, Oregon, in June 1979. It was only the second sperm whale stranding in North America; it was the fourth largest of seventeen such strandings worldwide since 1617.

The only recorded mass stranding of sperm whales in the western United States occurred in 1979 near Florence, Oregon.

Single strandings of sick or dying whales occur much more often than mass strandings, which are recorded most often among deepwater, gregarious whales with the most highly developed social behavior. One theory suggests that the whales stranded in Oregon were staying with sick, injured, or dying members who had headed for shore, as whales often do when in trouble, perhaps driven by a fear of drowning. Spectators at Florence tried to tow some of the whales back to sea, but all of the whales returned to the beach.

Because the 12-ton whales were still alive when discovered, testing of tissues and blood could be carried out before they died and their bodies decomposed. Researchers have not, however, determined the exact cause of the stranding. The whales' organs of echolocation proved free of ear parasites; such parasites can disturb balance, making it difficult for the animal to surface and breathe.

Another theory suggests that these sperm whales followed a school of spawning squid too close to shore. Squid were seen in the vicinity of the stranded whales, and the whales' stomachs were found to contain only squid beaks. Or the whales may have been fleeing killer whales, fierce predators feared by all the great whales. (See Orcas.)

The most complicated theory centers on geomagnetic fields in rocks. Whales may use geomagnetic clues to guide themselves through the sea, switching off other sensory systems such as echolocation and vision. When a magnetic valley coincides with a sand bank or beach such as the one in Florence—long, sloping, shallow, and lacking land formations to bounce back sonar echoes—a whale becomes disoriented, strays into shallow water, and strands.

WOLVES The gray wolf, or timber wolf (*Canus lupus*), is the largest of the wild dogs, the stock from which domestic dogs descended some 12,000 years ago. The shy wolves can weigh up to 175 pounds and measure 6½ feet, nose tip to tail tip.

The rarest of all Northwest mammals is the gray, or timber wolf.

Almost extinct in the Lower 48, gray wolves were classified as an endangered species in 1973 (except in Minnesota). The rarest of Northwest mammals, wolves never abounded in this region. Bounties on wolves began as early as 1850, and by 1900, 2 million had been killed. A few packs in the Olympic Peninsula and in the Okanogan area disappeared about 1910. By 1930 the gray wolves were nearly extinct, as a result of a wolf control program in the West encouraged by the federal government. Under this program, wolves were shot, trapped, and poisoned.

Now, gray wolves are making a limited comeback in the Northwest, although they propagate very slowly because breeding in a pack is the prerogative of the dominant male and female. The highly social wolves mate for life and if the female should be killed, the male takes over care of the pups.

GRAY WOLF

◆ After wolves had been absent for thirty years in Glacier National Park, a wolf pack that wandered into Montana from Canada produced a litter in the park in 1986. It had earlier produced several litters outside the park. Currently, some twenty wolves live in or near the park. Glacier National Park includes such predators as wolves in its policy of preserving and promoting a natural balance in the ecosystem.

◆ In the spring of 1990, a wolf den was discovered in Ross Lake National Recreation Area in Washington's North Cascades National Park. Wolf tracks had been spotted in previous years, but sounds of wolf cubs heard in 1990 were the first indication of breeding wolves in Washington since the early 1900s. Great care was taken not to disturb the wolves, who are quick to move dens.

Wolves normally prey on weak or young animals. Large animals can usually outrun or outfight them. Not efficient predators, wolves achieve a kill in only one of twelve tries.

TWO

PLANTS

· · · · · · · · · · · · · · · · · ·

From the fast-growing alder . . .
to mosses that nurture rain forests . . .
to the odd youth-on-age plant

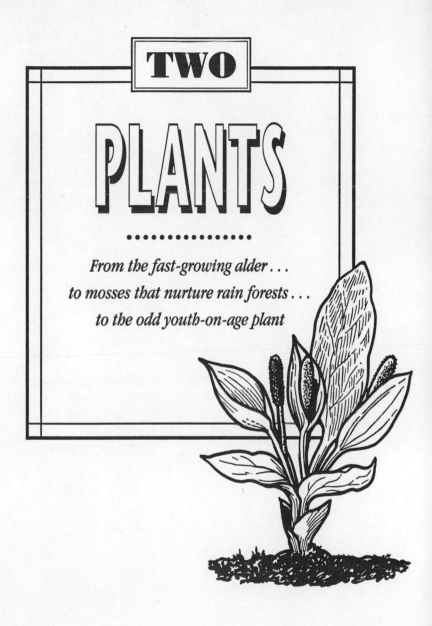

AGRICULTURE Agriculture first sent down roots in the Northwest as the fur trade began to decline. Mountain men and retired Hudson's Bay Company employees reluctantly took up farming, beginning in 1832 to settle around an area that became known as French Prairie, just north of what is now Salem, Oregon. Jason and Daniel Lee, the first American missionaries in the Northwest, arrived two years later, hoping to interest local native Americans in farming. In part because both coastal and Plains Indians already harvested a number of naturally growing plants—particularly camas bulbs—the missionaries' attempts to interest them in cultivating crops failed.

Northwest states lead the nation in the production of hops, apples, filberts, potatoes, barley, grass seed, winter pears, and sweet cherries.

◆ The Hudson's Bay Company created the Northwest's first agricultural enterprise in 1838, establishing Puget's Sound Agricultural Company. Located near a Hudson's Bay trading post close to what is now Tacoma, Fort Nisqually, the new agricultural company farmed land "between the headwaters of the Cowlitz Portage and Puget's Sound." Encountering poor soil that required heavy fertilization, the agricultural company eventually concentrated on raising cattle and sheep, which thrived on the rich native grass. However, they successfully harvested thousands of bushels of wheat, oats, barley, peas, and potatoes as well.

◆ Even before the construction of huge dams, extensive irrigation systems opened up arid land east of the Cascade Range to agriculture. One of the largest ditch systems in Idaho, the Ridenbaugh Ditch, was dug in the 1890s. It stretched for 50 miles, irrigating 25,000 acres. By 1909 Northwest farmers were irrigating 3 million acres, reclaiming entire valleys.

Today, planting in soil enriched by volcanic ash and irrigated by river water impounded by dams, Northwest farmers often lead the nation—and sometimes the world—in harvests of agricultural crops. Northwest fields, for example, provide half of the U.S. crop of alfalfa seed.

◆ Washington ranks second in the nation in diversity of crops, producing more than forty different commodities in sufficient quantities to warrant statewide record keeping. Farming employs more workers than does any other business in the state. Washington leads the nation in the production of apples, hops, winter pears, red raspberries, sweet cherries, spearmint oil, and carrots for processing.

◆ Washington's 60-mile-long Yakima Valley is one of the country's most fertile, and yet most arid, growing regions. The valley receives only 7 inches of rain a year, most of it during the winter, so valley crops depend upon irrigation. In most years Yakima County ranks among the nation's top five counties in crop productivity. Although the valley is especially noted for the quality and quantity of its fruit crops, its leading crop is wheat.

◆ Oregon leads the nation in the production of grass seed, peppermint oil, filberts, and all berry crops that grow on canes (such as raspberries). Oregon fields grow 90 percent of the nation's Easter lily bulbs and nearly 100 percent of the nation's filberts.

◆ Idaho ranks first in the nation in the production of potatoes and barley; the world's highest quality of barley for malting and livestock feed comes from Idaho. Canyon County, Idaho, is the nation's center of farm-crop seed production, with farmers in that county producing eighty different crops, more than any other county in the nation. They produce 85 percent of the country's snap bean seed and 90 percent of sweet corn seed. Crookham Seed Company in Caldwell, Idaho, is the world's largest producer of hybrid seed corn.

◆ In barley production, Montana ranks second in the nation, next to Idaho. Montana is second only to Texas for acres of land in farms and ranches—more than 60,600,000 acres. Much of that land grows wheat; despite extremes of temperature, Montana ranks fourth in the nation in the production of all types of wheat.

ALDER In its early stages, red alder (*Alnus rubra*) ranks as the Northwest's fastest-growing tree. In five years it can reach 15 feet; in ten years, 35 to 40 feet. Largest of the alders and most valuable of coastal hardwood trees, red alder is the only commercially harvested tree in the Northwest that is more abundant now than it was a century ago.

The sun-loving, fast-growing red alder is usually the first tree to appear in areas devastated by fires or clear-cuts.

After dramatic occurrences such as fire, volcanic eruption, and clear-cutting, red alder are usually the first trees to appear. Growing quickly during the first critical years after a disaster, these trees stabilize the soil and shelter conifer seedlings that eventually appear.

Nitrogen-fixing bacteria in the alder's root tissue nodules convert air nitrogen into soil nitrogen. These bacteria, along with the alder's rapidly decomposing, nitrogen-rich leaf litter, greatly improve soil quality and facilitate the growth of other trees.

ALGAE Although they are the simplest of the true plants, algae are responsible for some of the most dramatic natural events in the Northwest. When the microscopic *Gonyaulax catenella* (part alga and part animal) colors Northwest salt waters rust red, reproducing by the millions until the water "blooms" in what is known as a red tide, Northwesterners stop eating shellfish from those waters for fear of paralysis or even death. These algae also

"Red tides," "red snow," and even the vivid color of the large green sea anemone are all caused by algae.

put on spectacular bioluminescent displays, which early native Americans heeded as warnings not to eat shellfish for a while. In the mountains, colonies of another tiny algae produce "red snow," staining patches of old snowfields red.

Green and golden algae color the large sea anemone a vivid green. Living symbiotically with the anemone, the algae photosynthesize food, some of which the animal absorbs, and receive shelter and useful animal waste products in return. The anemone orients its body so that the algae within it receive the maximum amount of sunlight for photosynthesis.

◆ Northwest lichen lovers know that those scaly, leafy, or hairy gray-green growths so visible on rocks and trees are the result of an odd marriage between millions of algal cells and a mesh of fungal filaments. Since no fungus manufactures its own food, and all algae do, the lichen alga photosynthesizes for two, while the fungus provides shelter from wind and loss of water. Recent research has questioned this seeming symbiotic paradise, suggesting that the lichen fungus is actually parasitic on the alga.

APPLES Washington produces more apples than does any other state—more than half the nation's crop. Apples constitute one of Washington's primary exports.

Washington leads the country in the production of apples, providing more than half the nation's total supply of fresh apples.

◆ The apple reportedly got its start in the Northwest around 1824, when a sailing captain called at Fort Vancouver, bringing with him apple seeds from England. The result of those seeds is the region's oldest apple tree, which grows in Vancouver, Washington, and still produces fruit, although of uncertain variety and poor quality.

Twenty apple trees that were planted in about 1838 by the Puget's Sound Agricultural Company still grow along the Nisqually River. Often the sites of old farms, homesteads, and Indian settlements can be identified by the rare varieties of apple trees that still grow there. Pioneers on the Oregon Trail brought apple seeds to the Northwest in the late 1840s. The homesteaders planted apple orchards in the Hood River valley, which today is Oregon's largest apple-growing region. With its warm days, cool nights, and mild winters, it is one of the most productive orchard regions in the world.

◆ The highest price ever recorded for an apple tree was $51,000, paid in 1959 by a Missouri nursery for a single Starkspar Golden Delicious grown near Yakima, Washington.

ARBORETUM The Washington Park Arboretum in Seattle boasts the most diversified woody-plant collection in the West.

Something is in bloom almost every day at Seattle's Washington Park Arboretum, home to nearly 5,500 different kinds of woody plants.

Part of the scientific mission of any arboretum is to discover how many plant species from around the world will grow in a regional climate. Some 5,500 different kinds of bushes, shrubs, and trees—both native and nonnative—thrive in the University of Washington's 200-acre woody-plant museum. The arboretum showcases major collections of magnolias, cherries, and conifers. Something is in bloom almost every day of the year at the arboretum. More than sixty of its trees are the largest or tallest of their species growing in Washington.

Designed by the well-known landscape architecture firm, The Olmsted Brothers, the arboretum was part of a master plan developed in 1903 by the sons of the distinguished founder of the firm, Frederick Law Olmsted, Sr. (The senior Olmsted is famous for designing such sites as New York's Central Park and the Capitol grounds in Washington, D.C.)

AVALANCHE AND GLACIER LILY

Avalanche and glacier lilies are among the first flowers to bloom on alpine slopes, even pushing up through the last of the snow.

Among the Northwest's most accessible and earliest-blooming alpine and subalpine wildflowers are the white-petaled avalanche lily (*Erythronium montanum*) and the yellow-petaled glacier lily (*E. grandiflorum*). Averaging only 6 to 8 inches in height, the elegant lilies get a headstart on their short growing season at timberline by starting to photosynthesize and grow while still covered with snow. The warmth of their plant tissues helps them push leaves and flower buds up through the snow.

The blooming periods of the two lilies overlap, so in July hundreds bloom, side by side, in damp meadows on Cascade peaks in Washington and northern Oregon and east of the Cascades to the Rocky Mountains. With only a few weeks of sunlight between snowmelt in July and new snow in early autumn, the lilies must quickly produce leaves, buds, flowers, and seeds. Each plant can store up only enough energy to bloom and form seeds once in every five or six years.

GLACIER LILY

BARK

The most widely used bark of any Northwest tree comes from the cascara buckthorn, which provides the active ingredient in many laxatives.

Northwest Indian tribes once used the bark of many trees and shrubs for a variety of purposes. Bark of some trees still proves useful today.

♦ The most widely used bark of any Northwest tree comes from the cascara buckthorn (*Rhamnus purshiana*), a shrubby tree 10 to 20 feet tall. Four to five million pounds of the bark are collected and dried annually to be used by pharmaceutical companies in making laxatives. Even stripping the bark with bare hands can produce a laxative effect.

Northwest Indians used the bitter-tasting cascara bark to

make laxatives, yellow and green dyes, and a tonic. At times they deliberately gave a fatal overdose of the tonic.

Cascara trees have been exploited for so long that large specimens are scarce. After bark collectors girdle the tree and remove the bark in sheets, they fell the tree so that new shoots will grow, ready for harvest in several years. A peeled tree that is not cut down to the stump will die without producing new shoots.

◆ Medical researchers have found a substance in the bark of the scarce Pacific yew tree that yields taxol, a compound used to produce the only drug successful to date in arresting ovarian cancer. The drug may also prove effective against other cancers. Unfortunately, removing the thin bark of the yew kills the slow-growing tree, and attempts to make synthetic taxol have failed.

◆ The bark most widely used by Northwest coastal Indians was that of the western red cedar. After pulling the reddish bark from old-growth cedars and drying it for months, the Indians soaked it and tore the fibrous bark into narrow strips.

They then wove the bark strips into bags and baskets, plates and platters, sails, and matting for temporary houses. Bark served as warp in blankets and other textiles; the woof was spun from mountain goat hair or, occasionally, dog hair. The Indians also shredded the bark finely for cradle padding, towels, and diapers, or wadded it for burning as torches and kindling. A coarser grade, woven into clothing, produced waterproof skirts, capes, dresses, hats, ceremonial headbands, and leggings. Fiber from the inner bark furnished cordage for fishing nets and for rope to lash together red cedar timbers in longhouses.

◆ The thick bark of the ponderosa pine is more fire-resistant than the bark of any other Northwest tree. One healthy 250-year-old ponderosa pine felled in Idaho showed the scars of twenty-one fires.

◆ Black cottonwood bark is so hard that cutting it with a chain saw can produce sparks.

BEARGRASS The Northwest's only evergreen member of the lily family is beargrass (*Xerophyllum tenax*), which grows only in North America. Also known as basket grass, the plant is abundant in mountain meadows and on open slopes in all the Northwest states. Thriving in high country such as Montana's Glacier National Park and Oregon's Mount Hood, it also occasionally grows at sea level.

Beargrass blooms in large, dense plumes of creamy white flowers on stalks often more than 3 feet high. Plants bloom erratically, with good years and bad. Growth spurts occur after fires or

The Northwest's only evergreen member of the lily family, beargrass plants bloom erratically, with good years and bad.

logging, perhaps because of increased light. Each year, offset plants spring up from the thick rhizomes, develop for several years, bloom, and then die.

In the past, native Americans used the long, tough, grasslike leaves of beargrass for weaving capes, hats, and baskets; bundles of the stiff leaves were used in trade and given as gifts. Contemporary native American basket makers prize the beargrass growing near Queets, on Washington's Olympic Peninsula: the leaves are twice the length of beargrass leaves found elsewhere.

Although the leaves are too sharp-edged to appeal to any animal but the mountain goat, larger animals eat the stems and tender leaves at the base of the plant in spring and the blossoms and soft seedpods later in the year.

BERRIES The Northwest is blessed with a bounty of wild berries. Wild berry plants, some with prickles and thorns and some without, some prostrate and some growing as trees up to 40 feet high, grow in a variety of Northwest sites: streamsides, open woods, cut-over or burned areas, and mountain slopes up to 9,000 feet.

Northwest Indian tribes gathered and preserved for winter use more than twenty native berries.

The many birds that gorge on wild berries, as well as bears, may have given the first Northwesterners a clue as to the edibility of such native berries as thimbleberries and salmonberries, salal and Oregon grape berries, red, black, and evergreen huckleberries, strawberries, red and blue elderberries, blackberries and cranberries, kinnikinnick and juniper berries, serviceberries, chokecherries, hawthorne and mountain ash berries.

◆ Native people used leaves, bark, and twigs from berry plants for medicinal purposes, and often ate young shoots. Animals browse berry shrubs, and seek shelter in the often-prickly thickets. Bears and birds rely heavily on berries. Mountain men, early explorers such as Lewis and Clark, and early settlers, including the Astorians in 1811, staved off starvation by eating wild berries.

Gathering and preserving berries was as important a part of annual food gathering among all Northwest Indians as was the catching of salmon and the digging of roots. Accordingly, berries appeared in various tribal myths. A Klamath Indian myth claims that the first people were made from serviceberry bushes. Their straight slender shoots were used for arrow shafts by tribes from the plains to the coast.

Most of the berries the natives ate raw and also dried, often smoking on racks over small fires. They also cooked berries in steaming pits or cedar boxes, mixing the bitter or astringent berries with blander ones. The pulp was pressed into cakes or pounded with buffalo meat (on the plains) or salmon bellies (on the coast) into pemmican, along with fat, for winter rations. Whether raw or dried, berries were often dipped in whale or seal oil, which provided necessary fat in the diet. Natives made a preserve from some berries and stored it in watertight baskets placed in the mud of cold streams or in swampy areas.

OREGON GRAPE

Native people knew how to safely prepare such potentially toxic berries as red elderberries and such astringent berries as chokecherries. They ate the berries of ground-hugging kinnikinnick and smoked its dry leaves, becoming intoxicated from the smoke. They instinctively knew they needed the carbohydrates provided by seeds and pounded fleshy, dark red chokecherries together with their hard stones and shells. Lewis and Clark's journal entries describe a native bread made of serviceberries mixed with pounded seeds of balsam-root and lamb's-quarter.

♦ Salmonberries, borne on one of the most common berry-producing shrubs in Northwest fir forests, were not usually dried, because of their softness—like that of the thimbleberry. Indians ate them raw and made a beverage of salmonberries. Early explorers who suffered digestive upset from eating too much salmon ate salmonberries for relief.

♦ The tiny, delectable wild blackberry, also called dewberry, is the only blackberry native to the Northwest. It is as much a favorite today as it was long ago. Its small seeds and rich flavor make it one of the Northwest's most sought-after berries.

♦ Native people from both coast and interior camped each fall on the slopes of Washington's Mount Adams to pick huckleberries and to socialize. The women gathered berries while the men hunted large game. The savory berries were sun- or smoke-dried and mashed into cakes, which were stored in leaves or bark.

♦ Aromatic, although mealy, salal berries were popular with coastal Indians, who found them everywhere in coastal forests. They would pick a twig thick with berries, dip it in whale oil, and pull the berry-laden twig through the mouth. A syrup was often made from this much-prized berry. Loaves of mashed and dried salal berries often weighed more than 10 pounds.

♦ The berries of Oregon grape, the Oregon state flower noted for its shiny leaves and bright yellow flowers, were eaten fresh, mixed with other berries, and used to flavor soup. The berries yielded a blue dye, and roots a yellow dye used for basket materials, buckskins, and porcupine quills used for ceremonial garments and rattles.

BITTERROOT Montana's state flower, the bitterroot (*Lewisia rediviva*), has given its name to a mountain range, a valley, and a river in Montana. Its 2-inch-long, starchy tuber is nutritious, but tastes slightly bitter even after cooking. Bitterroot was the second most important food plant (after camas) gathered by Montana's Indian tribes. A sack of dried roots reportedly equaled a horse in value. Native peoples dug a year's supply of the roots at one time, always before the flowers opened.

The bitterroot has given its name to a mountain range, a valley, and a river in Montana.

The 3-inch-high plants are sometimes called rockroses because they seem to grow out of stone on ridges or rocky slopes. The *rediviva* in the plant's name refers to the ability of long-dried roots to sprout and grow.

BLACK COTTONWOOD The Northwest's largest broadleaf tree is the black cottonwood (*Populus trichocarpa*), which grows abundantly in all four Northwest states. Perhaps the largest poplar in the world, the tree grows to 175 feet in height and 4 to 5 feet in diameter. In summer, seed capsules spill tiny, cottony seeds into the air, the unmistakable sign of the cottonwood tree.

One of the tallest broadleaf trees in North America, the black cottonwood grows to a height of 175 feet.

Although it is a moisture-loving tree, the black cottonwood tolerates the widest range of rainfall of any Northwest tree—from more than 100 inches of rain on the coast to 6 to 8 inches inland. In the interior deserts it grows only along lakes and streams, serving as an indicator species for water-saturated or flood-prone land. The trunk, so waterlogged it can barely float, gushes water when cut down. The tree is too subject to rot to be valuable for timber and is good for firewood only when well dried.

Black cottonwood is a favorite nesting tree for a variety of birds. The big tree offers excellent support for the huge, unwieldy nests of larger birds such as blue herons, bald eagles, and ospreys.

BONSAI TREES Bonsai lovers can view the West Coast's largest public collection of miniature trees in the Pacific Rim Bonsai Collection, located at the Weyerhaeuser Company Corporate Headquarters in Federal Way, Washington. Specimens include more than fifty miniature trees. Some of the bonsai—"trees in pots" in Japanese—are more than 500 years old. The oldest is a 37-inch-high Chinese juniper grafted onto the trunk of a Sierra juniper dating from A.D. 990. A ponderosa pine from Colorado, only 30 inches high, dates back to 1380.

More than fifty "trees in pots," some older than 500 years, grow in the Pacific Rim Bonsai Collection, the West Coast's largest.

CAMAS The camas (*Camassia quamash*) sends up 2-foot stems with clusters of flowers that vary from iridescent pale blue to deep purplish blue. This showy plant, with its 1-inch, onionlike bulb, may have played the most significant role of any flowering plant in early Northwest history. Northwest tribes valued camas bulbs so highly that they battled one another over favored camas meadows. In 1878 settlers and members of the Bannock tribe went to war when the settlers' livestock rooted up and ate camas bulbs on the tribe's traditional camas lands.

Early Northwest native Americans so valued the tiny, onionlike bulbs of the camas that tribes waged wars over camas meadows.

Nez Perce Indians were harvesting their winter supply of camas in September 1805 when Lewis and Clark's half-starved group trudged across the Bitterroot Mountains into the Weippe Meadows. The Indians offered camas to the expedition. Many in the group became ill from eating too much camas; however, they later came to depend upon the bulbs for food.

Northwest native tribes often roasted the tiny bulbs, which taste like sweet potato, in rock ovens. In 1985 the largest, earliest, and best-preserved food-processing site in the interior Northwest, identified by huge quantities of rock once used for camas-roasting pit ovens, was discovered in northeastern Washington's Kalispell Valley near the Pend Oreille River. The fire-cracked rock was carbon-dated to 2000 B.C.

CARNIVOROUS PLANTS Four of the six U.S. genera of carnivorous plants grow in the Northwest: cobra lily, sundew, bladderwort, and butterwort.

In the Northwest, four species of carnivorous plants trap and digest insects to supplement their diets.

◆ Of these four plants, the cobra lily (*Darlingtonia californica*) is by far the largest and most spectacular. First discovered by a botanist with the United States Exploring Expedition, which arrived in Puget Sound in 1841, the cobra lily is the Northwest's only member of the carnivorous pitcher plant family. It has the most complicated leaf structure of any North American pitcher plant. Growing in nitrogen-poor soil, the cobra lily supplements its diet with insects.

The pale green, hollow leaf grows nearly 3 feet tall and catches its prey—wasps, bees, ants, flies, beetles—in a domed opening. Veined with red or purple and dotted with opaque spots, the leaf is shaped like the head of a striking cobra. Below the opening dangles a nectar-rich "fishtail," which lures insects. As insects gorge on the nectar, hairs slanting upward encourage them to enter the dome. Once inside, insects tire themselves by flying at what appear to be exits, but which are actually just the opaque spots on the dome. The slick surface of the inner dome and the long, stiff hairs, pointing downward here, prevent escape. The insects chute down the tube into a pool of lethal broth secreted at the base of the leaf.

In the pool, bacteria digest the soft body parts of the trapped insects. Plant walls and other areas below the dome absorb nutrients. As the tube fills with chitinous remains, it emits a strong smell of decaying insect.

One of the Northwest's most highly localized plants, the cobra lily lives only in wet, acidic peat or sphagnum bogs in southwest Oregon, growing at sea level along Oregon's coast and up to 8,000 feet in the Siskiyou Mountains. An 18-acre bog full of "cobras" forms the unusual Darlingtonia Botanical Wayside, located a few miles north of Florence, Oregon—at the northern limit of the lily's range.

COBRA LILY

◆ The tiny but sophisticated sundew (*Drosera rotundifolia*) has the most versatile glands of any carnivorous plant. These tiny flowering plants, common in the Northwest, grow in sphagnum bogs and also on moss atop floating logs, rising only a few inches high. Some 200 tentacles fringe a central leaf disk, which measures one-half inch across. A gland at the tip of each tentacle secretes a very sticky substance; this dewdrop of mucilage glistening at the end of a bright red stalk attracts and traps tiny insects such as gnats. The sticky leaf disk also acts as a flypaper trap, the mucilage on its surface suffocating the insect. Tentacles bend inward to secure the prey, in a cell-growth process similar to that in young plants bending toward light. They then move the insect toward the center of the leaf, where enzymes secreted by the tentacle glands and by other, shorter glands begin to dissolve the soft parts of the insect. Finally, the tentacles aid in absorbing the nutrients. One of the substances secreted is an antiseptic fluid that prevents the decomposition of the insect body from injuring the leaf.

◆ Tiny glands completely cover the fleshy, pale green leaves of the carnivorous butterwort (*Pinguicula vulgaris*). A drop of shimmering mucilage tips each gland, attracting and trapping insects. But the butterwort is not a passive flypaper trap. Its flow of mucilage increases as the insect struggles, and the leaf dishes slightly under the insect in a cell-growth response that pools the digestive fluids. The thin-edged leaves, already slightly rolled inward, curl in even more after catching an insect or two. This curling helps move the prey to the center of the leaf, brings more digestive glands into contact with the insect, and keeps rain from washing the insect off the leaf and from diluting the trapping and digestive fluids. The digestive fluid contains a mild antibacterial solution that prevents decay of the insect during the digestive process—a process that may take four or five days.

Butterwort grows near the ground in compact rosettes several inches across, with violetlike blooms. Found in damp mountain meadows as high as 7,500 feet, butterwort prefers mossy banks and moist rock crevices.

CEDAR None of our Northwest cedars are true cedars; those grow only in the eastern Mediterranean, North Africa, and the Himalayas. Our "cedars" share certain qualities, such as aroma and color, with those trees, but otherwise do not resemble them.

◆ The Northwest's longest-lived tree may be the Alaska cedar (*Chamaecyparis nootkatensis*), or yellow cedar, which can live to be 2,000 years old. Four fungi-killing chemicals in the heartwood make it unusually rot-resistant. Alaska cedar grows best in moist coastal forests at elevations of 2,500 to 6,500 feet. It is one of only a few conifers that grow almost exclusively west of the Cascades. One exception is a 10-acre grove in central Oregon at 5,500 feet; the grove is probably an Ice Age remnant from cooler, wetter times.

At timberline, Alaska cedar often sprawls like a shrub, growing on rocks in little or no soil. On Mount Angeles in the Olympic Mountains, a mat of Alaska cedar that is 50 feet across and 3 feet high may be 1,000 years old.

◆ The most useful native plant to Northwest coastal Indians was the western red cedar (*Thuja plicata*). In addition to the many uses they made of the bark, coastal Indians constructed coiled baskets from the tough, flexible roots, concocted medicines from cedar buds and tips, and scoured their bodies with the leaves and limbs.

Using jadite and shell tools, the Indians carved the easily worked red cedar into household boxes, large potlatch serving dishes shaped like reclining figures, animal masks, and totem poles. Red cedar artifacts 500 years old, recovered from the archeological dig at Ozette Village on Washington's Cape Alava, provide evidence of red cedar's resistance to rot.

Because the soft, straight-grained red cedar is one of the easiest of all woods to split, coastal Indians were able to cut dimensional lumber even with crude tools. Some of their boards were 3 inches thick, 2 to 3 feet wide, and 20 to 30 feet long. Red cedar provided posts, roof boards, and wall planks for tribal longhouses.

Red cedar dugout canoes enabled coastal tribes to become whalers, fishermen, travelers, and warriors. Their 60-foot-long war canoes carried tons of freight or thirty to forty warriors.

Red cedar ranks as the most rot-resistant of the conifers because of a preservative oil in the heartwood. Red cedars cut

Rot-resistant Alaska cedar can live up to 2,000 years; a felled western red cedar can remain nearly rot-free for 150 years on damp soil.

and left lying by pioneers, who scorned them, are still nearly rot-free after more than 150 years on damp soil.

Although not strong enough for heavy use, red cedar is free of pitch and remains durable when exposed to the severest climate; it is the lightest of all lumber when dried. Red cedar is the world's leading shingle and shake material, most of which is split from trees originating in Washington's Olympic National Forest.

◆ Of the four Northwest states, only Oregon has groves of Port Orford cedar (*C. lawsoniana*). The trees grow at low elevations in the state's southwest corner; Coos Bay marks the tree's northern limit. The fragrant wood, similar to that of Alaska cedar, is strong and easy to work. Port Orford cedar is the most endangered of all coastal Northwest conifers.

CENTER FOR URBAN HORTICULTURE

The only one of its kind in the world, the Center for Urban Horticulture teaches city dwellers how to raise gardens in an urban environment.

The University of Washington has developed a Center for Urban Horticulture in Seattle that is the only one of its kind in the world, dedicated to research and teaching about urban plants and their effects on humans. Opened in 1980, the center, with the aid of many local professional and amateur horticulturists, helps city dwellers raise gardens under the adverse conditions of the urban environment.

The 55-acre center includes greenhouses, demonstration and display gardens, a horticultural library, and a herbarium with dried specimens of Northwest cultivated plants.

◆ Seattle's moderate climate allows that city's gardeners to grow more plants than are grown in any other urban area in North America. Seattle hosts more than 400 amateur gardening groups.

CHANTERELLE MUSHROOM

Chanterelles thrive in the damp forests of Oregon and Washington, the nation's two leading producers of these delicately flavored mushrooms.

Ideal conditions in the damp forests west of the Cascades make Washington and Oregon the nation's largest producers of chanterelle mushrooms (*Cantharellus cibarius*), which grow best in tall, second-growth Douglas fir and hemlock forests. The flesh of the attractive, apricot orange chanterelles, often fluted like morning glories or vases, is a fall favorite of amateur mushroom pickers, who relish the meaty texture and nutty flavor. Yields fell as a result of overpicking in the late 1980s after exporters began to pay high prices for fresh chanterelles. (See Fungus.)

CLEMONS TREE FARM

The birthplace of commercial forestry's tree-farm system in the United States, Clemons Tree Farm covers more than 330,000 acres in Grays Harbor County near Montesano, Washington.

When the Weyerhaeuser Company began the farm in 1941, it was the first farm to grow trees as a crop. Before that time, reseeding was accomplished by aerial reforestation and by leaving a few seed trees standing after clear-cutting.

At the tree farm, managers chose seed from superior trees and encouraged fast growth by planting, fertilizing, weeding, and thinning. The best of the first crop of seedlings were cloned and crossbred, and second-generation seed from them is now planted.

Clemons Tree Farm has served as a model for 30,000 other U.S. tree farms.

Clemons Tree Farm has served as a model for more than 30,000 similar farms across the nation. In less than fifty years, the trees, most of them Douglas fir, have grown up to 140 feet tall and 2 feet in diameter.

DEER FERN

DEER FERN Among the many ferns that spring up in moist and shady Northwest coastal coniferous forests, only the deer fern (*Blechnum spicant*) produces two distinctly different types of fronds: one sterile and evergreen, the other fertile and seasonal. In spring and early summer, the sporebearing fronds rise nearly two feet above the rosette of short-stemmed evergreen fronds. The fertile fronds die down in late summer. The sterile fronds taper at both base and tip.

Of the common ferns that grow in Northwest coniferous forests, only the deer fern produces two different kinds of fronds.

More ancient than flowering plants, ferns have true roots, stems, and leaves but lack flowers, fruits, and seeds. They reproduce by spores, often borne on the backs of the fronds. Scattered by the wind, germinating spores give rise to a tiny plant completely different from the parent. This *prothallium* produces sperm and eggs that unite to create a new fern.

DEVIL'S CLUB

DEVIL'S CLUB No more formidable shrub exists in the Northwest than the profusely spined devil's club (*Oplopanax horridum*). A forest of yellowish, needle-sharp spines ⅜ of an inch long armor the thick stems. Spines also follow the veins on both upper and lower sides of the lobed, maplelike leaves, which can measure a foot across. Even the roots have spines. Hikers learn to give this plant a wide berth: its runners can trip the unwary, and contact with its vicious-looking spines causes painful swelling.

Needle-sharp spines cover the leaves, the stems, and even the roots of the formidable devil's club, which can reach heights of 10 feet or more.

Usually encountered in moist woods near streams, devil's club can reach a height of 10 feet or more as the huge leaves reach for the sun. In the fall, the shrub produces a cone-shaped cluster of bright red berries, attractive but inedible.

Northwest coastal tribes put this plant, a close relative of ginseng, to good use. They boiled the peeled bark and drank the infusion to cure colds, rheumatism, and tuberculosis. They dried the bark and ground it into a powder for use as perfume, baby talc, and deodorant. Indian shamans used the shrub in rituals for protection against supernatural beings. According to Indian legend, one hero threw a bit of devil's club in the path of a pursuing enemy, and at once, an impenetrable thicket of devil's club sprang up.

The creamy-white "petals" of the shade-tolerant Pacific dogwood, North America's largest native dogwood, are actually specialized leaves.

DOGWOOD   The Pacific dogwood (*Cornus nuttallii*), the Northwest's most shade-tolerant flowering tree, ranks as North America's largest native dogwood. Unique among hardwoods in preferring shade, it grows among huge conifers in dense, coastal forests. The creamy-white outer "petals," sometimes 5 inches across, are really bracts—specialized, petallike leaves. The true, yellow-green flowers cluster in the center.

Coastal Indians used the very hard, fine-grained wood to make bows, combs, and weavers' shuttles. Archeologists found such objects, 500 years old and perfectly preserved, at Washington's Ozette Village. (See Natural Features, Capes.)

Although it grows and even blooms underwater, eelgrass is not a seaweed but a flowering land plant, with true roots and stems.

EELGRASS   One of the few flowering plants that have returned to salt water, eelgrass (*Zostera nolti*) is a biological oddity. Unlike marine plants, it has true roots, stems, and leaves, and its seeds are enclosed in an ovary. Yet it has edged out into the sea, growing on mud and sand in quiet bays and estuaries. Its flowers bloom under water and its pollen and seeds are dispersed by water. Two of the most extensive "meadows" of eelgrass on the West Coast, if not in the world, grow in Washington waters at Willapa Bay and Padilla Bay. At Padilla Bay, near Bellingham, a 7,500-acre eelgrass meadow covers 75 percent of the mud flats. Eelgrass beds also thrive on the inner shore of Washington's Dungeness Spit.

The creeping rhizomes and roots of eelgrass stabilize the muddy soil while enriching it with decaying organic material. The beds shelter many lower intertidal and subtidal organisms: small snails and worms, shrimps, tiny sea urchins and anemones, and sedentary jellyfish and scallops, which in turn provide food for larger animals such as salmon and crab. Migrating and wintering waterfowl and shorebirds feed on the grass, its seeds, and the small animals living in the beds. Eelgrass beds are estimated to support 16 species of plants, 191 invertebrate species, 76 fish species, and 237 bird species.

FILBERT One of the nation's first commercial filbert orchards began in the Northwest in 1903 when pioneer farmer George Dorris planted fifty trees in rich soil along the middle fork of the Willamette River. The 250-acre Dorris Ranch is now a living-history farm and is listed on the National Register of Historic Places. The orchard still yields a crop of nuts each autumn.

A small area in Oregon's Willamette Valley produces 98 percent of the world's filberts.

Ninety-eight percent of the world's commercial filberts are produced in a small area in the Willamette Valley, most of them in the community of Dundee, which grows the world's largest and most oil-rich filberts.

The filbert (*Corylus cornuta*) ranks as one of the Northwest's largest deciduous shrubs, 9 to 12 feet high. This wild relative of the garden filbert, also called hazelnut, produces small, hard-shelled, edible nuts.

FIR The majestic Douglas fir (*Pseudotsuga menziesii*), the most abundant tree in the Northwest, grows to a greater size than any other tree in the world except the sequoia. The tallest on record, felled in 1895, reached 417 feet. A century ago, 300-footers were common.

The Douglas fir grows taller than any other Northwest tree; the tallest Douglas fir on record reached 417 feet.

Not a true fir, the Douglas fir resembles hemlock, balsam fir, and spruce. Botanist David Douglas, for whom the tree was named, called it a "false hemlock with foliage like a yew tree." It rates as the best-adapted western tree, tolerating more types of forest than any other species. It is one of the fastest-growing conifers west of the Cascades, with leaders sometimes shooting up 5 feet a season. Its thick bark resists forest fire damage.

Douglas fir is the most important commercial tree in the nation, yielding more timber than any other species in North America. Noted for its strength and lightness, Douglas fir was the wood used when replacement masts were needed for restoration of the frigate *Constitution* in 1925.

♦ The grand fir (*Abies grandes*), which grows only in the Northwest, is the second-fastest growing tree both east and west of the Cascades, sometimes growing 3 feet in one year. Douglas fir tops it on the coast, western white pine in the east. The most common of the Northwest's true firs, it thrives inland as far as western Montana, where it grows on moist mountain slopes below 6,000 feet. There, the shade-tolerant grand fir may reach 200 feet in height.

The beautifully symmetrical tree, with its stiffly horizontal branches, emits a strong balsamy fragrance. Young trees spurt balsam gum from resin blisters. An unusual barrel shape distinguishes its upright, 4-inch cones, borne near the top of the tree.

They remain green or greenish purple at maturity.

◆ The noble fir (*A. procera*) surpasses in size the other forty species of true fir in the world. Even average noble firs grow to 75 feet, while large ones will reach well over 200 feet or more, with trunks 3 to 6 feet in diameter. In deep woods, noble firs self-prune their dead lower branches, allowing their trunks to develop mast-straight. Intolerant of shade, noble firs grow slowly at first. They may require ten years to reach a height of 4 feet, but eventually they surpass their neighbors.

Noble firs are more resistant to insects, wind, and breakage from heavy snow than are other true firs, and they grow well even on rocky soil when moisture is present. Nobles live longer than most true firs—600 to 700 years. They are prized for Christmas trees and landscaping because of their dense foliage and pyramidal form. Their barrel-shaped cones are larger than those of other firs, 4 to 7 inches long and 2½ inches thick. The strong yet light wood of the noble fir provided the material for the frames of Royal Air Force Mosquito bombers during World War II.

Noble firs are one of the few Northwest trees that show evidence of the passing of pioneers along the Oregon Trail. On the south slope of Mount Hood at Laurel Hill, the trunks of a few nobles still bear scars made by rawhide ropes that travelers in the mid-1800s tied around the trees to brake the descent of wagons down the steep Barlow Road.

◆ Although subalpine fir (*A. lasiocarpa*) must survive in the harsh environment of the upper edge of the timberline, and although it is susceptible to almost every disaster that can befall a tree, it grows more abundantly than any other true fir in western North America. Everything seems bent on destroying it: budworms, snow molds, and high winds that dry out any foliage not protected by snowdrifts. Ice and rot can weaken or break the very brittle trunk during harsh winters with temperature extremes. The thin, resiny bark and pitchy cones burn easily; Lewis and Clark saw Indians set them afire as a spectacle. Even after the snowpack melts, fresh snow and frost endanger the tree's new growth. Although these firs bear a large seed crop, very few seedlings sprout, and even fewer survive.

Yet, a great many subalpine firs withstand these adverse conditions to grow in the snow, in rocky places, and in narrow, cold-trapping canyons of Northwest mountains. Although the fir cannot compete with larger trees at lower elevations, several features assure its survival in the harsh timberline environment. The fir may assume the form of a shrub less than 2 feet high. When it grows taller, its spire shape and very short, tough branches shed

DOUGLAS FIR

snow, preventing overloads from accumulating on and breaking the branches. Deep snow protects and insulates the lower, ground-sweeping branches, which can propagate by layering, sending down roots where they touch the ground. Eventually, a grove of trees encircles the parent tree.

FLOWER BULBS Millions of tulips and other bulbs bloom each year in the rich soil of Washington's Skagit Valley, some of the nation's most productive farmland. The Washington Bulb Company ranks as the biggest tulip company in the world, selling both cut flowers and bulbs. Commercial bulb fields covering 1,500 acres explode with color in the spring, attracting thousands of camera-toting visitors. Surprisingly, even Holland imports Northwest flower bulbs.

Oregon is home to the world's largest grower of tall bearded iris and the largest lily-growing company, while Washington has the world's largest tulip-growing company.

♦ In Canby, Oregon, 20 miles south of Portland, 50 acres of dahlias constitute the Northwest's largest dahlia tuber farm.

♦ In the Willamette Valley, Cooley's Gardens is the world's largest grower of tall bearded iris. A family business begun in 1928, Cooley's sells iris all over the world. More than 400 varieties of iris, ranging in color from green-yellow to near-black, cover 257 acres.

♦ The world's largest lily-growing company, Melridge's Oregon Bulb Farms of Sandy, Oregon, has developed seventy varieties of lilies, some of which grow 6 to 7 feet high. On its 400 acres in Sandy and its six other leased farms, Melridge can produce 14 million lily bulbs a year for propagation and for potted plants.

FLOWERING PLANTS Some of the rarest plant species in the western United States, even in the world, grow in microenvironments in the Northwest. Rare species of alpine flora, isolated long ago above continental glaciers, now survive only on mountains or canyon cliffs. Plants that migrated north during warm periods survived in isolated pockets during the periods of cold that followed.

Rare plant species, some of which grow nowhere else in the world, cluster in microenvironments scattered throughout the Northwest.

The Northwest has seven especially rich concentrations of rare flowering plants.

♦ Rising from the middle of the Olympic Peninsula like high-elevation islands, Olympic Mountain peaks provide an isolated environment where plant and animal species have followed unique evolutionary paths for thousands of years. Hardy perennials that survived the Ice Age on rocky outcroppings above the glacial sea now bloom in this harsh alpine environment above 5,500 feet. Some of the plants found here grow nowhere else in the world.

Best known is Piper's bellflower (*Campanula piperi*), one of the rarest and most beautiful of all western bellflowers, with clear blue flowers ½ to 1 inch wide. Scattered on high, rocky talus slopes, the plant grows no taller than 2 inches, rooting in fine crevices that protect it from the strong winds. Because it needs abundant moisture, this bellflower often grows near the toe of a glacier.

Other rare plants found in the Olympic Mountains are Flett's violet (*Viola flettii*), a true violet and an endangered plant that is also found in Washington's Cascade and Wenatchee mountains; Olympic Mountain butterweed, a deep-rooted member of the sunflower family that grows only in very deep soil; and the daisy-like *Senecio flettii*, which grows only on Mount Angeles, often on talus.

Most widely scattered of the Northwest's rare plants may be the Olympic onion (*Allium crenulatum*), which is found on high Olympic peaks, in the Wenatchee Mountains, and in southwest Oregon on the two highest peaks of the Coast Range—Saddle Mountain and Mary's Peak. It is often found in gravelly areas and among other rare alpine flora. The onion has rosy pink flowers, narrow leaves that sometimes curl in at the tip, and a distinctive onionlike odor from the bulbs and crushed leaves.

◆ Among the twenty plant species that grow only in Washington, ten are found only in the Yakima River Basin. One of them, *Erigeron basalticus*, a low-altitude perennial fleabane with pinkish purple, daisylike flowers, clings to crevices on basaltic cliffs in the Yakima Canyon.

◆ The extremely rare, giant coastal bog lily (*Lilium occidentale*) thrives among low, dense shrubbery only 100 yards from the Pacific Ocean in Bastendorff Bog. Located in Coos County, the bog supports Oregon's largest population of the rare lily. Its bright scarlet blossoms perch atop stems 5 to 6 feet long.

◆ Washington's Wenatchee Mountains, which intersect Mount Stuart in the Cascades and run southeast to the Columbia River, are home to more plant species of limited habitat than any other place in the state. The region may have escaped Ice Age glaciation, forming a high island where vegetation could survive.

Among other rare species protected in the Tumwater Canyon Botanical Area near Leavenworth is *Lewisia tweedyi*, rarest and largest of the *Lewisias*. This striking flower grows naturally only in the Wenatchee Mountains, blooming at elevations of up to 5,000 feet on slopes or in rock crevices where natural drainage keeps the crown dry. Flower stems 6 inches long bear up to five saucer-shaped blooms each, with petals 1½ to 3 inches across.

The blossoms vary in color from salmon pink to apricot to pale yellow, contrasting vividly with the cluster of evergreen leaves. A thick, fleshy taproot extends 3 feet beyond the few inches of soil into talus slopes and rock crevices. The hardy plant withstands temperatures between minus 30°F and 100°F.

Larkspur Meadows Preserve spreads over more than 230 acres in the Wenatchee Mountains, protecting the largest known population of two of Washington's rarest plant species—the Wenatchee larkspur (*Delphinium viridescens*) and the Oregon checkermallow (*Sidalcea oregona* var. *culva*). Both grow exclusively in this relatively small area of the Wenatchee Mountains.

♦ Southwestern Oregon's Klamath-Siskiyou area, where coastal fog meets arid interior air, is a botanist's dream, containing one-fourth of Oregon's rare or endangered plants.

In the same part of Oregon, the Kalmiopsis Wilderness is home to *Kalmiopsis leachiana,* one of the world's rarest shrubs. This small, seldom-seen rhododendronlike plant, a member of the heath family, was discovered in 1930. Often only 6 to 12 inches high, the plant grows almost exclusively in a small area of the Siskiyou National Forest below 5,000 feet. A pre-Ice Age relict, the *Kalmiopsis* roots in cracks and crevices on steep hillsides in the rain shadow of coastal mountains; a few of the shrubs grow near the Umpqua River. The shrub bears clusters of ¾-inch pink blossoms set off by glossy, dark green leaves. The rugged 80,000-acre Kalmiopsis Wilderness was established to protect this and other rare plants, as well as more than 1,400 other species of flora.

Away from the coastal fog belt, in Josephine and Curry counties, the rare *Iris innominata* grows. Not discovered until 1928, its typical iris blooms, in colors of bronze, yellow, or purple, are veined in a deeper tone of the main color.

KALMIOPSIS

♦ Washington's Bald Hill Preserve is located at the southern edge of the Puget Sound lowland and encompasses an exceptional diversity of habitats and plants—more than 200 species typical of glacial outwash prairies. Rarest plants in the 291-acre preserve, bought by The Nature Conservancy in 1987, are the threatened giant *Trillium albidum* and Nuttall's quillwort, once believed extinct in Washington.

Nearby stand old-growth coniferous forests with Douglas firs up to 8 feet in diameter and more than 250 years old; white oak woodlands and savannahs; rock outcrops, cliffs and boulders; open, grass-covered "balds"; riparian deciduous forests, wetlands, and a lake. Grand fir, western red cedar, bigleaf maple, Pacific dogwood, Pacific madrone, and western hemlock all thrive in the richly varied habitats.

♦ In the unique and rich floral area at the Columbia River Gorge, alpine plants flourish at sea level, survivors of the last Ice Age. The climatic extremes of the gorge—dry at the east end, wet at the west end—create unusual growing conditions. Of more than 800 plant species in the Columbia River Gorge, 58 are rare or endangered, and 9 grow nowhere else in the world.

Toward the east end of the gorge on both sides of the river, the rare *Penstemon barrettae* Gray displays its 1½-inch-long, purplish blooms on basaltic cliff faces, talus slopes, and flat rocky soil. It survives with the help of roots that fan out 4 feet and thrust 2 feet deep in search of water and food. Its leathery leaves, 1 to 5 inches long, are the showiest of all penstemon leaves— silver green in summer, purplish bronze in winter.

On the Washington side of the gorge, nine rare plant species grow in one of the area's densest concentrations of rare plants. A few specimens of the obscure buttercup (*Ranunculus reconditus*) survive on dry hillsides. About 1,000 plants of the Columbia River milkvetch (*Astragalus columbianus*), believed extinct in 1975 after Priest Rapids Dam was built, were discovered in 1980 growing between Hanford Reservation and the Yakima Firing Range. The Hanford Nuclear Reservation provides habitat for at least twenty-two rare plants and animals.

FORESTS The first forests in the coastal Pacific Northwest were lodgepole pine (*Pinus contorta*). As the climate grew cooler and moister, the pine were replaced by today's hemlock, cedar, and Douglas fir. The Pacific Northwest's forests are predominantly evergreen because the mild climate allows the trees to photosynthesize all winter, enabling them to outgrow the deciduous trees, which are inactive while leafless.

Forests— predominantly evergreen—comprise 55 percent of Washington's total acreage, 49 percent of Oregon's, 41 percent of Idaho's, and 24 percent of Montana's.

♦ Oregon has the largest amount of forested land of the four Northwest states, with 29,810,000 forested acres covering 49 percent of the state's total acreage. Washington ranks second with 23,181,000 forested acres, but is first in total percentage of its land forested at 55 percent. Idaho comes in third with 21,726,600 forested acres, 41 percent of the state's total area. Montana, fourth largest state in the nation, has the smallest acreage in forests, 12,559,300 acres, and the lowest percentage of total land forested, 24 percent.

♦ Washington and Oregon have the densest and most extensive coniferous forests in the world, with trees that live longer and grow larger than those anywhere else. They reach their prime at 350 years. The Northwest is also unexcelled in the world for its large and long-lived *individual* trees of many diverse conifer species; ten genera are represented in coastal forests alone.

◆ Oregon has the largest number of national forests in the Northwest—thirteen forests totaling 15,607,738 acres. The Northwest's largest national forest is Idaho's Boise National Forest, with 2,650,000 acres. Idaho's Challis National Forest ranks second with 2,535,590 acres. Montana's ten national forests (several of which straddle the state's borders) contain 65 percent of Montana's trees. More than 98 percent of the state's trees are softwood.

◆ The biomass (total volume of standing and downed wood) of Northwest old-growth forests is greater than that in any other place in the world and is triple that of tropical rain forests. Downed Douglas fir logs make the most lasting contribution to the biomass because they may remain on the ground without rotting for 300 years.

◆ In 1990, in the largest acreage and dollar transaction in its history, The Nature Conservancy's Washington Chapter purchased and eventually sold to the U.S. Forest Service one of Washington's largest remaining old-growth forests. For $10.5 million The Nature Conservancy acquired from Crown-Pacific Company a roadless tract of 1,200 acres at Noisy Creek east of Mount Baker. Douglas fir, western hemlock, western red cedar, and Pacific silver fir up to 850 years old and 13 feet in diameter dominate this living museum. The forest is home to many wildlife species, including the endangered grizzly bear and possibly the gray wolf, and is designated semi-primitive, rather than wilderness.

◆ The huge, old-growth forests of the Northwest store more carbon per acre than do any other terrestrial systems, including tropical rain forests; thus, they help combat the greenhouse effect and clean the air of pollutants. They also create soil, reduce flooding, offset summer droughts, minimize soil erosion, and provide habitat for nitrogen-fixing lichens. These forests support sixty-four vertebrate species of wildlife, more than any other North American area except the Sierra Nevada.

◆ Oregon boasts the world's only major stands of Port Orford cedar, the Northwest's only myrtle groves, and the world's most northerly stand of redwoods—all in its southwest corner. Washington contains more than half of the world's western red cedar, and 40 percent of its western hemlock.

◆ Although western red cedars are primarily concentrated in the moist coastal Northwest with its mild winters, cedar trees form surprisingly lush stands inland in northern Idaho and northwestern Montana. Along Idaho's Selway River, the cedars of

Moose Creek Grove are 8 to 9 feet in diameter. In Idaho's Roosevelt Grove on the west side of Priest Lake, ancient cedars measure up to 12 feet in diameter. Montana's 100-acre Ross Creek Cedar Grove Scenic Area shelters 400-year-old red cedars 175 feet high and up to 8 feet in diameter. Near Libby, Montana, along Grant Cedars Nature Trail, stand some of the country's finest groves of virgin cedar and other huge trees.

◆ Three distinct types of forests are now growing in the devastated area on Mount St. Helens in a controlled experiment. In one type, nature provides the seedlings with no human help. Only a few willows and alders grow there now. In a second forest, Weyerhaeuser Company planted 19 million Douglas firs in holes dug through the volcanic ash into the old soil. Some of these trees reached more than 20 feet in height within ten years after planting. The U.S. Forest Service planted the third forest on 14,000 acres with 9 million mixed trees: noble fir, pine, cottonwood, Douglas fir, and hemlock. Although growing more slowly than the Weyerhaeuser trees because of less intensive care, they represent a true forest with mixed species.

◆ In 1989 foresters surveying in the Willamette National Forest discovered a grove of some of the Northwest's largest Douglas firs, with 500-year-old trees 270 to 310 feet high. This classic old-growth forest also contains hemlocks, western red cedar, nurse logs, and snags.

Fossilized leaves, seeds, nuts, and stems—40 to 60 million years old—are preserved in Oregon's John Day Fossil Beds National Monument.

FOSSILS In 1990 an unusual magnolia leaf was found compressed in shale in an ancient lake bed at the Miocene Period Clarkia deposit near Moscow, Idaho. Although the leaf had died at least 17 million years ago, it was still green and contained undamaged strands of DNA, the genetic code of life. For the first time in the history of evolutionary science, researchers, using a new technique of biotechnology, were able to extract from the ancient leaf a tiny sample of undamaged DNA, to make multiple copies of a single molecule of it, and to compare the genes to the corresponding genes in a modern species. That green magnolia leaf from Idaho showed that seventeen mutations in magnolias, five of them significant, had occurred since the leaf fell into the lake.

◆ One of the few places in the world where seeds, leaves, nuts, and stems of fossil plants are all preserved in the same location is at Clarno, northernmost and oldest (40 to 60 million years) of the three units that comprise Oregon's John Day Fossil Beds National Monument. The Painted Hills Unit also has plant fossils, but none with so many plant parts present. Plant species familiar today, such as walnut, grape, pistachio, palm, and water lily, were preserved when huge amounts of volcanic ash erupted from nearby volcanoes, covering and smothering plants and animals in the area.

Fossilized leaves and seeds in the middle and upper ash layers at John Day reveal a drastically different climate in that part of Oregon 30 million years ago—one that was warm and moist, supporting lush vegetation and subtropical forests with flowering trees. Leaf imprints have been found of palm, ginkgo, magnolia, avocado, and fig trees.

♦ In Oregon's Clear Lake, headwaters of the McKenzie River, boaters and divers can easily view a forest of Douglas fir and western red cedar trees, 2 to 3 feet in diameter, submerged in the crystal clear water. The forest was inundated more than 4,000 years ago when a lava flow from Belknap Crater in central Oregon flowed west into the Upper McKenzie River valley, damming it. Although the branches are gone, the tree trunks are still erect, waterlogged but preserved in the icy, spring-fed water.

FUNGUS With more than 3,000 species of large fruiting fungi, the Northwest ranks as a world center of mushroom diversity. Mycological Society exhibits in the Northwest routinely display more than 200 varieties of labeled local mushrooms. Although three dozen are edible, only about two dozen varieties are choice. Among these are morels, chanterelles, oyster mushrooms, and matsutake.

More than 3,000 species of fruiting fungi grow in the Northwest; the boletus is one of the largest, weighing as much as 10 pounds.

Northwest mushrooms begin appearing in late March at sea level and continue at high elevation into June. Fall season begins after the second good rain, usually in August, and lasts until freezing.

♦ Idaho and other inland areas bear prolific crops of very large mushrooms such as *Boletus edulis,* one of the most popular edible mushrooms among collectors. Often weighing 4 or 5 pounds, the *boletus* may grow to record size in inland coniferous forests—up to 10 pounds in weight and 12 inches across the cap. The firmer, younger ones are tastier than the giant specimens.

♦ The world's largest officially recorded tree fungus (*Oxyporus nobilissimus*) was found in 1946 in Mount Rainier National Park. Measuring 56 by 37 inches, it weighed more than 300 pounds. The nonedible, woody fungus—one of a few fungi species that are perennial—was growing at the base of a western hemlock in an old-growth forest, its preferred habitat. The record specimen showed thirty-five annual growth layers.

MOREL

GINKGO PETRIFIED FOREST Washington's Ginkgo Petrified Forest State Park near Vantage contains more tree species than any other petrified forest in the world. The more than 200 species and 50 genera identified there include hemlock, Douglas fir, pine, spruce, crabapple, hickory, gum birch, ash, myrtle, magnolia, buckeye, cypress, chestnut, sycamore, three species of elm, nine of oak, eight of walnut, and ten of maple—as well as many water- or moisture-loving species that no longer grow in the Northwest. The petrified trees include a maple 50 feet high, a spruce 100 feet high, an oak 6 feet in diameter, and sequoias 10 feet in diameter.

Wahington's Ginkgo Petrified Forest contains more tree species than any other petrified forest in the world.

Petrified remains of a gingko tree found in the area gave the park its name. The only surviving member of a group of ancient trees, the gingko first appeared 160 million years ago during the Jurassic period, and no longer grows wild anywhere in the world. Some gingko trees planted in Ginkgo Petrified Forest State Park are thriving.

Ten million to twenty million years ago, before the Cascades rose and cut off the moist ocean air, the climate in eastern Washington was often warm and moist. Lakes and swamps were abundant, and tropical shrubs and trees flourished.

The trees now fossilized at the Gingko Petrified Forest site fell from hills or floated down rivers into lowland swamps and lakes. Whenever a red-hot lava flow encountered lakes and swamps, it cooled rapidly, forming pillow basalt around the watersoaked trees, which were often buried in mud. Later flows, which poured out over a period of 10 or 15 million years, repeated the process, burying successive layers of ancient trees and sealing them against decay.

Over the centuries, silica-bearing groundwater gradually seeped through the lava and penetrated the buried logs, precipitating opal and chalcedony. These forms of silica replaced the cellulose in the wood, faithfully preserving cell structure and even growth rings. Such minerals as iron and manganese in the groundwater produced brilliant colors and strange designs in the petrified wood.

After the Cascades were uplifted, eastern Washington became arid. Erosion by ice sheets and by scouring floods eventually cut through many layers of lava, exposing the petrified trees. No one knows how many other forests lie below this one.

GRASSES The least known and appreciated element in the Northwest's plant heritage is grassland. Bison could not have existed in the numbers they did without Montana's nutritious and extensive grasslands. Three-fifths of the eastern part of Montana consists of plains—high, rolling prairies, grazing land rich in such grasses as blue grama, bunch, bluestem, and needle.

◆ The Inland Empire of eastern Washington and Idaho's Panhandle lead the nation as producers of bluegrass seed because of their climate and disease-free strains of seed. Much of the crop is exported.

◆ Oregon ranks first in the nation for total production of grass seed, with the Willamette Valley producing 50 to 60 percent of the seed used worldwide. Some of the world's largest crops of ryegrass seed grow near Albany. The state grows mainly Derby Perennial Ryegrass, one of the finest turf grasses known. Its quick recovery makes it the grass of choice for Super Bowl games and major golf tournaments around the world.

◆ Several rare grassland communities, including combinations of threatened or endangered Idaho fescue, three-tipped sagebrush, and antelope bitterbrush, are protected in Washington and Oregon on preserves purchased by The Nature Conservancy. They include 180-acre Barker Mountain Preserve and 339-acre Davis Canyon, both in Okanogan County, Washington.

◆ The dry, Palouse bluebunch wheatgrass prairies of Oregon have been listed as critically imperiled. One of only three known vestiges of this once-flourishing grassland lies at the junction of two narrow canyons in the Columbia Basin and provides a haven for the burrowing owl—threatened in the state—and the long-billed curlew, which is a candidate for federal listing.

HEMLOCK Washington's state tree, the western hemlock (*Tsuga heterophylla*), is the most abundant coastal conifer in the Northwest. As the Northwest's most shade-tolerant conifer, the western hemlock thrives in the shade of the huge trees with which it grows. Its closely set branches produce the densest shade of any conifer.

At age 25 to 30, the western hemlock produces more seeds than do all associated trees—as many as 8 million an acre each year. The small, light seeds can travel half a mile in a light wind, germinating and thriving on mineral soil, moss, decay, litter, rotten stumps—wherever there is moisture—and producing a crop of seedlings greater than that of all other conifers. Because western hemlock is not drought-resistant, its seedlings cannot survive in clear-cuts. Under other adverse conditions, however, the seedlings will develop very slowly for decades and then spurt in growth when conditions improve. In time, western hemlock dominates a coastal forest that is undisturbed by fire or logging.

Oregon ranks as the country's largest producer of grass seed, while eastern Washington and the Idaho Panhandle lead the nation in the production of bluegrass seed.

The Northwest's most abundant coastal conifer, the western hemlock scatters as many as 8 million seeds an acre each year.

Although not a huge tree, reaching only 100 or 150 feet in height, the western hemlock often grows in such dense stands that an acre of hundred-year-old trees on a good site can yield more timber than an acre of less-crowded, larger Douglas fir. The strong wood—fine textured, straight grained, and pitch-free—saws without splintering. Western hemlock supplies cellulose that goes into rayon yarns and plastics, and its long, strong fibers are excellent for pulp.

♦ The mountain hemlock (*T. mertensiana*) endures the harshest conditions of any Northwest tree. Living almost exclusively in the uppermost forest zone, it survives the continent's deepest and wettest snow—up to 50 feet a year—as well as heavy spring runoff and abundant rainfall. Its long, slender branches droop as they load up with snow and spring back when they suddenly release their load.

When moisture is sufficient, mountain hemlock seeds sprout quickly, even on glacial moraines at timberline or on recent lava flows. In extremely harsh conditions, the tree can reproduce by sending down roots from the layers of lower branches.

Mountain hemlock grows at an elevation above 6,000 feet on the rim of Crater Lake and abounds in the Bitterroot Mountains of northern Idaho and Montana. Under the best conditions, the mountain hemlock is an attractive tree that can soar to 100 feet or more, producing bushy, blue-green clusters of plump needles somewhat similar to those of spruce. Under timberline conditions, however, it often creeps and sprawls, growing less than 6 feet high, gnarled and scrubby.

HOPS Washington leads the nation in the production of hops (*Humulus bipulus*), which usually rank among the state's top five or six most valuable exported crops. Together, Washington, Oregon, and Idaho grow nearly 99 percent of the nation's supply of hops.

Idaho, Oregon, and Washington grow nearly 99 percent of the nation's supply of hops.

Puyallup, Washington, once reigned as the hop center of the world. After a blight in the 1880s ruined hop crops in Europe, Puyallup hops were in great demand. The blight eventually hit the Puyallup hops, ruining crop after crop, and then the Panic of 1893 devastated the economy. Europeans resumed hop production, and growers in the Yakima Valley—where hops are not as susceptible to mildew as they are in rainy western Washington—began to dominate the hop market. The Prohibition era temporarily ruined the market for hops in the United States.

Easily damaged by cold, fog, or rain during harvest, hops require specialized care and critical timing, irrigation or abundant rainfall, and well-drained, loamy soil. The Yakima Valley, with its drier climate, plentiful irrigation water, and fertile volcanic soil, eventually became the new hop capital, with the greatest concentration of hop fields in the world. The Yakima Valley normally supplies more than 70 percent of the hops used by U.S. beer makers—about 40 million pounds. At Toppenish, Washington, the world's largest hop field covers 790 acres.

◆ With a root system 15 feet long, young hop vines can grow 6 inches a day in the fertile Yakima Valley. Propagated by root cuttings from underground stems, the vines cling by strong, hooked hairs to strings suspended from trellises 16 to 18 feet high.

The aroma and bitter taste that hops impart to beer come from sticky, yellowish granules on the mature cones. The loose, papery cones, 2 to 4 inches long, are kiln-dried on slats at a low temperature and then cured in a cooling house.

Yakima hops are famous for the mellow flavor of their essential oils, bitter resins, and tannins. Quality hops, both bitter and aromatic types, are the most expensive ingredient in beer and ale. The art of "hopping" is critical to the production of good pilsner and ale.

INDIAN PIPE

The saprophyte Indian pipe (*Monotropa uniflora*) sends up its clustered white stalks 4 to 10 inches high only in densely shaded, low-elevation, old-growth coniferous forests with moist, humus-rich floors. The nodding, translucent stalks are covered with overlapping white scales; the end of each stalk resembles an inverted pipe bowl.

Indian pipe grows in shade too dense even for ferns.

Like all saprophytes, Indian pipe lacks chlorophyll and so needs no sunlight. It draws nutrients from decaying plant material, aided by a symbiotic relationship with mycorrhizal fungi that sheath its root hairs and reach out several feet underground, expanding the root system. The host provides carbohydrates the fungi cannot produce. The plant grows in shade so dense that often not even ferns appear nearby. As the seedpod matures, the stem straightens, blackening with age.

As ancient forests are cut, Indian pipe is losing its habitat and becoming increasingly rare.

INDIAN PIPE

JUNIPER

Western juniper (*Juniperus occidentalis*) may hold the record for tree longevity among trees that grow in the Northwest. A gnarled, 3-foot-high western juniper in Utah has survived 3,000 years. Very slow growing, these trees often measure only 1 foot in diameter after three hundred years.

*The slow-growing
western juniper is one
of the Northwest's
longest-lived trees,
typically surviving for
500 to 1,000 years.*

Junipers can grow in areas too dry for ponderosa pine, surviving under hostile conditions in Columbia River canyons of southern Washington and northern Oregon, and in northeast Oregon on isolated pinnacles, bluffs, and mesas. Able to survive on only 8 inches of precipitation a year, the hardy, gnarled little juniper is often the only tree growing in Oregon's arid high desert.

Juniper cones differ from the cones of other conifers. The mature cone, purplish or bluish with a white waxy covering, resembles a berry. Traces of cone scales, however, can be seen on the surface, formed by the fleshy scales fused together. Since male and female cones are often produced on separate trees, not every tree forms fruit. Cones remain on the tree for about 14 to 16 months, all winter, unable to fall and germinate until they undergo certain internal changes. They provide valuable winter food for birds, which in turn disperse the 1 to 3 seeds normally inside each cone. Humans value the cone's resinous flavor in gin. Gin-makers prefer the immature fruit produced by female flowers, which is richer in oil and resinous flavor than that of the male cone.

Native Americans drank a juniper-berry tea as a remedy for colds, sore throats, respiratory troubles, and tuberculosis.

Although the western juniper grows mainly in Oregon and California, it reaches its northernmost limits near Pasco in southeastern Washington. Here the state's largest grove, a scattering of older trees with few seedlings, barely survives among active sand dunes. In 1984 the Washington Wilderness Act created the Juniper Dunes Wilderness to protect the trees and Washington's largest and most active inland dunes.

◆ The Rocky Mountain juniper (*J. scopulorum*), very similar to the western juniper although requiring a little more rain, grows throughout most of western North America. It thrives in dry valleys and in the high plains and buttes of western Montana, with a few groves in northern Washington east of the Cascades and northeastern Oregon. Some grow in the rain shadow on Washington's San Juan Islands.

Like the western juniper, Rocky Mountain juniper grows slowly, preferring full sunlight. Often scraggly and gnarled in poor sites, Rocky Mountain junipers can grow up to 50 feet tall in eastern Oregon when they are sheltered and rooted in good soil. Those growing at high elevations—as high as 9,000 feet in some cases—come to resemble living snags after hundreds of years of storms and blizzards strip off their bark and foliage.

The reddish, fragrant wood of both juniper species, knotty

and long lasting, makes good fence posts and pungent fires.

KELP Of the nineteen genera and forty species of kelps along the Pacific Coast—more than in any other ocean—80 percent thrive in the Pacific Northwest. Only a few other areas in the world can top Northwest waters for number of genera and species and for the profuse growth of individual algae. The Northwest coast—particularly the Washington coast with its diversity of habitat—is especially rich in marine algae.

Breaking records for plant growth achieved in a single season, the bull kelp will grow as much as 120 feet from spring to winter.

The kelps prefer cold, shallow salt water and rocky coasts in a temperate zone. They thrive in the waters of Washington's outer coast, the Strait of Juan de Fuca, and the San Juan Islands. Groves of huge kelps shelter numerous marine animals and serve as food for many others. Sea urchins can devastate the vast beds if uncontrolled by predators such as starfish and sea otters.

◆ A marine algae, the bull kelp (*Nereocystis luetkeana*) ranks as the Northwest plant that achieves the most growth in a single season. It is an annual seaweed that overwinters as an almost microscopic plant. Attached by its holdfast to rocks 20 to 50 feet deep, bull kelp begins to grow in the spring and may reach more than 120 feet in length before winter storms tear it up.

One long stipe (stem) extends from the holdfast, ending in a hollow, gas-filled bulb that can grow as large as 6 inches in diameter. This bulb floats 32 to 64 thin but tough blades (leaves) 9 to 12 feet long, which hang down like a drapery. The holdfast serves only as an anchoring mechanism so that, even after being torn loose, a plant can still reproduce and grow as long as light is sufficient and water is circulating. Groups of large kelp plants, often called trees of the sea, form huge underwater forests.

◆ The giant kelp, *Macrocystis integrifolia,* a perennial that also grows in Pacific Northwest waters, achieves its greatest growth in the intense sunshine of California. *Macrocystis,* unlike bull kelp, sends forth several heavily branched stipes with many smaller floats, each supporting a single blade 1 to 2 feet long.

◆ These brown algae rank among the most complex of the seaweeds, with the highest differentiation of tissues of any algae. Much simpler than land plants, they do not need water- or nutrient-supply systems or strong stems. The sea provides most of their needs directly, supporting the blades and bathing them with water.

BULL KELP

◆ Coastal tribes dried kelps for winter food, often fermenting them first to improve digestibility. The strong, flexible stipes provided fishing lines to catch cod and halibut; the hollow floats made convenient vessels for storing fish oil. For centuries the huge kelps supplied the world with its main source of iodine. California harvests *Macrocystis* for algin, which is used for thickening in such products as ice creams, salad dressings, medicines, and paints. The Northwest has never successfully exploited its kelps.

The western larch and alpine larch, among North America's only native deciduous conifers, turn golden yellow before shedding their needles each fall.

LARCH   In the fall the needles of the western larch (*Larix occidentalis*) and the alpine larch (*L. lyalli*) turn golden yellow and then drop. Only one other native conifer in North America is deciduous. Abundant in all the Northwest states, western larch ranks as the world's largest larch, reaching 180 feet in height and 3 to 4 feet in diameter. It is the only one of the world's ten larches that does not grow at timberline in high mountains.

Except for sequoias, the western larch produces the largest proportion of straight, limbless trunk in relation to its height of any North American tree. When it is very young, the western larch grows faster than other trees in the Northwest interior, a trait important to its survival since it requires full sunlight. Some of the western larches growing in western Montana are 900 years old. Contributing to the tree's long life is its thick, fire-resistant bark.

Western larch provides one of the heaviest and densest woods of any Northwest conifer, yet the wood is easily split and worked. Few other softwoods are so hard, straight, heavy, and durable. Early settlers used the wood for telegraph and telephone poles, for railroad ties, and in mines.

♦ Although shedding its needles each fall saves the western larch from damage by most insects, one pest has become widespread and uncontrollable since the 1960s. The tiny larch casebearer is the larva of *Coleophora laricella,* a small silvergray moth. The larva eats its way into the soft larch needles that appear in the spring, then carries the needle around its body as a portable home, or case. Even though the larch grows another crop of needles, tree growth suffers drastically from repeated defoliation.

♦ The alpine larch, a conifer that grows only in the high mountains, sheds its yellowed needles much earlier in the fall than the western larch. It buds in early June, even when half-covered with snowdrifts. Its buds differ from those of the western larch in being covered with woolly hairs. The lower limbs of alpine larch saplings retain their green needles all year.

The cold-loving tree grows only in the interior of the Northwest, high in the Rocky Mountains and Bitterroots of Montana and Idaho, or on high ranges east of the Cascades. It grows where the weather is too cold or the soil too rocky for most other trees, at elevations so high that snowbanks in the area may never melt. The alpine larch shines as a pioneer, sometimes sprouting on completely bare boulders and rock piles recently deposited by glaciers and avalanches. Roots reaching deep into rock crevices anchor it firmly against strong winds. Avalanches can flatten a young alpine larch again and again, but it will always rebound.

Although slow growing, the alpine larch always maintains an upright posture; even though its trunk may twist, the tree never deforms into matted growth. One 2-inch-high tree proved to be not a seedling but a 10-year-old! At altitudes of 6,000 to 8,000 feet, the alpine larch may barely reach 3 feet high at an advanced age; yet, in sheltered locations, alpine larch can reach 50 feet or more. An exceptionally large alpine larch found above Washington's Lake Chelan at 6,200 feet has reached 94 feet in height and more than 6 feet in diameter.

MADRONE The Pacific madrone (*Arbutus menziesii*) is the tallest North American evergreen broadleaf. Two madrones in Seattle's Seward Park rank as Washington's champions at 97 and 111 feet in height, but madrones can also be scraggly and even shrublike. No other broadleaf evergreen tree grows so well and so abundantly north of the Columbia. The slow-growing tree is especially long-lived for a hardwood, living to be 200 to 250 years old.

North America's tallest evergreen broadleaf tree, the Pacific madrone reaches heights of 90 to 100 feet and lives for 200 to 250 years.

The madrone grows well at low altitudes along the coast in Washington and Oregon, where winters are mild. The largest trees often grow near salt water on high bluffs, tolerating dry, rocky soil. The leathery leaves keep water loss at a minimum and insulate against the cold. Madrones abound in the Puget Sound area, along Hood Canal, and in Washington's San Juan Islands. They also grow well in Oregon's Willamette Valley, far from the ocean.

PACIFIC MADRONE

This relative of the rhododendron litters more than any other Northwest tree. The thick, lustrous evergreen leaves shed constantly throughout half the year, especially in midsummer. The reddish brown bark of older trees sheds in ragged strips, but rewards the viewer with new, bright red twigs and a colorful underbark that is first green and then red.

Although a hardwood tree, madrone wood lacks commercial value except as firewood. When cut close to the ground or burned, the tree sends up shoots from the stump that grow into new madrones.

The largest leaves of any Northwest native tree, measuring 8 to 12 inches across, cover the branches of the bigleaf maple.

MAPLE The largest leaves of any native Northwest tree cover the bigleaf maple (*Acer macrophyllum*), the largest maple species in North America. The giant leaves, measuring 8 to 12 inches across and arranged so that they do not shade one another, are deeply and unevenly five-lobed. Held on stalks 6 to 12 inches long, the leaves stir and even spin in the wind. In autumn they blaze orangish red.

These huge deciduous trees, which can reach 8 feet in diameter, prefer the moist lowlands of western Washington and Oregon. In rain forests, moss, lichens, and licorice ferns heavily drape the massive, spreading limbs of bigleaf maples, whose large branches and often rough bark offer secure attachment.

Nearly 500 perennial herbs are cultivated in the University of Washington's medicinal garden, the largest of its kind in the Western Hemisphere.

MEDICINAL GARDEN The University of Washington maintains on its campus the largest medicinal garden in the Western Hemisphere. In 1911 Charles Johnson, dean of the university's pharmacy school, began the garden on just 1 acre, intending it for the use of faculty and students of pharmacy. But during World War I, the garden was planted with digitalis and belladonna to meet the demand for medical supplies. The garden thrived in the days when pharmacists mixed most of their own medicines. When World War II shut off imports of important drugs, the medicinal garden again grew the essential plants.

Now some 500 perennial herbs grow in classic, rectangular beds in the 2-acre garden. The majority of plants either have current medicinal value or were once used as medicines, many in the Middle Ages. Plants ranging from subtropical to subarctic thrive there.

Among the medicinal plants in the garden are thyme, once used to treat low-level urinary tract infections before antibiotics were discovered; cardamon, which disguises the bad taste of many medicines; foxglove (*Digitalis purpurea*), still vital in heart medicines for arrhythmia and congestive heart failure; and cascara tree and senna shrub, used for laxatives.

As many as 6,000 pounds of mosses, lichens, and other epiphytes, or air plants, may grow on a single acre of land in the Olympic Peninsula rain forests.

MOSSES, LICHENS, AND OTHER EPIPHYTES Olympic Peninsula rain forests produce the most epiphyte species (seventy-seven) and the most individual epiphytes of any area equal in size in the Lower 48. Forty or fifty varieties of mosses, lichens, liverworts, and other epiphytes drape trees, rocks, and logs in almost every Olympic Peninsula coniferous forest. The number of species would be greater except for occasional summer droughts a month or two long that discourage other species. Epiphytes—air plants—manufacture their own food, extracting water for the process from the well-saturated air in old-growth forests; the host, often a sturdy bigleaf maple, provides only support. Nitrogen-fixing lichens are also common in such old forests. Tree roots absorb nutrients captured in mats of mosses and lichens, while mosses growing under trees benefit from rainwater enriched by minerals leached from the tree leaves.

Rain forests provide varying habitats for species that prefer to grow at different levels. Some epiphytes grow only on the crown of a bigleaf maple; others only on branches, trunks, near tree bases, or on fallen logs. Still others are less particular, growing anywhere and everywhere. The hairlike moss that hangs in long festoons from tree branches in rain forests or other wet coastal woods is usually *Isothecium stoloniferum.*

A rain forest may produce 6,000 pounds of epiphytes per acre.

When wet, epiphytes on only one huge bigleaf maple can weigh nearly a ton.

♦ The endangered moss *Limbella fryeii* is known to exist in only one place in the world—Sutton Lake Marsh on Oregon's central coast. The lake surrounds the marsh on three sides. The rare moss grows at the bases of willow and crabapple trees.

♦ A freshwater moss grows in Crater Lake's pristine waters at the greatest known depth of any such moss in the world—325 feet. Very few plants can manufacture food by photosynthesis in waters deeper than 200 feet because of limited light penetrating beyond that depth, but Crater Lake's deep waters are unusually clear. (See Natural Features, Crater Lake.)

MOUNT ST. HELENS PLANT LIFE
The most unexpectedly rapid return of plant life after a disaster occurred on Mount St. Helens after the 1980 eruption. Scientists initially believed that the eruption had so sterilized the soil that no plants would grow there for years. Within four months, however, plant life appeared in many areas. Some plants seeded themselves naturally, aided by wind or mud, finding depressions in the ash caused by rain and its runoff. Others sprouted from underground corms undamaged by the scorching volcanic blast.

Within only four months of the 1980 Mount St. Helens eruption, nearly 230 of the original 300 plant species had returned to the devastated area.

First came fireweed, always quick to appear in burned-over areas. Surprisingly, some small trees and other plants had survived, protected by heavy layers of snow on north-facing slopes. Among these plants were a few clumps of lupine in the blast area. Such plants as lupine and red alder, which can convert atmospheric nitrogen gas into soil nitrogen, began to improve soil fertility. A student working for the U.S. Forest Service built a fence around the first lupine that poked up through the ash. That one plant eventually seeded some 160,000 offspring.

Even delicate avalanche lilies sprouted from their protected underground corms. Some plants remained alive under the ash for as long as three years, resuming growth after rain and melting snow washed away the deep ash. Contrary to expectations, ash stimulated rather than stunted plant growth, holding soil moisture like a mulch.

The first fall rains in 1980 brought small black mushrooms (*Anthracobia melatoma*), which evidently found organic material in the ash. By breaking down such material, the fungi helped build soil for higher plants. Farther down the mountain, shell fungi soon appeared on trees blown down by the blast; their mycelia apparently had been insulated deep inside the wood.

Two years after the blast, noble fir seedlings appeared. Mycorrhizal fungus, a soil fungus essential to the survival of many conifers, returned, allowing conifer seedlings to grow in the deep ash where soil and the fungi were buried. All plant life thrived during the wet, cool summer of 1983. Of nearly 300 species formerly growing in the area, 230 had reappeared by that time.

Soil fertility was increased by decomposition of the bodies of large animals that had died in the blast and by the many mounds of deep, rich earth pushed up by pocket gophers, who had survived underground.

Roosevelt elk quickly returned, feeding on the more than 17 million seedlings planted in areas outside the Mount St. Helens National Monument. The elk, dispersing seeds through droppings, seeded their trails as they moved across the area.

Millions of trees had died, particularly in the Red Zone nearest the mountain, where they were stripped of limbs, snapped off, or uprooted. Many were Douglas fir, with trunks 6 feet in diameter. On the north-facing slopes where snow had buried trees, the tops of small trees were burned off, but the roots, trunks and lower branches, protected by snow, remained unharmed. Some trees planted after the blast have grown in height to more than 20 feet.

Some grasses and trees were planted to stabilize the mudflow, but no planting was allowed within the 110,300 acres of national volcanic monument area. There nature is being allowed to heal itself in a rare outdoor laboratory. Unfortunately, human visitors increasingly interfere with the natural processes.

OAK Among all the tree species that grow in the Northwest, the sole representative of the oak family is the Oregon white oak (*Quercus garryana*). This tree displays the distinctive oak shape, with gnarly limbs and spreading crown.

Oaks, among the most abundant and widespread trees in the world, thrive in dry habitats and rocky soils where most conifers do not grow well. Their leathery leaves with hairy undersides retain moisture. On rich bottomlands the slow-growing oak can thrive for 500 years, reaching 75 to 90 feet in height and 5 feet in diameter.

At one time, thousands of oaks grew in Oregon's Willamette Valley and Douglas County, in oak savannahs where native peoples regularly burned the land as a way of herding deer into feeding grounds. They depended on the acorns for food. But as settlers thronged in, the burning stopped and other trees sprang up, shading out the oaks.

Oregon white oaks also grow in Washington on dry, rocky sites in the San Juan Islands, in Sequim, in the semiarid Yakima Valley, and at the eastern end of the Columbia Gorge, where they adopt a scrubby form. In 1988 The Nature Conservancy bought a 206-acre site on Waldron Island in the San Juan Islands, creating a new preserve that supports one of western Washington's finest oak woodlands.

The oak produces hard, fine-grained white wood of excellent quality. Harder and stronger than cedar, the wood is twice as heavy, with heartwood equally rot-resistant.

The Oregon white oak is the Northwest's only native oak and the second-largest oak in the West.

OHME GARDENS Ohme Gardens, located in eastern Washington just northwest of Wenatchee, was originally planted by the Ohme family for their own pleasure. So many people wanted to share that pleasure that the Ohmes opened the gardens to the public. Lookouts from the desert bluff on which the gardens are located, 600 feet above the Columbia River, provide sweeping views of the river and the Wenatchee Valley.

The Ohme family began landscaping the gardens soon after Herman Ohme bought an apple orchard in 1929 and built a home on a rocky promontory included with the property. Over nearly fifty years, despite their lack of formal training, the Ohmes landscaped the bluff. They planted alpine meadows around weathered volcanic rock formations and transplanted such trees as cedars, hemlock, and spruce from both sides of the Cascades. The Ohmes pumped water from the Columbia River to irrigate the gardens and added twin pools with waterfalls flowing into them.

Despite an annual temperature range of more than 100°F,

Miniature alpine meadows and conifer forests thrive in the Ohme Gardens, 600 feet above the Columbia River, despite a temperature range of 100 degrees.

the gardens, which have been expanded over the years to cover nearly nine acres, display a surprising variety of plants. Ferns and mosses carpet miniature conifer forests; cacti and sedums cling to cliffs; penstemon, thyme, and phlox accent open spaces.

ORCHIDS The phantom orchid (*Eburophyton austiniae*) ranks as the most elusive and one of the most beautiful of the Northwest's forty varieties of orchids. Seldom seen, the orchid is limited to the Northwest, where it grows in the Olympic Peninsula, the Cascades, and west central Idaho.

Forty orchid species, subspecies, and varieties grow in the Northwest, including the rare phantom orchid, found nowhere else in the world.

The rare phantom orchid always grows in dense and undisturbed conifer forests where little sunshine intrudes. Because of the orchid's lack of chlorophyll, stems, flowers, and sheathlike leaves are usually pure white, except for a touch of golden yellow on the lower lip of the flower. Stems 8 to 20 inches long bear fragrant spikes of five to twenty waxy, translucent, ½-inch blooms. Deriving nourishment from decaying vegetation with the help of symbiotic fungi, this lovely saprophyte rarely flowers, perhaps once in seventeen years.

The orchid family ranks as the second most numerous plant family. Each plant produces millions of seeds and ensures cross-fertilization with chemical, structural, and timing devices, including the use of scent to lure specific insects.

♦ The spotted coralroot (*Corallorhiza maculata*) and the striped coralroot (*C. striata*), members of the orchid family, display an interesting flower structure adapted for cross-pollination by insects. Like most orchids, the coralroot forms one lower petal shaped differently from the sepals and other petals; this broad lip encourages pollinating insects to land. As an insect gathers nectar from the orchid, two pollen masses projecting above the lip dust the insect, while the pollen it gathered from a previous bloom is transferred to the sticky stigma. Both striped and spotted coralroots send up from their knobby, branched rhizomes smooth pinkish stems 10 to 14 inches long, with a few fleshy scales or clasping purplish bracts instead of leaves. The striped coralroot, with white sepals and petals striped with purple, is the showiest of its family. The many-flowered stalk of the spotted coralroot bears orchid-shaped flowers about ½ inch long, resembling the flowers of the rare phantom orchid except for their pinkish color and distinctive three-lobed, red-spotted white lip.

Occasionally a colony consists of as many as 1,000 striped coralroots growing in the moist soil of dense coastal coniferous forests, sometimes as parasites on conifer roots.

PHANTOM ORCHID

PINE The inland lodgepole pine (*Pinus contorta* var. *latifolia*) is the only conifer that bears cones adapted to forest fires. A heavy layer of resin coats some of the 2-inch-long cones on each tree, sealing the seeds into the protective scales. During a forest fire, heat melts the resin and the seeds fall out into the ash-enriched soil. The resulting seedlings gain a headstart on those of other trees. On a single acre after a burn, thousands of lodgepole pine seedlings sprout, eventually forming a dense stand of trees. In such dense stands, the trees are stunted from being crowded and grow like identical poles, 50 feet high with trunks only 5 to 6 inches in diameter. But at high altitudes, where they grow alone, each lodgepole is shaped differently by wind and snow.

The thick, fire-resistant bark of the ponderosa pine and the lodgepole pine's special cones, which open only during intense heat, enable these species to survive forest fires.

In addition to sealed cones, each lodgepole produces unsealed cones, which release seeds normally in years without forest fires. Sealed cones often hang on a lodgepole pine for many years, the seeds still viable even when bark encases the cones.

Lodgepole pines are North America's most abundant and widely distributed commercial trees, growing mainly east of the Cascades to the Rocky Mountains. The slow-growing lodgepole pine requires 100 years to reach 50 or 60 feet in height and 3 feet in diameter; however, it may start producing cones after only six years, earlier than most conifers.

This pioneer tree moves quickly into meadows or into swampy land filled with silt and grass. It can survive drought, soggy or humus-poor soil, and intense heat as well as temperatures well below freezing. But the resinous wood and cones make it vulnerable to fire, as do the dense stands with dead limbs bristling on every tree. Lodgepole pines do not self-prune their dead lower branches. Thus, when trees die, these dead limbs hold them upright, forming "ghost forests."

The lodgepole is named for the use native Americans made of the trees as supporting poles for tepee lodges. The Indians cut the trees in spring, let them dry all summer until they were very light but still strong, and then covered them with animal skins to form lodges. For traveling and carrying goods, Indians put together a drag sled called a travois, made of two long poles with a skin stretched between. Later, settlers constructed telegraph and telephone poles and log buildings from the pines.

♦ The ponderosa pine (*P. ponderosa*), also called western yellow pine, resists fire and drought better than any other Northwest tree. Able to survive on far less water than other conifers, it grows almost exclusively east of the Cascades, where only 8 to 10 inches of rain fall each year. The ponderosa's root system, deep and extensively branched, is the most efficient of all pines. A 4-year-old tree only 1 foot high will send down a taproot 5 feet long.

These hardy trees, which live to be 400 to 500 years old, can tolerate a ground surface of up to 162°F. The pines seal fire scars with pitch, thereby keeping out decay and insects. The very thick bark of older trees allows them to survive many fires.

Ponderosa pine is the West's foremost lumber pine, except on the Northwest coast, where Douglas fir reigns. Because of its clear, even grain, the wood is used for interior finishing work and door and window frames. This pine grows very slowly for the first ten or fifteen years and bears abundant crops of cones only after about fifty years. Forgotten chipmunk caches account for 85 percent of its seedlings.

◆ The largest cones of any Northwest conifer grow on the sugar pine (*P. lambertiana*). The huge cones, 10 to 16 inches long with a diameter of up to 3½ inches, hang from a 6-inch stalk very high in the tree. A tree 150 years old may bear a hundred or so cones each year. Even after they open in October to let the seeds escape, the cones hang on the tree until the next summer. The tree is named for a sweet, edible resin that it exudes to cover wounds made by fire.

No other pine in the world sends up such a long trunk that is so free of limbs and has so little taper. Nor does any other tree produce so much lumber per acre. This tallest and largest of the more than 100 pine species ranks as fourth greatest of all American trees in size, after the two sequoias and the Douglas fir. Its straight grain makes it useful for pipes in church organs. Early settlers favored its timber for bridges and barns, flumes and sluice boxes.

◆ The western white pine (*P. monticola*) bears only a few pitchy cones a year, but its cones rank second in size among the cones of Northwest conifers. Squirrels and tree-nursery managers prize the heavy cones, which can grow up to 10 inches long, for their abundant seeds. Western white pine can be identified by the small, regular squares deeply scoring its mature bark. The long trunk yields some of the most valuable wood in the Northwest, strong but lightweight, with very straight grain.

Idaho once boasted the world's most extensive stands of western white pine, but many of the trees have been converted into matches or claimed by blister rust. Fortunately, the great forest reserves formed during the conservation era of Theodore Roosevelt and Gifford Pinchot in the early 1900s have protected many white pine. The largest stand of white pine in the nation stretches for 83 miles through the former St. Joe National Forest, which is now part of Idaho Panhandle National Forest. The western white pine champion, however, grows in Oregon, in the mountains near Medford. It is 239 feet tall and 6½ feet in diameter.

POTATOES Although potatoes, which originated in Peru, grow almost everywhere in the world, nowhere else do they grow as bountifully as in the Northwest.

Idaho, with more acres planted in potatoes than any other state, is home to the nation's largest potato-processing industry.

◆ Idaho ranks first in the nation in number of acres planted in potatoes (three times as many as Washington) and in value of total production. Washington comes in second. In yield of potatoes per acre, however, Washington leads the world, producing nearly 25 tons per acre. Oregon is second. Russet Burbank potatoes make up 80 percent of the crop.

◆ Early Spanish explorers brought potatoes from Peru to the Northwest in the late 1600s and gave some to native people on the coast. Makah Indians on the Olympic Peninsula still grow that long, narrow potato, which is drier and denser than the modern potato.

In 1841 the United States Exploring Expedition stopped in the Northwest to survey. When the expedition's commander, Lt. Charles Wilkes, U.S. Navy, visited the ruined site of Oregon's Fort Astoria, which had not been inhabited since 1824, he found potatoes still growing in the garden.

The Nez Perce Indians planted potatoes in Idaho in 1836, at the suggestion of Idaho's pioneer missionary, Henry Spalding.

◆ Idaho, famous for its Russet Burbank potatoes, was the first state to grow them in commercial quantities. Idaho possesses excellent conditions for growing the hybrid potato: high-elevation climate, fertile river valleys, abundant water from the Snake River, and sandy volcanic soil.

RUSSET BURBANK POTATO

Although Idaho once monopolized potato production, Oregon and Washington have now taken over a significant share of the market. Central Washington and Oregon have the same ideal growing conditions as Idaho, including the sandy loam consisting principally of volcanic ash. Washington boasts a longer growing season than Idaho and an equally ample supply of water—from the Columbia River.

◆ Idaho's potato-processing industry rates as the nation's largest, handling two-thirds of the nation's processed potatoes. Idaho potatoes made the owner of Jack Simplot Enterprises one of the nation's richest men. During World War II, from 1942 to

1945, his converted onion-drying plant produced 33 million pounds of dehydrated potatoes for the military. Today 4 to 5 million pounds of potatoes a day pass through only one of his eight plants and the business is valued at more than $550 million. In less than an hour, a potato is sorted, washed, steamed, peeled, blanched, dip-frozen, fried, and frozen again.

◆ Washington potato producers provide about half of the nation's frozen potato exports. Potatoes routinely rank among Washington's five most valuable food exports. Eighty-five percent of Washington potatoes end up in chips, fries, hash browns, and country fries.

RAIN FOREST The rain forests of the Pacific Northwest, which contain the largest stands of old-growth conifers south of Alaska, form an important part of the world's temperate-zone, coniferous rain forests. They are concentrated in a 50-mile section of the Olympic Peninsula in three glaciated river valleys: the Queets, Quinault, and Hoh. The coniferous rain forest growing along the Hoh River is one of the world's largest and most impressive.

The Northwest's rain forests earn their name, with some 150 inches of rain falling over nearly 100 days each year.

The special ecosystem in the forests supports numerous species of birds, amphibians, and flowering plants, some of which are found nowhere else in the world. Across the forest floor stretches a mantle of mosses, lichens, club mosses, and liverworts—a mantle that is thicker, heavier, and more diversified than the mantle of any other temperate-zone rain forest. In these cool, moist forests, Sitka spruce grow much larger than anywhere else in their range. Western hemlock, Douglas fir, and western red cedar also grow to record sizes here. (See Tree Champions.)

A unique combination of factors accounts for the existence of Northwest rain forests. Ocean fog and frequent clouds lock in the damp air, maintaining high humidity. Rain falls at an annual rate of more than 150 inches, the highest anywhere in the contiguous United States, sweeping over the forests from the Pacific Ocean and falling gently for about 100 days a year. Lush undergrowth and leaf canopies help keep the air cool and moist by blocking out sunshine from the forest floor. Huge fallen nurse logs support tree seedlings that could not otherwise compete with lush groundcover. Hundreds of feet of glacially deposited gravel and rock drain the deep layer of rich forest soil, while the broad, gently sloping walls and floors of the U-shaped glacial valleys minimize root erosion.

RHODODENDRONS Washington, which named the wild *Rhododendron macrophyllum* its state flower, and Oregon lead the world in rhododendron production and hybridization. The two states grow the world's greatest variety of the showy genus (which includes azaleas) in a rainbow of colors: white, purplish blue, pink, red, yellow, purple, and orange. The rhododendron genus, whose name in Greek means "tree rose," comprises an exceptionally large group of more than 1,000 species (with more always being discovered) and an additional 2,000 named varieties.

Northwest rhododendrons range in size from dwarfs 6 inches high to 30-foot-high trees.

The acidic soil and moderate coastal climate of the Northwest prove ideal for rhododendrons. Native rhododendrons grow on the western slopes of the Cascades at elevations of 3,300 to 5,000 feet, and on the Oregon and Washington coasts; they are especially prolific on the Olympic Peninsula and Whidbey Island.

The shrubs vary in size from rock garden dwarfs 6 inches high to tree rhododendrons (*R. calophytum*), native to China, which grow to 20 and 30 feet in the Northwest and to 80 feet in China.

Five hundred pure species are hardy in the Northwest, thriving at temperatures as low as about 10°F. Another 300 species, mostly from Asia, are semitropical to tropical and require a greenhouse or coolhouse in winter. Some of the most fragrant varieties grow only indoors.

Bigleaf varieties, grown mostly as a curiosity in the Northwest, include *R. sinogrande*, whose enormous leaves can be 30 inches long and 12 inches wide. Its flower trusses are nearly the size of basketballs.

In both Oregon and Washington, hundreds of backyard hobbyists, in addition to large commercial growers, raise rhododendrons by the acre. Hybridizers breed for color, early blooms, height, shape, tolerance to sun and shade, hardiness (one rhododendron is hardy to minus 25°F), and fragrance, which can be intensely sweet. There is even a species with whitish leaves that turn chocolate brown and bear woolly fuzz on one or both sides.

◆ The Rhododendron Species Foundation Display Gardens at Weyerhaeuser Corporate Headquarters in Federal Way, Washington, feature one of the world's most comprehensive collections of rhododendron species (not hybrids) native to North America, Europe, Southeast Asia, and the Far East. More than 2,200 different varieties, which have been labeled and classified, thrive in a 24-acre botanical garden that also includes heathers, lilies, ferns, maples, and rare plants.

◆ Puget Sound rhododendron breeders send newly developed

hybrids to Meerkerk Rhododendron Gardens on Whidbey Island, operated by the Seattle Rhododendron Society. There growers test and evaluate new hybrids for five years before propagating them commercially. During blooming season visitors can tour the gardens.

RHUBARB Washington's fertile Puyallup Valley now grows 100 percent of the nation's hothouse rhubarb and 75 percent of its field-grown rhubarb. Rhubarb rates as a $2 million crop in the valley, where growers harvest more than 5 million pounds each year. Only the stalks are edible; oxalic acid-laden roots and leaves can make humans sick and can kill livestock.

Rhubarb growers in Washington's Puyallup Valley harvest more than 5 million pounds a year and produce 100 percent of the nation's hothouse crop.

Hothouse growers force the winter crop of rhubarb by growing special fields of "mother plants" outdoors for two or three years without pulling any stalks, allowing the roots to store up energy. Then the huge root clumps are dug up and brought inside dark hothouses, where they send up pale pink stalks that are harvested when they are 18 inches tall.

SKUNK CABBAGE The skunk cabbage (*Lysichitum americanum*) bears the largest leaf of any Northwest plant. This Northwest native, one of the earliest spring plants, sports a leaf that is often more than 3 feet long and a foot wide. One leaf reportedly measured 56 inches long and 29 inches across.

Skunk cabbage leaves, the largest to grow on any Northwest plant, often reach 3 feet in length and a foot across.

The leaves spring up from the base of the plant several weeks after the yellow spathe (hood) appears. The spathe, not a bloom but a colored bract (a petallike leaf), encloses a fleshy club crowded with hundreds of small, green true flowers.

Skunk cabbage requires abundant moisture; thus, it often grows in swampy lowlands, but also in coastal forests and at elevations of up to 4,000 feet in the Cascades.

Skunk cabbage is related to the taro, the Polynesian food plant. Northwest Indians used its huge leaves with the fleshy midribs for berry and water containers, to make a cure-all infusion, and to cover and flavor camas bulbs in cooking pits. They applied heated skunk cabbage leaves and spathes to rheumatic joints and painful wounds and swellings.

SKUNK CABBAGE

All parts of the skunk cabbage contain calcium oxalate crystals, which cause an intense burning sensation and irritation of mouth and throat when the plant is not properly cooked. Native Americans steamed or roasted the spathes and roots for several days before eating them; they ground the dried roots into flour. Bears eat the entire plant and deer browse the leaves without any apparent ill effects.

SPRUCE Engelmann spruce (*Picea engelmannii*) grows in the widest elevation range of any Northwest tree—from sea level in the rain shadow of the Olympic Mountains to 9,000 feet in the interior Northwest.

Sitka spruce, the Northwest's largest spruce and one of the world's largest trees, yields wood that is stronger pound for pound than steel.

Slow-growing and very tolerant of shade, this spruce can take advantage of the growing space opened up when other trees die. The Engelmann spruce can grow to 120 feet, towering over other trees. Yet at timberline, it may assume a shrubby form. At the highest part of its range, the Engelmann spruce is dwarfed and often sprawling. But in sheltered sites, even at high altitude, it can reach 80 or 90 feet. Wind storms are likely to break it off because of its height and dense crown. Lightning scars mark the trunks of most Engelmann spruce in high country.

♦ Sitka spruce (*P. sitchensis*) is the largest Northwest spruce. Only five trees in the world, incuding the Sitka spruce and the Douglas fir, pump sap and nutrients 300 feet high.

In valley bottoms Sitka spruce grows quickly—175 feet in its first 100 years. It seldom thrives more than 12 miles inland, preferring the mild and wet coastal winter of the Olympic Peninsula, where it benefits from more than 150 inches of rain a year. By the time it is 800 years old, a Sitka spruce can reach a height of 300 feet with a trunk measuring 8 to 10 feet in diameter above the swollen base—if not damaged by storms. Unlike other conifers, which grow at ever-higher elevations in the southern part of their range, the Sitka spruce rarely grows above an elevation of 1,500 feet anywhere.

Sitka spruce furnishes excellent raw material for paper pulp. Its wood surpasses most other woods in resonance and fidelity to pitch, a quality that makes it ideal for piano sounding boards.

Of all wood in the world, Sitka spruce tests first in strength-to-weight ratio; pound for pound, it is stronger than steel. During the two world wars, the aircraft industry used Sitka spruce extensively, valuing the strong but light wood for its ability to absorb shock and its ease of repair. Loggers cut a great amount of Sitka spruce in Washington and Oregon during the two wars, but, because plane manufacturers demanded unflawed wood, as much as 90 percent of the cut was wasted.

This spruce rapidly replaces itself through seedlings that grow atop stumps, on rotting logs, and on the huge roots of fallen trees. Many Sitka spruce display stilted, aboveground roots 6 or 7 feet high, which formed when the roots straddled a rotting nurse log as they reached down into the soil for nourishment.

♦ Weeping spruce (*P. breweriana*) ranks as the rarest of the spruces; with its drooping branches and slender cones, it is unusually beautiful as well. Also called Brewer spruce, it grows in one of the most inaccessible and least visited spots in the Northwest, the Brewer Spruce Research Natural Area, in the Kalmiopsis Wilderness of Oregon's Siskiyou Mountains. The tree—a pre-Ice Age relic of a swampy, subtropical era—now grows 50 to 70 feet in height, mostly on cold north slopes in hollows at the heads of canyons. The weeping spruce grows only on serpentine soil. (See Natural Features, Serpentinite Rock.)

Seven of the nation's thirteen tallest trees grow in Washington and Oregon.

TREE CHAMPIONS Seven of the thirteen tallest trees in the nation grow in Washington and Oregon. In addition, many Northwest trees hold records for being the largest individual trees within their species.

Olympic National Park rain forests grow the largest known individual trees of four species: Alaska cedar, subalpine fir, Douglas fir, and western hemlock. Oregon boasts fifty-six national champions of fifty-two different species. Oregon also has a champion big-tree hunter, Frank Sesock, who has discovered more than twenty-two champion trees.

The following selected list of Northwest trees that are the largest of their species is based on records compiled by The Washington State Big Tree Program and the National Register of Big Trees. Championship status is determined not only by height but by the total mass of each tree. Total mass is calculated by adding together one point for each foot of height, one point for each inch of circumference measured 4½ feet above the ground, and one point for each 4 feet of crown spread. Trees within five points of each other are ranked as co-champions. The following list gives only height and location.

The list changes as champion trees die, are dethroned— sometimes by losing height after a lightning strike—or are destroyed. A Hoh River vine maple champion was felled during logging operations in the early 1980s. Oregon, which chose the Douglas fir as its state tree, has had two world record Douglas firs, but each has blown down—twice returning the record to Washington.

SPECIES	HEIGHT IN FEET	LOCATION
Alder, mountain	50	Clear Lake Reservoir, WA
Alder, red	104	Clatsop County, OR
Alder, white	70	Nez Perce N.F., ID
Birch, water	53	Wallowa County, OR
Birch, western paper	81	Bellingham, WA
Buffalo berry, silver	22	Malheur County, OR

SPECIES	HEIGHT IN FEET	LOCATION
Cascara buckthorn	47	(Three Oregon specimens)
Catalpa, northern	86	Walla Walla, WA
Cedar, Alaska*	120	Olympic N.P.(Lake Quinault), WA
Cedar, Port Orford*	219	Siskiyou N.F., OR
Cedar, western red*	178	Olympic Peninsula (Hoh River), WA
Cherry, bitter	104	Vashon Island, WA
Cottonwood, black	155	Willamette Mission State Park, OR
Crabapple, Oregon	79	Nisqually Wildlife Refuge, WA
Dogwood, Pacific	60	Clatskanie, OR
Dogwood, western	19	Seattle, WA
Fir, Douglas*	298	Olympic N.P. (Hoh Trail), WA
Fir, grand*	251	Olympic N.P. (Duckabush River), WA
Fir, noble*	238	Gifford Pinchot N.F., WA
co-champion	272	Mount St. Helens, WA
Fir, Pacific silver	203	Forks, WA
Fir, subalpine*	129	Olympic N.P. (Cream Lake), WA
Hawthorn, oneseed	64	Volunteer Park, Seattle, WA
co-champion	39	Olympia, WA
Hawthorn, shining	22	U.W. Campus, Seattle, WA
Hazelnut, California	47	Carkeek Park, Seattle, WA
Hemlock, western*	202	Olympic N.P. (Wynoochee trail), WA
co-champion	241	Olympic N.P. (Hoh River), WA
Larch, alpine	95	Wenatchee N.F., WA
Laurel, California	88	Siskiyou N.F., OR
Laurel, English	33	Seattle Center, Seattle, WA
Maple, bigleaf	101	Jewell, OR
Maple, Douglas	65	Ahsahka, ID
Maple, vine	92	Olympic N.F., WA
Mountain ash, Sitka	50	Gardiner, OR
Spruce, Engelmann*	179	Payette Lake, ID
Spruce, Sitka*	206	Seaside, OR
co-champion	191	Olympic N.P. (Lake Quinault), WA
Willow, Sitka	34	Coupeville, WA
Yew, Pacific	54	Gifford Pinchot N.F., WA

*Denotes world champion

WHEAT Winter wheat routinely ranks in value as Washington's number one or number two crop and as its top export crop.

Some of the world's finest spring wheat is grown near Great Falls, Montana, using dry farming methods. In good years, the value of Montana's wheat crop exceeds that of Montana's total mineral output.

The first wheat combine in the Northwest was used in 1898

The nation's largest wheat farm is a 90,000-acre spread in Montana, the state that produces some of the world's finest spring wheat.

near Davenport, Montana. The huge machine, which combined cutting and threshing, revolutionized wheat growing. Pulled by thirty horses in five rows of six horses each, it reduced the average threshing crew from twenty to six men.

One of the first self-propelled wheat combines, powered by steam, was built in Oregon's Asotin County in 1911. It required an engineer, a fireman to tend the boiler, and two men to follow the combine—one to pick up thrown belts, the other to put out the fires they started.

◆ The nation's—and possibly the world's—largest wheat farm is a 90,000-acre spread near Hardin, Montana.

WIND RIVER TREE NURSERY One of the largest federal tree nurseries in the nation, Wind River Tree Nursery covers 302 acres on which 21 million trees a year can be planted. The U.S. Forest Service established the nursery in 1909 east of the Bonneville Dam at Carson, Washington, near the Columbia River to provide a source of tree seedlings after disastrous forest fires in the Northwest during the summer of 1903.

As many as 21 million trees may be planted each year at the 302-acre Wind River Tree Nursery.

The Forest Service also established an arboretum to test various tree species for their adaptability to Washington soil and climate. Fifteen of Washington's largest nonnative trees grow in Wind River Arboretum. They include such exotics as the Crimean black pine, giant sequoia, Serbian spruce, and Polish larch. The state's champion chinkapin (70 feet tall) and sugar pine (96 feet tall) grow there.

WINE GRAPES Certain regions of the Northwest have nearly ideal conditions for wine grape growing: sandy loam over rocky volcanic soil for good drainage and heat retention; long summer days (with two more hours of light each summer day than in California); and cool nights that add a desirable tartness. Despite these favorable conditions, vinifera grapes were not planted in the Northwest until 1960.

Barely 30 years old, the wine-grape-growing industry in the Northwest is one of the nation's largest, with Washington consistently ranking as the country's second-largest producer of vinifera grapes.

◆ For the past several years Washington has ranked as the nation's second-largest producer (after California) of vinifera grapes and premium wines. Over a ten-year period, 1980 to 1990, the state increased its wine grape acreage from 2,500 to 11,000 acres; it now has more land devoted to the production of wine grapes than any other Northwest state. It boasts the most wineries in the Northwest, jumping from only six in 1982 to one hundred in July 1990. Washington's yield per acre of wine grapes is twice that of New York state.

Most of Washington's wine grapes are planted in the arid

south-central part of the state in the Yakima Valley and Lower Columbia Basin. This area is just north of the 46th Parallel—nearly the same latitude as the Bordeaux and Burgundy regions of France.

The Cascade Range shelters the area from the heavy rainfall of western Washington. In June the grapes receive seventeen hours or more of not-too-intense sunlight each day, so that they ripen with a good sugar-acid balance. Washington grapes are tarter and crisper than California grapes, with more intense flavor and aroma, and a more pronounced varietal character. Some 80 percent of Washington's wine grapes are white, predominantly white riesling.

WINE GRAPES

♦ Some of Idaho's wine grapes grow at the highest grape-growing altitude of any Northwest vineyards, up to 3,000 feet. Most of the wine grapes—riesling, chardonnay, and cabernet sauvignon—grow in the southwest, 40 miles west of Boise.

♦ Oregon raises one of the most difficult-to-grow wine grapes, pinot noir. Oregon growers have recently begun planting pinot gris, a new European variety that is rarely grown in the United States. Most Oregon vineyards are much smaller than those in Washington and Idaho and are often family operations.

♦ Two Northwest areas, Yakima Valley and Walla Walla, have received federal recognition as official viticultural areas. A third, larger official viticultural area, the Columbia Valley, encompasses the Yakima Valley and Walla Walla areas.

YEW The Pacific yew (*Taxus brevifolia*) is one of the slowest-growing trees in the world. A yew with a trunk 5 to 10 inches in diameter and up to 30 feet tall may be 300 to 700 years old. In spite of its flat, evergreen, needlelike leaves, the yew is not a true conifer and is classified in its own family. It is unusual in producing new growth that remains light green all year and in enclosing its seed, not in a cone, but in a small, fleshy aril, a red and waxy structure that is open at the apex.

One of the slowest-growing trees in the world, a 300-year-old Pacific yew, may have a trunk 5 to 10 inches in diameter.

The Pacific yew grows predominantly in the Northwest. It requires shade and grows especially well in dense, mature Olympic Peninsula forests, where it can reach 75 feet in height. Major stands of yew also grow in Oregon's Willamette and Umpqua national forests and in Idaho's Nez Perce National Forest.

Fine-grained yew wood is springy, durable, and strong. A beautiful wood, it displays rosy red heartwood and pale yellow sapwood. The thin bark of the fluted and twisted trunk continually sheds papery scales, revealing the rosy inner bark.

Historically, Northwest Indians valued Pacific yew for making spoons, boxes, drum frames, digging sticks, clubs, harpoon shafts, log-splitting wedges, bows and arrows, and canoe paddles. Settlers used the wood for fence posts, tool handles, and— because of its colorful heartwood—for furniture.

Yew wood has had little modern commercial value. But, researchers recently have discovered that yew bark contains a cancer-fighting chemical. Whereas yews were once indiscriminately cut in logging operations, they are now being spared so that the bark can be harvested.

Buds formed at the base of the leaves of the youth-on-age or pig-a-back plant become independent plants.

YOUTH-ON-AGE PLANT One of the oddest of the Northwest's native plants is youth-on-age (*Tolmiea menziesii*), sometimes called pig-a-back plant. On this unique plant, small buds form at the base of the hairy, heart-shaped leaves and grow into independent plants. Flowers appear at the top of stems that can be more than 2 feet high. Youth-on-age prefers moist soil in woodlands or along steam banks and is rarely found east of the Cascades.

THREE

NATURAL FEATURES

. . . .

From agates that would be thunder eggs . . .

to the River of No Return Wilderness

AGATES Agates are the Cinderella stone of the Northwest. Their handsomely banded and patterned interiors are usually concealed by a rough exterior. The four Northwest states, especially Oregon, lead the nation in amount and variety of agates and agatized wood.

Agates and agatized wood are more plentiful in the Northwest than in any other part of the country.

Agate pebbles are scattered along ocean beaches in southern Oregon, where winter storms constantly unearth new ones, and in stream or gravel riverbeds in Montana and Idaho, often on hillside terraces above streams. In gemstone-rich Idaho, agates with plumes of white, red, yellow, and blue are found in veins a foot wide at Graveyard Point. Agate hunters uncover scarce Ellensburg blue agates in eastern Washington's Teanaway Ridge and in the Ellensburg Formation. Idaho, too, offers the prized blue agates. Montana takes pride in red-and-white banded agates and in moss agates with fernlike patterns.

THUNDER EGG

♦ Most of the nation's thunder eggs—large agates in nodules that geologists call "septarian nodules," and which can be as large as grapefruit—are found in arid central Oregon north of Bend in such places as the Ochoco Mountains. The welded ash ledges of a 30-million-year-old rock layer known as the John Day Formation contain large numbers of thunder eggs. The knobby, ridged exterior of a nodule often conceals a handsome interior marked with a star shape; no two thunder eggs are exactly alike.

♦ Agates can form in the cavities and veins of any rock, but the Northwest's abundant silica-rich lava, with its many gas cavities, provides the ideal matrix. Groundwater circulating through the lava very slowly precipitates out silica minerals—quartz, opal, chalcedony (a translucent blue or gray quartz)—that eventually fill the cavities over many thousands of years. More thousands of years may pass before the filled nodules erode out of the ash beds and become available for the rockhound to saw open.

AMBER The only amber on the West Coast is found on Tiger Mountain, a remnant of a very old mountain range near Issaquah, Washington. Transparent and yellowish with a resinous luster, the amber is 35 to 50 million years old. Amber is not a mineral but an organic compound, the fossilized resin or gum of ancient trees. Rockhounds find the Issaquah amber, in pieces that vary in size from sandgrain to 2 inches in diameter, in and near fragments of carbonized wood in rock and coal outcroppings, and also as isolated nodules in gray shale and sandstone bedrock. The local amber contains bubbles and bits of fiber, but no fossil insect remains. Because it fractures so readily, Issaquah amber is seldom used in jewelry.

Amber is not a mineral, but rather a fossilized resin.

*Idaho's Snake Plain
Aquifer, one of the
world's largest, holds
hundreds of times
more water than any
of the state's surface
reservoirs.*

AQUIFER Idaho's Snake Plain Aquifer, underlying the plain north of the Snake River, is one of the world's great aquifers. Extending almost 100 miles northeast from Hagerman Valley, it holds hundreds of times more water than any of Idaho's surface reservoirs, making it one of the state's most valuable resources. Many thin layers of basalt lava interbedded with silt, sand, and gravel as deep as 3,000 feet form the aquifer. Minor folding and faulting have greatly increased its permeability.

Water that flows off central Idaho's lofty mountain ranges, which receive heavy winter precipitation, drains into the deeply fissured and porous aquifer. Thousands of years ago, the rivers flowed above ground to join the Snake. But repeated lava flows in the area filled the channels of the rivers again and again, forcing them to cut new channels, forcing even the Snake River into a great curve to the southwest. Unable to maintain their new channels, such rivers as Lost River and Little Lost River went underground and found their ancient channels, now filled with porous lava.

The subterranean rivers race along under the lava plain, aided by the downwarping of the plain, which is due, in part, to the enormous weight of lava and water. After traveling more than 90 miles, the rivers finally emerge as springs, cascades, and waterfalls on steep canyon walls along the north bank of the Snake River, culminating in the Thousand Springs at Hagerman. Each year, those underground rivers of the aquifer add 200 billion cubic feet of much-needed water to the Snake River below Milner Dam where, during periods of maximum irrigation, the river would be almost dry except for the aquifer water.

*Weirdly shaped
sandstone spires,
sculpted by wind and
rain, mark Montana's
badlands regions.*

BADLANDS One of the most spectacular of Montana's badlands, Makoshika State Park, near the Yellowstone River, contains 8,834 acres of weirdly eroded sandstone and mudstone columns capped with hard sandstone that protects the softer material below. Surface runoff and splashing rain have eroded the soft stone, which is pale gray and soft brown, into such shapes as spirals, pyramids, matterhorns, and buttresses.

♦ Medicine Rocks State Park, another badlands 10 miles north of Ekalaka, Montana, displays 316 acres of weathered sandstone so soft that grains easily brush off. Dozens of oddly shaped, steep-sided formations—some of them ridges 80 feet high and buttes with flat tops 25 to 80 feet across—remain from an old bed of sandstone, which may have formed from ancient sand dunes. Holes of all sizes honeycomb the chalky white formations. Since no evidence of stream erosion exists, the sculpting force must have been wind. Each formation is surrounded by a small, moat-like depression that was evidently excavated by strong winds.

BALANCED ROCK One of Idaho's best-known landmarks, Balanced Rock, looms on a bluff above Salmon Falls Creek Canyon. The 40-foot-high, top-heavy chunk of weathered lava rests on a base only 1 foot by ½ foot by 3 feet. The formation resembles a huge stone mushroom with a thin stem.

In Idaho, a 40-foot-high chunk of lava balances precariously on its small base.

BATHOLITHS The Idaho Batholith, largest of nearly a dozen large granitic intrusions in Idaho, ranks as the most extensive granite mass in the Northwest and possibly the nation. It extends 250 miles long and 100 miles wide across most of central Idaho and into western Montana. Intruded nearly 100 million years ago, it forms one of the most dominant features of central Idaho, uplifted into high, jagged mountains such as the glacier-sculpted Sawtooths or exposed by erosion on the Snake River Plain. There the Snake, Selway, Salmon, and Lochsa rivers have cut huge canyons, exposing a belt of granite 80 miles long that covers 16,000 square miles.

A gigantic intrusion of granite, uplifted into mountain ranges and cut into deep canyons, stretches across 250 miles of central Idaho.

The formation of the batholith was related to the violent inter-action between the continental plate moving westward and the oceanic plate moving eastward at a time when the western edge of the North American continent was just beyond Idaho's present border with Washington. As the heavier ocean plate dived under the continental plate, the friction between the two melted the edge of the oceanic plate about 60 miles under the surface. That very hot rock rose toward the surface to form batholiths and plu-tons (small batholiths). Both plutons and batholiths form the core of most Northwest mountains.

A batholith, like lava, originates as molten rock that wells up deep in the earth. But whereas lava, erupting to the surface through faults and fissures, cools too rapidly to form crystals, the batholith cools slowly underground, crystallizing and forming granite. Sometimes only part of a mass of rising molten rock cools underground, and the rest erupts.

♦ Most of Idaho's ore deposits and gemstones formed in strata near the margins of the batholith, with different mineral com-pounds precipitating out at different temperatures. Similar pre-cipitation of minerals resulted in rich ore deposits associated with plutons and batholiths in all four Northwest states. (See Gold and Silver, and Minerals.)

♦ The Idaho Batholith might still lie deep below the surface except for the extraordinary journey of the continental rock that covered it. That 10-mile-thick layer of continental crust grew unstable because of the great mass of fiery magma bulging up beneath it. Great slabs of it broke up, skidding along on the still-molten lava and traveling—over a period of a million years—50 miles east into western Montana, leaving the batholith exposed. Huge pieces of that crust slid on top of each other, forming two great Montana mountain blocks—Sapphire Block and the Pioneer Range.

♦ Montana's huge Boulder Batholith, formed from different magma than the Idaho Batholith, lies between Butte and Helena and is responsible for the rich gold and silver ores discovered in that area. This magma, which crystallized very near the surface, also erupted to build the Elkhorn Mountains.

BAYS On the Oregon coast at Depoe Bay nestles one of the smallest natural harbors in the world, a harbor within a harbor. Some 20 million years ago, sediment-carrying waves ground out a rectangular niche in basalt lava along the coast. Later wave action exploited a weak spot in the niche and scoured out a passage nearly 50 feet wide. The waves continued to grind away lava, carving out a 6-acre lagoon beyond the passage. Now deep-sea fishing boats anchor in that harbor, sheltered in a rocky amphitheater. Watching the boats maneuver through the narrow passage in a rough sea is a spectator sport for tourists.

The Pacific Ocean carved out a tiny harbor within a harbor at Depoe Bay and built a 20-mile-long sand spit that protects the shallow waters of Willapa Bay.

♦ The most pristine river estuary in the Lower 48, Willapa Bay in Washington's extreme southwest corner is almost completely shielded from the rough waters of the Pacific by 20-mile-long Long Beach Peninsula. The mile-wide sandy spit formed during the last 8,000 years as ocean currents carried north a portion of the enormous sand deposits that the Columbia River dumped at its mouth. The peninsula, which absorbs the shock of 40-foot-high breakers and winds of 140 miles an hour on the ocean side, no longer increases in length; dams on the Columbia River trap most of the sediment upstream. During the last Ice Age, when the sea level was 300 feet lower, the shallow bay formed part of Willapa Hills. At low tide, much of Willapa Bay consists of mud, with 15,000 acres of that mud housing oysters.

The bay surrounds Long Island, part of the 11,000-acre Willapa National Wildlife Refuge. Long Island, with an area of 4,700 acres, is the largest island of its kind on the West Coast, accessible only by private boat.

BEACHES The world's only driftwood beaches occur on Puget Sound and the Pacific Northwest coast. Such beaches form only where an ample number of trees grow near the water, as in Oregon and Washington, and only where the winds are onshore, pushing floating objects toward shore, where they strand.

The world's only driftwood beaches extend along the shorelines of the Pacific Northwest.

Although some driftwood floats in from distant points, most originates locally. Many logs lost from log rafts in Puget Sound or the Columbia River are carried out to sea and later wash up on ocean beaches. With time, the logs acquire a silvery sheen and satiny texture.

◆ Washington's 28-mile-long sandy Long Beach Peninsula, which shelters Willapa Bay, boasts the longest natural beach in the nation, with some 13 to 15 miles of sand hard-packed enough for cars to drive on.

◆ Ruby Beach on Washington's Olympic Peninsula displays swaths of colorful sand. Wave action grinds pinkish sand from garnet crystals on the beach; the crystals may have been carried to the beach by Ice Age glaciers that plucked them from sandstone outcroppings in the Olympic Mountains. The sorting action of the waves concentrates the relatively heavy garnet sand.

◆ Beaches along the Oregon coast often display black sand, ground from dark volcanic rock. In southern Oregon, much of the black sand comes from igneous rocks—patches of old ocean crust—in the Klamath Mountains. These rocks contain magnetite (the magnetic oxide of iron), red garnet, chromite, zircon, and ilmenite (a titanium mineral)—denser minerals than the quartz and feldspar commonly found in sand. Streams bring these minerals—plus small amounts of gold and platinum—to the coast, where ocean waves neatly sort each mineral by weight into curving swash marks. Attempts at mining the beach ores have not proved profitable.

BEACON ROCK Beacon Rock, rising 848 feet above the Washington shore of the Columbia River Gorge, 5 miles west of Bonneville Dam, ranks as the West's highest monolith—a single rock formation detached from bedrock, protruding from the earth's surface. This solidified core of a volcano may be 9 million years old, its volcano active during the uplift of the Cascades. Erosion of the outer surface of ejected material left only the hardened plug standing.

Beacon Rock, the West's highest monolith, rises 848 feet above the Columbia River.

Charles Ladd, a Portland banker, bought Beacon Rock in the early 1900s to save it from being quarried. A narrow ¾-mile trail to the summit zigzags along fifty-two switchbacks and crosses twenty-two wooden bridges spanning fissures in the huge rock. The summit offers impressive views of Mount Hood, Mount Adams, and the Columbia River.

The most westerly point in the Lower 48 is Washington's Cape Alava.

CAPES Washington's Cape Alava on the Olympic Peninsula extends farther west than any other land in the Lower 48, a few hundred feet farther than Cape Flattery. The whale-hunting Makah Indians occupied Ozette Village on Cape Alava for several thousand years. Discovery in 1970 of artifacts that severe winter storms had washed out of a beach ledge prompted excavation of the area. A decade of excavations at Cape Alava revealed five flattened Makah longhouses buried under claylike mud from a series of mudslides 500 years ago. Recovered from the community dwellings were some 60,000 artifacts. The mud and waterlogging perfectly preserved even objects made of wood and fiber, such as mats, blankets, and cradles. The Makah Cultural and Research Center in Neah Bay displays 500 of the choicest artifacts.

◆ At the tip of the Olympic Peninsula, Land's End lookout on Cape Flattery marks the most northwesterly land in the Lower 48. A rough, ½-mile trail leads to the edge of a sheer cliff with wave-battered rocks below. Nearby Tatoosh Island boasts one of the Northwest's oldest lighthouses, built in 1857 near the treacherous entrance to the Strait of Juan de Fuca.

◆ Many of the capes jutting into the sea along the Oregon coast are former volcanoes. Twenty million years ago, when most of the Oregon Coast Range was underwater, lava poured out profusely onto the coast and ocean floor. Basalt dikes 4 feet thick cutting through Yaquina Head mark it as a former volcano. Cape Perpetua and Heceta Head consist of cemented fragments of volcanic rock and tuff.

◆ A narrow winding road, the Three Capes Scenic Loop Road, leads off the main Oregon coastal highway to Capes Lookout, Meares, and Kiwanda. Some 15 million years ago, a huge flow of basalt lava formed 700-foot-high Cape Lookout, often said to be the most scenic cape on the Pacific coast. At the wave-assaulted base of the massive cape, which may once have been an offshore volcanic island, sea-cooled pillow basalt contrasts strikingly with layers of lava that spilled out on land. Cape Meares was formed by basalt lava that erupted at about the same time.

◆ The wave-sculpted cliffs of Cape Kiwanda originated in a beach with multicolored sand, which was later submerged, compressed into rock, and then uplifted. Sand dunes rise from the cape, and miles of sandy beach stretch south of it. Ordinarily, the surf would quickly reduce a sandstone cape into sand again, but a large basaltic sea stack just offshore of Cape Kiwanda protects it by absorbing the force of the waves. Sheltered by the sea stack, fishing boats can be launched directly into the open surf here,

TATOOSH LIGHTHOUSE

one of the few places in the nation where this occurs.

◆ The light-colored cliffs of Cape Blanco make it the most visible point from sea on the Oregon coast. Martin d'Aguilar, an early Spanish explorer, discovered and named the cape in 1603. Cape Blanco was the first point in Oregon to appear on a map of the Northwest, one of only three physical features on Gerhard Mueller's map of the Pacific Coast of 1764. The others were the Strait of Juan de Fuca, depicted only as a break in the coastline and indicated on the map as "Entrance discover'd by Juan de Fuca in 1592," and "The River of the West," shown extending far inland into a totally blank interior. This river was presumably the Columbia, whose entrance d'Aguilar discovered in 1603, although he did not enter it.

◆ Cape Foulweather, named by Captain James Cook in 1778, offers a veritable museum of lava types: volcanic rock usually found near the vent or on the flanks of a volcano; lava flows that erupted on land and pillow basalts that erupted underwater; volcanic ash that settled from the air, and some that settled from ocean currents. Formerly an offshore volcanic island, the cape uplifted at the same time as Oregon's Coast Range.

CAVES See Lava Tube Caves; Limestone and Marble Caves; and Sea Caves.

CITY OF ROCKS The towers, tubs, bottles, and other fanciful figures eroded from granite in Idaho's unusual Silent City of Rocks marked an important stopping place for early wagon travelers across the continent. Below the "city," now protected within a national reserve, lay Emigrant Canyon, where the Salt Lake Alternate joined the California Trail.

Early travelers who stopped to rest at this "city" of weather-carved rocks etched names and messages into the granite stones.

On the weirdly shaped rocks in southwestern Idaho, some of them rising 250 feet, thousands of emigrants carved out or used axle grease to write names, dates, and messages. They bestowed on the rocks such descriptive names as Dragon's Head, Old Woman, and Bathtub Rock—a 200-foot-high rock with a concave top that catches rain. The weather-carved rocks, which originated in an enormous, isolated granite dome, cover 25 square miles within a series of eight canyons.

COAL Most of eastern Montana sits on top of the largest coal deposit in the world, the vast Fort Union Coal Formation. Estimates of its size range from 1.3 trillion to 50 trillion tons. One seam of coal alone, 14 feet thick and close to the surface in the Fort Kipp coalfield of the Fort Union formation, is estimated to

Eastern Montana rests on top of the world's largest coal deposit.

contain 300 million tons.

The low-sulfur coal, most of it lignite, lies in relatively thick veins just under the surface and can be strip-mined. Once, coal powered the railroad locomotives that pulled freight trains nearly a mile long over the Rockies and Cascades. Now, most of the coal produces electric power for export to Oregon and Washington, where native coal is low-grade and often hard to mine because of extreme tilting and folding of coal veins.

In the 1880s, Lake Coeur d'Alene provided a watery highway for goldminers.

COEUR D'ALENE LAKE
Idaho's Lake Coeur d'Alene is sometimes counted among "the five most beautiful lakes in the world." More than two dozen bays indent its 56-mile length, which is shaped like a sprawling, highly ornamented M. The Coeur d'Alene Mountains provide a soaring backdrop. A number of large rivers running into the lake provide boaters, whether by canoe, sail or power, with extensive waterways to explore. Although a road encircles it, and a huge sawmill and the city of Coeur d'Alene spread along its shores, much of the meandering lake remains unspoiled.

Historically the city of Coeur d'Alene was a jump-off place, the end of the stagecoach line during early gold rush days after the 1881 discovery of gold in the Coeur d'Alene Mountains 40 miles to the east. The huge lake provided a waterway for ships to carry freight and passengers to the mines. Two steamers built during the winter of 1883 and 1884, the *Coeur d' Alene* and the *General Sherman,* made numerous trips up the lake and into the Coeur d'Alene River to the head of navigation near Cataldo. From there, prospectors took the "jackass trail" to the mines. The steamship business continued to thrive after lead and silver were discovered and timber operations began.

COEUR D'ALENE LAKE

Today, with seventeen boat launching sites, Lake Coeur d'Alene offers a plethora of boating pleasures, with side trips up rivers that empty into the lake, such as the Spokane River, the St. Joe River, and the Coeur d'Alene River, which is navigable for 24 miles with channels into seven of nine lakes along the river.

Basalt, layered during millions of years of recurring lava flows, covers the Columbia Plateau with one of the world's deepest lava beds.

COLUMBIA PLATEAU BASALT
One of the world's deepest lava beds covers the Columbia Plateau of eastern Washington and northeastern Oregon. No one knows how deep it is, but a well drilled 16,000 feet deep near Yakima, Washington, failed to pass through the comparatively recent Columbia Plateau basalt flows into the ancient ash beds, old lava flows, and sedimentary rock that undoubtedly underlie eastern Washington. Lava flows obscure much of the Northwest's geological history, hiding

boundaries of previous events.

Thirteen to twenty-five million years ago, the lava welled up quietly from fissures several miles long in northeastern Oregon and southeastern Washington, covering much of the surrounding area. The flows continued over a period of about four million years and reached some of west-central Idaho and part of southwestern Washington and northwestern Oregon. Both Oregon and Washington display dikes where lava solidified in the fissures after eruptions. The depth of separate flows varied from a few feet to more than 200 feet, with the very thin lava tending to pond most thickly in eastern and central Washington. In eastern Washington, only the Okanogan Highlands in the northeastern corner stood above the lava. The weight of that incredible accumulation of basalt lava caused extreme subsidence in the Columbia Plateau.

Seldom before or since has lava flowed in such volume, covered so extensive an area (200,000 square miles), or recurred with such long intervals between flows. Hundreds of thousands of years passed between flows, long enough for soil and lakes to form, forests to grow and die. The sequence can be read in road cuts and in gorge, canyon, and coulee walls: black for basalt, white for lake sediment, and red for tropical laterite soil, which formed on top of lava layers during moist, warm periods and was later covered with more lava.

◆ A single flow, the Roza Flow, ranks as the largest known prehistoric lava flow: 300 miles long, covering 15,400 square miles. The 15-million-year-old flow can be traced from Grand Coulee east to Spokane, south to Pendleton, and southwest into the Columbia River Gorge.

Other flows raced into the northern end of the Willamette Valley, on to Portland, and then west to the Pacific, extending 40 miles underwater. Flows on slopes may have reached 25 miles an hour velocity.

◆ These lava flows played an important role in shaping the land east of the Cascades. They filled in canyons and other low spots, dammed streams, encased or carbonized trees, turned lakes and rivers into steam, and created new lakes and swamps. Repeated flows forced the mighty Columbia to alter course, making a half-circle in Big Bend country, and built part of the extensive Snake River Plain. (See Snake River Plain.)

COLUMBIA RIVER The Columbia River ranks as the Northwest's longest and largest river, flowing 1,243 miles from its source in British Columbia to the Pacific Ocean. Six miles wide at

*Water from the
Columbia River,
largest of the West
Coast rivers flowing
into the Pacific,
dilutes the ocean
as far as 300 miles
offshore.*

its mouth near Astoria, it is the largest of the West Coast rivers flowing into the Pacific.

◆ Among the rivers of the Lower 48, the Columbia rates fourth in volume of discharge, averaging 265,000 cubic feet a second. The huge amount of water dilutes the ocean as far as 300 miles offshore, giving sensory clues to salmon and steelhead returning to spawn. Early explorers noted the discoloration as they sailed past, but massive sandbars disguised the river mouth.

◆ Because the Columbia originates in British Columbia's Columbia Lake at an elevation of 2,650 feet—a region rich in glaciers and snow—the river's discharge stays fairly continuous throughout the year. Unlike most rivers, the Columbia, fed by heavy snowmelt, peaks in spring and early summer when farmers most need irrigation water.

◆ The Columbia and its tributaries comprise the principal river system of the Cascade Range, draining the entire chain from British Columbia to central Oregon. Drainage from parts of seven states feeds the river system, including all the waters of northwest Montana, which drain into the Columbia via the Clark Fork and Kootenai rivers. The watershed totals more than 259,000 square miles, an area larger than France. The Columbia's main tributary is the Snake, itself a major river 1,038 miles long.

◆ Unlike most other Northwest rivers, the Columbia did not seek the path of least resistance around obstacles and high ground when the rising Cascades threatened to alter its route. Instead, it cut through a relatively low part of the Cascades at Wallula Gap in Horse Heaven Hills. The river may have been dammed behind the rising mountains, forming a series of temporary lakes each time one of the Spokane Floods occurred; but eventually it cut through the lava as it poured over and eroded the edge of the basalt cliffs. With the help of torrents of floodwater, the river has deepened its gorge until, in some places, it flows 4,500 feet below the plateau rim.

◆ The powerful river has been diverted temporarily by ice dams and by the Spokane Floods, and permanently at least twice by massive flows of basalt. Columbia Plateau basalt flowing north forced the Columbia to make the wide arc of the Big Bend in northeastern Washington, undoubtedly turning the river into steam where water and lava met. The river marks the western boundary of the Columbia Plateau lava, flowing between the lava plain and the older rock of the Okanogan Highlands and the Cascade Range. Today's Columbia River Gorge represents a detour of the ancestral Columbia north of the original channel, now hidden under Mount Hood. (See Columbia Plateau

Basalt and Spokane Floods.)

COLUMBIA RIVER GORGE
Scenically and geologically, the 85-mile-long Columbia River Gorge rates as one of the nation's natural wonders. Essentially a sea-level mountain pass, and the only "road" available in early days, the Columbia River Gorge marks the only significant break in the Cascade-Sierra Nevada chain.

Sharply tilted lava layers in the walls of the 4,500-foot-deep Columbia River Gorge provide clues to the rising of the Cascade Range.

Within the gorge, which varies in width from 5 to 8 miles and plunges to 4,500 feet, the river winds past sheer cliffs scoured clean of soil by a rampaging flood-swollen river, past smooth-sided shrinkage columns of basalt, waterfalls cascading over steep river-cut cliffs, erratic rocks stranded high on basalt ledges, ancient and modern landslides that once blocked the river on the north side, and lava layers tilted almost on end as the Cascade Range pushed upward. The river passes 700-foot-high Crown Point, part of a huge lava flow that filled the more southerly canyon of the ancestral Columbia millions of years ago, forcing it to detour into the modern gorge. East of Hood River the gorge opens up, displaying expansive ledges of plateau basalt on either side.

The steep, river-gouged walls of the Columbia River Gorge allow geologists one of very few glimpses into Columbia Plateau basalt. Clearly visible are great arches and sags in the layers of lava, which were steeply tilted and tightly folded as the Cascade Range was uplifted 2 to 5 million years ago.

◆ The Columbia Gorge encompasses two distinct biological and climatic regions. Rain may be falling at the western end while the sun is blazing at the eastern end. Western hemlock and Douglas fir heavily forest the Pacific end, giving way to dry-country ponderosa pine and Oregon white oak in the east. Dry, often bitterly cold air from the eastern interior collides with moist, warmer ocean air. The narrower parts of the gorge funnel the wind through at a steady 15 to 25 miles an hour, providing some of the best wind-surfing waters in the world.

COLUMBIA GORGE
WINDSURFER

◆ In 1986 Congress formed the Columbia River Gorge National Scenic Area, protecting about 85 miles of the scenic gorge from unsuitable development and growth. The scenic area extends from Troutdale in the west to The Dalles in the east.

COLUMBIA RIVER MOUTH
The Columbia River ends at one of the world's most treacherous river mouths and sandbars. Erratic currents and winds up to 160 miles an hour have earned the river mouth and bar the nickname "Graveyard of the Pacific,"

*More than 2,000
shipwrecks have
occurred off the
mouth of the
Columbia River, the
"Graveyard of the
Pacific."*

with more than 2,000 shipwrecks and 1,500 deaths to its dis-
credit. Because of a "tidal sloop" of short, steep waves at the
mouth, ships with only a 35-foot draft can hit bottom in 60 feet of
water. Storm waves 25 feet high batter South Jetty. The river
mouth proved so dangerous to early sailing ships that the first
lighthouse on the Northwest coast was built there in 1856 at Cape
Disappointment.

◆ The raw material for the Columbia bar, and for Pacific
beaches and sand spits, came from huge amounts of sediment the
river carried and dumped at its mouth. The Columbia used to
dump more sediment into the Pacific than any other Western
Hemisphere river—7.5 million tons a year—gouged from
Cascade volcanoes by glaciers and carried into the Columbia by
tributaries. Now, 11 major dams and more than 100 dams on
tributaries trap most of the silt—and tame a once-wild river.

*Crater Lake, formed
when ancient Mount
Mazama collapsed, is
the nation's deepest
lake and one of the
world's clearest.*

CRATER LAKE The nation's deepest lake, second deepest in
the Western Hemisphere and seventh deepest in the world, lies
within Oregon's only national park. At an elevation of 6,176 feet,
Crater Lake nestles within a volcanic caldera that measures
6 miles across and has walls 4,000 feet high. The lake reaches
a maximum depth of 1,932 feet, with an average depth of
1,500 feet.

◆ The water in Crater Lake is some of the clearest in the world.
In no other lake does light penetrate so deeply, enabling freshwater moss to grow at greater depths than in any other lake
on earth. Depth and clarity intensify the peacock blue of the
lake's waters.

◆ The water level in the lake, which has no known inlet or
outlet, varies less than 3 to 5 feet a year. Evaporation, seepage,
and snowmelt from an annual snowfall of 50 feet maintain the
water level. A snowfall of 155 inches in November 1984 broke a
50-year-old park record for one month's snowfall. One day in
February 1971, 3 feet of snow fell, setting a new one-day record
for the park.

◆ Crater Lake fills the caldera of ancient Mount Mazama, a
former southern Cascade Range volcano that was one of Oregon's
highest peaks, perhaps 12,000 feet high. More than 6,700 years
ago, in some of the most violent eruptions known in the
Cascades, Mount Mazama spewed out the largest amount of
pumice ejected by a recent Cascade volcano. As a result, the
volcano summit collapsed into the caldera now occupied by
Crater Lake.

Later volcanic activity on the lake bottom created Crater

Lake's distinctive Wizard Island. That cinder cone, which displays Mazama's youngest rocks, rises 2,750 feet from the caldera floor, but only 760 feet of it is above water. Cinders, volcanic bombs, and scoria fragments litter the slopes of Wizard Island, whose base has been broadened by eruptions of blocky lava.

The oldest visible Mazama flow is 161-foot-high Phantom Ship, part of a peak built earlier than the main mass of Mount Mazama. It could be part of Mount Mazama's conduit system. The rock of this well-known Crater Lake formation and the rock through which it cuts may be the oldest in the park.

CRATERS OF THE MOON
Idaho's Craters of the Moon National Monument displays in 83 square miles an extraordinary variety of young basaltic volcanic features. Part of a much larger lava field, and geographically part of the Columbia Plateau, Craters of the Moon lies at the northeast corner of the Snake River Plain at an elevation of 7,576 feet. Most of the eruptions that formed the various volcanic features of the area, dating from 1,000 to 15,000 years ago, occurred quietly along fissures of the Great Rift. (See also Columbia Plateau Basalt and Snake River Plain.)

Cinder cones, spatter cones, lava bombs, and fumaroles cover the 83 square miles of Idaho's Craters of the Moon National Monument.

Craters of the Moon includes some of the nation's most recent lava flows—flows 500 to 1,600 years old. With only 10 inches of rain a year, erosion of the lava is minimal. Freezing and thawing have split crater walls and rubble into grotesque forms. Surprisingly, 200 species of plants and 2,000 species of insects thrive in the seemingly sterile lava.

♦ The monument's Big Cinder Butte is pure basalt, one of the few such cinder cones in the world; at a height of 800 feet, it is also the world's largest. Along with thirty-five other cinder cones in the area, it formed when molten, gas-charged rocks fountained into the air, hardened into cinders, and built the symmetrical cones as they fell.

♦ The region's spatter cones, some of the largest and most symmetrically shaped of their kind in the Lower 48, resulted from the eruption of pasty lava that stuck together in clots and fell near the eruptive vent.

TWISTED TREE AT
CRATERS OF THE MOON

♦ Lava bombs—blobs of lava shaped and solidified in the air— litter the lava fields of Craters of the Moon, ranging in size from several inches to several feet, and in shape from ribbons and spindles to pancakes and footballs.

Also presenting evidence of varied volcanic activity in Craters of the Moon National Monument are 100 fumaroles, broad lava rivers atop other lava flows, natural bridges, several types of tree molds, a unique cobalt blue flow of "squeeze up" lava, and lava tube caves more than 800 feet long and up to 30 feet in diameter.

DRY FALLS Once the world's largest waterfall, Washington's Dry Falls flowed nearly 10,000 years ago, filled to overflowing by the Columbia River swollen by floods identified by scientists as the world's largest, the Spokane Floods. Before each flood, a lobe of the Purcell Trench Glacier formed a dam that impounded Montana's gigantic Glacial Lake Missoula. Each time that ice dam broke, the backed-up water surged out, enlarging the Columbia River to flood stage. Torrents of water plunged over three deeply notched, horseshoe-shaped cliffs 400 feet high and 3 miles along the crest. Those floods, which may have recurred forty times, although not always so dramatically, enlarged what was at first probably only a shallow gorge but is now known as Lower Grand Coulee.

The world's largest waterfall once swept over 3 miles of horseshoe-shaped cliffs at Washington's Dry Falls.

Rock-encrusted icebergs carried in the tumultuous, silt-charged floodwater chewed away both the coulee walls and the lip of the falls, which consisted of easily eroded, cracked basalt. During the height of flooding, the coulee was filled to overflowing. But as the water continued to work on the collapsing lip of the falls, the great cataract retreated farther and farther upstream, leaving behind Lower Grand Coulee, eventually enlarged to its present-day length of nearly 17 miles. When the ice sheet receded, no longer damming the river, the floods ceased, no more water ran through the coulee, and Dry Falls were truly dry. Only deep plunge pools at the base of the falls now glint with water. (See Spokane Floods.)

The Okanogan glacial lobe reached its southernmost position near Dry Falls, leaving behind many basaltic and granitic erratics. The low hills of Withrow Moraine, made of glacial rubble, mark the southern edge of that ice lobe.

DUNES The most extensive group of active coastal sand dunes in the nation stretches along the Oregon coast for more than 100 miles and extends 3 miles inland. Some of these dunes are as tall as 600 feet. Nowhere else in the world has so much ocean-related sand piled up. The 40-mile-long Oregon Dunes National Recreation Area between Coos Bay and Florence protects the tallest dunes.

The tallest landlocked sand dune in North America rises 470 feet above the desert in southwestern Idaho.

Oregon's dunes began to form about 13,000 years ago during the last glacial period when ocean water was swollen with sediment-laden glacier melt. Today rivers carry to the ocean sand eroded from exposed sandstone bedrock in the Coast Range.

Offshore currents distribute the sand along the coastland, and tides, waves, and wind move the sand among the dunes.

Oregon's coastal sand dunes support 175 species of bird life, along with reptiles, mammals, and insects. Wildflowers thrive on the edges of inner dunes. Just below the surface, the sand, which retains subsurface water, maintains a cool 60°F.

♦ Oblique dunes, named for crests that are oriented obliquely to both northwest and southwest winds, occur only in Oregon. These narrow, parallel ridges of sand average 550 feet from crest to crest and rise to 165 feet. Although their average length is 3,600 feet, a few stretch for nearly a mile.

♦ Living dunes can move 6 to 18 feet a year in the direction of the prevailing wind. The Oregon dunes encroach on roads and forests, killing trees by burying them. Dunes have created a chain of freshwater lakes east of the coast highway by damming the mouths of seventeen of the smaller rivers between Florence and Coos Bay. Prime dune-building time is winter, when coastal storm winds blow up to 100 miles an hour.

Early in the twentieth century, an attempt to stabilize the dunes was made by planting European beach grass on some dunes near river mouths. The grass spread rapidly, and shrubs and trees soon took hold as well. The planting has created fore-dunes up to 25 feet high that parallel the shore, drastically reducing the amount of sand moving inland to feed the dunes.

♦ The tallest landlocked sand dune in North America rises in 2,840-acre Bruneau Dunes State Park in southwestern Idaho, soaring 470 feet above a nearby desert lake. Two of the most prominent dunes in the area cover 16 acres. The dunes are unique in the Western Hemisphere for rising not at the edge of their natural sandy basin but from the center. The temperature in the arid region ranges from 0°F to 110°F.

♦ In southern Idaho's sagebrush country, a rare sand desert 2 miles wide stretches for 30 miles west of St. Anthony. The active dunes, 10 to 100 feet high, shift constantly in the wind.

♦ Some of Washington's largest and most active inland dunes have accumulated in the state's smallest wilderness area. Juniper Dunes Wilderness protects a 7,100-acre area 15 miles northwest of Pasco, with dozens of square miles of dunes ranging from 200 to 1,200 feet wide, and rising to 130 feet. Warm desert winds blow incessantly, tidily sweeping loose sand into dunes. The sand blows off nearby prehistoric lake beds and sandbars along the Columbia River. The greatest concentration of western juniper trees in Washington grow in the dunes, their northernmost limit. In addition to the junipers, a sparse plant cover of grasses and shrubs protects many of the dunes. Although water is scarce, coyotes, kangaroo rats, and mule deer wander through Juniper Dunes.

◆ In the desert country of Washington's Quincy Basin rise some unusual crescent-shaped sand dunes. Dunes of this type, known as Barchans, are formed when the wind consistently moves the sand from the same direction. In Quincy the dunes migrate eastward, with the horns of the crescent pointing in that direction.

DUNGENESS SPIT The longest natural sand spit in the United States, Dungeness Spit, curves out into the Strait of Juan de Fuca for nearly 6 miles between Port Angeles and Sequim. On the western outer shore of the 100-yard-wide spit, which is exposed to the strait and the prevailing winds, the rough surf often carries in driftwood, which sprawls in chaotic heaps down the center of the spit. Along the inner eastern shore, protected by the spit, lies calm, shallow, 556-acre Dungeness Bay, with an enclosed harbor, tideflats, and saltwater marsh. The spit and adjacent tide line form Dungeness National Wildlife Refuge. Lying within the rain shadow of the Olympic Mountains, the spit receives only 15 inches of rain a year.

A smaller finger, Graveyard Spit, hooks away from the main spit, turning toward the land and forming a small, very shallow inner lagoon. Along that shore, luxuriant beds of eelgrass attract tens of thousands of migrating shorebirds each spring and fall. Many species winter there.

◆ One of the Northwest's oldest lighthouses (1857), the first on Washington's inland waters, stands ½ mile from the tip of Dungeness Spit. It marks a landform so low in elevation that early sailing ships often did not see it until they grounded on its shores.

◆ Dungeness Spit grows about 15 feet a year. Wind and water currents lengthen the spit by depositing sediment from the mouth of nearby Dungeness River and clay, silt, sand, and gravel eroded from steep sea cliffs along the strait.

EARTHQUAKES One of the strongest earthquakes ever recorded in the Lower 48 occurred in August 1959 in Montana's Madison River Canyon, 28 miles northwest of West Yellowstone. Registering 7.8 on the Richter scale, the quake, with eleven major shocks, was felt by people in eight states. It ranks as one of the West's most dramatic physical disasters, taking place during the height of camping season at 11:37 P.M., while campers slept.

The quake, which was followed by major aftershocks, opened two major faults, the larger one along the north shore of Hebgen

Dungeness Spit, the longest natural sand spit in the nation, curves nearly 6 miles out into the Strait of Juan de Fuca.

An earthquake measuring 7.8 on the Richter scale rocked western Montana in 1959.

Lake, where Hebgen Dam impounds the Madison River. The lake bed was tilted, its south shore raised 8 feet. At the more spectacular Red Canyon fault scarp, the earth was ripped open for 15 miles and vertical displacement of the crust reached 20 feet. The quakes also caused numerous blowholes, some as large as 15 by 50 feet, as compressed water was forced up through layers of sand.

Waves 20 feet high surged down the 7-mile-long lake and poured over the dam in a wall of water.

The night of the earthquake, hot spring activity some 50 miles away in Yellowstone National Park changed more drastically than it had in all the years since 1872, when the park was created. The quake triggered eruptions in hundreds of springs, nearly half of which erupted for the first time in their known histories. Others shortened the lengths of their eruption intervals but played twice as often. One minor geyser temporarily became major; another erupted continuously. Across from Old Faithful, which was barely affected, Giantess Geyser blew for 100 hours instead of its normal 30.

Madison River Canyon Earthquake Area was created, the first area ever established in the United States to preserve earthquake-caused features.

◆ Montana has registered 2,973 quakes since records were first kept in 1935. Most of them (2,945) occurred before 1947. In the northern Rockies, as in Oregon's basin and range province, a maze of faults, generally trending northwest, moves blocks up to form mountain ranges and drops others down to form broad basins, often generating earthquakes by the movements. Most Montana earthquakes concentrate in a zone south from Helena through Yellowstone National Park.

◆ An earthquake in Idaho's Thousand Springs Valley in October 1983 triggered the largest upsurge of groundwater ever recorded following an earthquake in the United States. Registering 7.3 on the Richter scale, the earthquake released 400 billion gallons of water from the Snake Plain Aquifer. Water shot 10 to 20 feet into the air, flooded roads, and formed a shallow lake. Compressed water was forced up through sand, forming a string of forty blow-hole craters; the largest was the size of an Olympic swimming pool. Old Faithful, some 300 miles away, lengthened its interval between eruptions by 8 minutes. Big Lost River and five other rivers in neighboring valleys doubled their flows.

The floor of Thousand Springs Valley vibrated so strongly that Lost River Fault, a seam in the earth's crust that runs for 10,000 feet, suddenly opened up. Within 15 seconds, a rupture 25 miles long and 10 miles deep cut through gravel eroded from Borah Peak, Idaho's highest mountain at 12,655 feet. That peak gained a foot in elevation as Lost River Range was uplifted. Thousand Springs Valley subsided 4 feet.

♦ The most severe earthquake in Washington's recorded history, 7.1 on the Richter scale, shook the southern Puget Sound area on April 13, 1949. A second shock, nearly as strong, followed seconds after the first. During the quake, which centered along a deep fault line near Olympia, cracks opened in the earth in Seattle near Green Lake and in the University of Washington Huskies' practice football field. Debris that fell from buildings buried cars; water tanks and mains burst. More than 1,000 homes and other buildings suffered millions of dollars of damage. Eight people died as a result of the quake.

ECLIPSE In 1979 thousands of eclipse watchers and astronomers from the United States and Europe flocked to the small Columbia River town of Goldendale, Washington. Goldendale, noted for its clear skies and lack of light pollution, had been chosen as the Official Eclipse Observing Station for the last total solar eclipse visible in the United States in the twentieth century. It occurred at 8:16 A.M. on February 26, 1979.

Thousands flocked to Goldendale, Washington, to watch the 1979 total solar eclipse.

Professional astronomers had visited Goldendale before. During the previous total solar eclipse, on June 8, 1918, they had come to the small town, bringing their portable instruments. For the 1979 eclipse, astronomers were able to work in an observatory built in 1973 on a 150-acre site north of town.

Rain clouds obscured the sun until five minutes before the eclipse began. The sky cleared just long enough for viewers to see the total eclipse; then rain clouds returned.

ERRATICS Orphans among Northwest rocks, huge boulders called erratics rest on mountain slopes and valleys far from their sources. Isolated and not at all resembling surrounding rocks, erratics give clues as to how the landscape was sculptured. The rocks could have been carried only in icebergs floated on powerful floodwaters or in the flowing ice of continental glaciers. They were picked up from debris at the base of cliffs or at the edge of the Columbia Plateau, or torn from canyon walls. As the ice sheet or the iceberg carrying them melted, the erratics were stranded far from home bedrock.

Erratics, or "orphaned rocks," lie scattered across the Northwest landscape, transported far from their origins by ancient floods and ice flows.

♦ Erratics lie scattered by the hundreds over the Columbia Plateau, from Grand Coulee Dam down to Pasco Basin. Some are perched 1,100 feet high on mountainsides; others are displayed in roadcuts of glacial till—unsorted sediment that a glacier has dropped. Distinctive erratics of pink or red sandstone originated in western Montana. Largest and most dramatic of all the erratics are the haystack rocks that loom up in hayfields of eastern Washington. The huge blocks of black basalt were plucked from the northern rim of the Columbia Plateau by the passing ice sheet and dropped farther south, near Withrow Moraine.

ERRATIC ALONGSIDE
FARMHOUSE

◆ Icebergs that once floated in Glacial Lake Missoula dropped huge boulders on the site of what is now the University of Montana campus at Missoula. Glacial ice brought to northeastern Montana colorful erratics of red and gray granite and streaky red and black gneiss that it had picked up in northern Manitoba.

◆ Hundreds of erratics are stranded in Oregon's Willamette Valley, 100 miles south of Ice Age glacial margins. Icebergs carried the erratics into a temporary lake that formed in the northern Willamette Valley after water backed up behind an ice jam in the Columbia River Gorge north of Portland. Because the lake was 400 feet deep, these erratics are found at elevations of 400 feet or lower. Erratic Rock State Park near McMinnville was created around a single huge slate erratic.

◆ The Olympic Mountains are studded with so many massive granite boulders on their north slopes, that geologists once thought the mountains contained a granite core and were of volcanic origin. But the Puget Lobe of glacial ice transported those granite erratics from British Columbia mountains, dropping them at elevations as high as 3,000 feet, the greatest height the ice reached on Olympic Mountain slopes.

FAULTS One of the nation's highest and one of the world's largest fault scarps, Abert Rim, extends for 30 miles along a fault in south-central Oregon. An 800-foot lava cliff caps the tilted escarpment, which rises a total of 2,500 feet above the floor of Alvord Desert.

Abert Rim, in Oregon, ranks as one of the nation's highest and one of the world's largest fault scarps.

Like other tilted blocks in the region, Abert Rim slopes up gently on one side, and drops steeply on the other. Deep internal pressure fractured the many eastward-tilting layers of basaltic lava that make up Abert Rim. A strong earthquake then either thrust the fractured lava up along the western side of a crustal fracture or dropped the valley below it.

◆ One of the continent's largest exposed faults, Oregon's Brothers fault zone, shows up in satellite photographs as a major, deeply fractured line of faults. North of Brothers fault zone, the lava plateau is intact, unfaulted. South of it, the plateau is broken into often-huge fault-block and fault-scarp mountains, which are separated by fault-block basins. The Brothers fault zone extends from Bend to southeastern Oregon and then curves south into central Nevada. Crustal movement along it is so recent that erosion has barely rounded the edges of the fault scarps.

◆ Steens Mountain in southeastern Oregon's Alvord Desert ranks as the highest fault block in the nation, at 9,670 feet. A fault block is a mountain-sized piece of the earth's crust, bounded on two or more sides by faults, and thrust up by movement along those faults. Rising almost without foothills above grassland and sagebrush, Steens is a classic fault block, rising above the many others found in Oregon's basin and range province. The mountain's western side rises gently, gaining 5,000 feet in 20 miles; in contrast, the nearly perpendicular eastern side rises abruptly to that height in only 3 miles. The segment of crust that formed Steens Mountain includes some 100 lava flows, part of a volcanic plateau that stretches for several thousand square miles east of Abert Rim. On the eastern flank of the mountain, dikes that are the source of some of these flows are visible—fissures in which the last lava of a flow solidified.

◆ Idaho's Great Rift National Landmark is the longest and deepest open volcanic rift on the North American continent. This zone of weakness follows a series of geological faults through which much of the basalt lava of Snake River Plain rose 2,100 years ago. It stretches for 46 miles, through and beyond Craters of the Moon National Monument. Never violent, flows from the rift were quiet or sputtering, the source of the highly varied lava formations in that rugged region.

◆ One of Montana's major areas of faulting, the Lewis and Clark fault zone, runs from Washington's Okanogan Valley to the Boulder Batholith west of Helena. This area contains most of Montana's active faults, cutting through older ranges and into new ones still rising. Most of the faults in the zone have not moved for a few million years. The rich Coeur d'Alene mining district follows this fault zone through northern Idaho.

FLATHEAD LAKE Montana's Flathead Lake is the largest natural freshwater lake west of the Mississippi. It is 28 miles long and 5 to 15 miles wide, large enough that strong winds can whip up whitecaps on it. With a shoreline of 185 miles and a surface of 189 square miles, the lake is bordered by six state parks and includes within it Wild Horse Island State Park. Flathead Lake is scenic as well as large, with the snowcapped Mission and Kootenai mountain ranges towering over it.

Monster sightings have been reported at Montana's Flathead Lake, the largest freshwater lake west of the Mississippi.

◆ Flathead Lake is noted for its excellent year-round fishing, especially for bull trout (formerly called Dolly Varden) native to the Flathead River drainage. Flathead Mackinaw trout can weigh more than 40 pounds. Of twenty-six species of fish now in the lake, eleven are native. Each year fishermen catch 300,000 fish there. Sightings of a monster in the lake are frequent, and in 1955 a fisherman caught one—a 7½-foot, 181-pound sturgeon. He played the big fish from 9 P.M. until 3 A.M.

◆ The west side of Flathead Lake marks the end of the northwestern branch of the active Intermountain Seismic Zone, which passes through Yellowstone National Park. As a result of activity in this zone, small tremors often shake Flathead Valley.

◆ During the last Ice Age, a lobe of glacial ice filled present-day Flathead Valley. As the lobe receded, depositing great amounts of glacial material, it left behind a huge mass of ice. Glacial deposits accumulated around but not on the surface of the remaining ice. When the ice chunk melted, it left a depression in the glacial deposits, which formed the bed of Flathead Lake.

FLATHEAD RIVER The South, Middle, and North forks of the Flathead River form the longest river system in the nation protected under the Wild and Scenic Rivers Act. These rivers flow through 219 miles of Montana's ruggedly beautiful backcountry. The Flathead River drains from huge Flathead Lake at Polson, winding though a series of steep-walled canyons. During May and June, water floods past the 200- to 500-foot-high, perpendicular walls of the Flathead River Gorge at the rate of 500,000 gallons a second.

The Middle, North, and South forks of the Flathead River form the longest river system protected under the National Wild and Scenic Rivers Act.

◆ The lobe of glacial ice that once filled Flathead Valley left behind a moraine that blocked the Flathead River's former valley, called the Big Draw. That forced the river into its present channel, flowing west and then south from Flathead Lake. The Big Draw contains deep deposits of glacial outwash gravels left by meltwater pouring off the lobe of ice. Surprisingly, these 10,000-year-old outwash deposits are scarcely eroded and are still clearly stream channels.

FOREST FIRES The Northwest's most disastrous forest fire, the Bitterroot Fire of 1910, incinerated forests in northeastern Washington, western Montana, and much of northern Idaho in a swath 160 miles long. The fire burned over 3 million acres of forest land, destroyed 8 billion board feet of marketable timber, most of it white pine, and claimed eighty-five lives. More than 3,000 men, many untrained in firefighting, fought more than 1,700 separate fires.

The 1910 Bitterroot Fire destroyed more acreage and took more lives than any other Northwest forest fire on record.

The fires began in June, and by early August they seemed under control. Then hot, dry winds caused fires to flare up in the Bitterroot Range along the Idaho-Montana border until most of the forests of northern Idaho were aflame. By August 20 the "blow up" had become a fire storm impossible to control. Flames shot thousands of feet into the air. Hundreds of firefighters were trapped within fire zones, surviving in the middle of hot creeks, in burned-out areas, or in mine tunnels so hot that supporting timbers burst into flames. On the last day of August, the winds calmed, humidity climbed, and the rains began, finally extinguishing the great fire.

◆ In a series of disastrous forest fires that occurred in the Northwest in the summer of 1902, a total of 110 separate fires broke out from Eugene, Oregon, to Bellingham, Washington, covering 700,000 acres and killing thirty-six people. Twelve billion board feet of timber, mostly old-growth Douglas fir, were lost to flames. The largest fires, known as the Yacolt Burn, blazed in forests in Washington's Clark and Skamania counties. During the day the sky was so black from smoke and ashes that people carried lanterns on the streets.

Fires continued to break out for years afterwards among the half-burned trees and snags. The Forest Service established the Wind River Tree Nursery to provide trees for reforestation of the burnt forests. (See Plants, Wind River Tree Nursery.)

◆ In 1933, 1939, and again in 1945, forest fires devastated Oregon's Tillamook Burn area. The 1933 fire was fought by 1,800 men and burned 380 square miles containing 10 billion board feet of marketable timber. The two later fires destroyed most of the trees that had survived the first fire. The reforested area now boasts trees 40 feet high, including western hemlock, Douglas fir, and western red cedar.

BURNED FOREST

GEMSTONES Almost every county in Idaho, "The Gem State," offers gemstones for the rockhound. Idaho boasts the most varied assortment of gemstones in the Northwest—more than eighty varieties, including beryl, zircon, malachite, topaz, and tourmaline. Rockhounds willing to rough it can find emeralds in the north, sapphires in the mountain lakes region; rubies, garnets in six colors, aquamarines, and industrial-quality diamonds in central Idaho; and garnets everywhere. One of the nation's best gem-hunting areas is Hells Canyon, where the Snake and Clearwater rivers meet.

◆ Idaho is one of only two places in the world where precious four- or six-rayed star garnets, the state's official gemstone, are

Idaho, "The Gem State," is one of only two places in the world where four- and six-rayed star garnets are found.

found. In 1981 a 2-pound garnet was sluiced out of clay and rocks at Emerald Creek.

◆ In North America only Idaho continues to mine fire opals commercially. Opals discovered in Idaho at the turn of the century equaled in color any opals in the world. Fire opal sometimes is found encrusting fossil bones unearthed in the state.

◆ Washingtonians find amethysts of good color in Walker Valley, a few miles southeast of Mount Vernon. Fire opals are occasionally found near Pullman, where they were mined around 1891. Bright red realgar crystals from Green River rank among the finest such crystals in the world. Washington's Tiger Mountain boasts the only amber found on the West Coast, although it is not of gem quality. (See Amber.)

◆ Oregon takes pride in its agates, jasper, bloodstone, geodes filled with quartz crystals, green garnet and green jasper known as "Oregon jade," pink rhodonite, and fire opals. Serpentinite rock in the Klamath Mountains sometimes yields striking aggregates of red garnets and green jadite or jade. Some beaches yield jade pebbles and garnets.

◆ Montana has long ranked as the top state in the nation for gem sapphires. In the state 400,000 sapphires were sluiced out from 1899 to 1900. Of these sapphires, 25,000 were suitable for faceting. Today the state provides nearly half of the world's sapphires. Although Montana sapphires range in color from cornflower blue to green, red, and aqua, the most valuable stones glow electric blue. Yogo Gulch sapphires are valued for their deep blue untinged by green; no other source exists for stones of this color.

First discovered in Montana by placer miners sluicing gold, sapphires are still mined in the state by sluicing and hydraulic operations. Because the sapphires of Yogo Gulch are found in an intrusion of rock, the mines in that area work hard rock—the only sapphire mines in the world to do so. Miners let the rock soften out in the weather for several years before they break it up and wash out the stones. Elsewhere, the stones are found in stream gravels or soil and are washed out.

◆ Montana gemstones also include agates, rubies, amethysts, industrial diamonds, and garnets. In several mountainous areas of Montana, a reaction between granite magma and the limestone it penetrates produces rock called skarn, filled with large garnet crystals and other minerals. Garnets often erode out of this skarn as loose stones. Garnets found in Ruby Range, named by miners who thought the garnets were rubies, are exceptionally clear and of good color.

Klamath Falls, Oregon, heats public buildings and private homes with its subterranean geothermal reservoir, the most extensive one underlying any city in the Western Hemisphere.

GEOTHERMAL The most extensive subterranean geothermal reservoir of natural steam and hot water underlying any city in the Western Hemisphere lies beneath Klamath Falls in southwest Oregon. Scarps rise on either side of the city, which lies in a trough that was dropped along a fault. Hot rock lies at a shallow depth beneath Klamath Falls, and the ancient lake beds that underlie most of the Klamath Lake lowlands form a watertight lid over the hot rocks, trapping hot water.

Native Americans and early settlers bathed and cooked with water from the many hot springs that used to issue freely in the area, but the 500 wells drilled in the hot spring belt for private and public use have dried up the springs by diverting the water.

For nearly a century Klamath Falls has made extensive and varied use of its geothermal energy. Early residents piped the hot water directly from springs into their homes. Later, they drilled wells and then submerged coils through which city water could run and be heated. That process saved pipes in the home from being corroded by the mineral-impregnated geothermal water.

The first commercial use of geothermal water in Klamath Falls began in 1911 when geothermally heated water was piped into radiators and the basement swimming pool of a newly built, four-story hotel, the White Pelican. Now, geothermal water heats Klamath Falls apartments, public buildings, and homes; keeps sidewalks, driveways, and a critical highway section snow-free; cures concrete and pasteurizes milk.

◆ Boise, Idaho, began to use geothermal energy in the late 1880s, when city officials authorized the drilling of two wells for hot water to supply the huge swimming pool and hot mineral baths of their new natatorium. When the wells unexpectedly produced a bonanza of 800,000 gallons a day of 170°F water, far too much for natatorium use, the city decided to use the excess for heating homes. In 1892 they constructed the nation's first municipal geothermal water system, delivering hot water to 244 homes along Warm Springs Avenue from wells only 400 feet deep. Geothermal water later heated some of Boise's commercial and public buildings. For more than a century, the original two wells have produced abundant water at the same temperature and flow.

An ancient lake—the largest the world has ever known—once inundated many of the river valleys of western Montana.

GLACIAL LAKE MISSOULA The largest lake that ever existed in the world, Glacial Lake Missoula, formed 10,000 years ago. Ice several thousand feet high from the Purcell Trench Glacier dammed the valley of the Clark Fork River in Idaho near present-day Pend Oreille Lake. Without an outlet, water from the river backed up in many of Montana's river valleys, eventually

covering 2,300 square miles with 500 cubic miles of water—
more than the combined total of every stream in the world today.
When the ice dam broke, a wall of water as high as the dam
rushed out, inundating the area with the largest floods for which
there is geological evidence. The ice dam later re-formed, the
lake filled again, and the dam broke again; the cycle repeated
itself as many as forty times.

GLACIER NATIONAL PARK The geologic history of
Montana's Glacier National Park is color-coded, with the strikingly varied colors of different formations of ancient Precambrian
rock more than a billion years old easily identifiable on cliff walls
throughout the park. Most of the park was created by a mammoth 2-mile-thick slab of billion-year-old Precambrian Belt rock
that moved 35 to 50 miles along the Lewis overthrust fault,
thereby covering a much younger layer of sedimentary rock only
65 to 100 million years old. Mountains in the park are well
known among geologists for their exposure of the ancient rocks;
a single mountain may display two to four of these formations.

Faulting has exposed Precambrian rock more than a billion years old on cliffs in Glacier National Park.

The oldest formation, just above the fault and prominently
appearing as white sandy cliffs in some parts of the park, consists
of about 2,500 feet of Altyn limestone, light buff when weathered,
and full of sand grains. Next comes Appekuny green, made up of
3,000 feet of green mudstone, shales, and argillites, especially
noticeable in the eastern part of the park. Contrasting vividly with
it, especially after rain, the next 3,000 feet or more of red mudstone form the Grinnell formation, filled with ripple marks, mud
cracks, and raindrop impressions. The red color is due to abundant iron oxide cementing the sand and mud grains together.
Between the two a layer several hundred feet thick intermixes the
red and green. Near the top are 4,000 feet of gray limestone, the
younger Siyeh Formation, found on the park's highest peaks in
the Lewis and Livingston ranges. On the very top, where they have
not eroded away, rest the youngest rocks, Shepard tan and Kintla
red mudstones. The bright red of the Kintla formation caps high
peaks along the continental divide.

GLACIERS Washington boasts by far the most extensive network of glaciers—135 square miles of them—in the Lower 48.
Of the more than 1,000 glaciers discovered when the nation's
glaciers were mapped during the International Geophysical Year
in 1957-1958, Washington glaciers covered 75 percent of the
total area. Between Snoqualmie Pass and the Canadian border,
519 glaciers cover more than 97 square miles. The Olympic

The most extensive network of glaciers in the Lower 48 mantles the mountain ranges of Washington.

Mountains contain 60 glaciers, the North Cascades more than 300. Washington's Cascade and Olympic mountains are endowed with huge glaciers because of their many high peaks, their cold temperatures, and because of moisture-laden Pacific winds that dump more than 50 feet of snow a year on the highest peaks.

♦ Although the Olympic Mountains do not reach as far north or as high as do the Rocky Mountains and the Cascade Range, Olympic glaciers, fed by extraordinary amounts of snow, are large. Seven glaciers up to 900 feet deep wrap around two-thirds of Mount Olympus, the highest peak in the Olympics. Longest is the Hoh, at 3½ miles. During the last Ice Age, Olympic glaciers filled their valleys and reached to the sea; they joined the lobes of ice in Puget Sound and the Strait of Juan de Fuca.

♦ Mount Rainier possesses the most extensive system of glaciers of any single U.S. peak outside Alaska, with twenty-five named glaciers and fifty smaller ice patches and secondary glaciers forming an irregular star radiating from the summit. Some forty-one glaciers originate in high cirques or summit ice fields. The largest glaciers hug the north and east slopes, protected from the sun.

During the last glacial period, the valley glaciers of Mount Rainier extended for 15 to 40 miles. The mountain's longest and largest glacier today, deeply crevassed Emmons Glacier, measures only 5 miles long. Rainier's great height probably allowed it to keep its glaciers even during warmer intervals between ice ages.

♦ Mount Rainier's Carbon River Glacier, over 4½ miles long, contains the mountain's thickest ice—705 feet at 6,200 feet elevation. The glacier has scoured out the largest cirque found on any Cascade peak, with walls rising 3,600 feet to summit ice. Carbon River Glacier terminates at the lowest elevation—3,000 feet—of any glacier in the Lower 48.

♦ Nisqually Glacier on Mount Rainier ranks as one of the world's most accessible glaciers, by car or by foot. It is easily visible from the Nisqually River Bridge on the road between Longmire and Paradise, and from Paradise itself. It was the first U.S. glacier discovered, in 1857 during an ascent of Mount Rainier, and is the best documented glacier in the Western Hemisphere, with photographs dating back to 1884 and records of its size to 1857. Between that date and 1944, it retreated 4,131 feet. The trimline on vegetation in the area documents its many advances and retreats. Now 4 miles long, Nisqually Glacier continues to recede, melting readily because of its southern exposure and low terminus, at 4,000 feet.

◆ In the scenic Beartooth Range in Custer National Forest, not far from Yellowstone National Park, Montana boasts a glacier unique in the world—Grasshopper Glacier. About 300 years ago, strong winds blew a large swarm of grasshoppers onto glacial ice. Winter snows then entombed the insects, and they became part of the glacier. Now the frozen grasshoppers, having flowed through the glacier, are melting out at its toe.

GOLD AND SILVER

Gold was first discovered in the Northwest in 1852, in Deer Lodge Valley in Montana and in Jacksonville in southern Oregon Territory. Jacksonville became the first boomtown of the Northwest, richest of the Siskiyou mining camps. Washington's first gold strike came in 1854 on the upper Columbia at Fort Colville. (See also Minerals.)

Gold was once so plentiful in Montana that miners occasionally found it clinging to the roots of overturned trees.

◆ The early strikes in Montana failed to attract many prospectors because of the state's lack of roads and isolated location. The second gold strike in 1958 at Gold Creek again failed to lure many miners. But the Mullan military wagon road from Fort Benton, Montana, to Fort Walla Walla in eastern Washington was completed in 1860. Primitive as it was, the road opened up Montana to mining.

In 1863, after gold was discovered at Alder Gulch—which later became Virginia City, Montana—10,000 miners worked Montana's recently discovered placer deposits. The area was nicknamed the "hundred million dollar placer." Because placer mining—the washing out of loose gold—required no elaborate equipment, Montana soon boasted 500 mining camps.

Ten million dollars in gold was taken from 17-mile-long Alder Gulch during its early years. From a single hillside across the gulch from Virginia City, gold worth $5 million was sluiced out. Gold was so plentiful in Montana that sometimes miners found it clinging to the roots of overturned trees. In one claim near Pony, chunks of quartz rock were so full of gold that the prospector mashed it out with a pestle. For each 100 feet of pay dirt worked in Confederate Gulch—only ½ mile long and 200 to 300 feet deep—a prospector could earn up to $100,000 by sluicing.

PANNING FOR GOLD

◆ Montana's mining millions, gold and silver, include: Elkhorn, $14 million; Garnet's Nancy Hanks mine, $10 million; Mammoth's mines, $14 million; Drumlummon Mine, $50 million; Alta Mine, $32 million. Wickes, with huge smelters and refineries, processed $50 million in silver and gold.

◆ Butte, Montana, ranks as one of the richest mineral areas of the world. It began as a placer gold camp in 1864, but also contained huge quartz veins filled with silver minerals waiting to be exploited. By the late 1870s, Butte was the largest mining town in Montana Territory. When the silver veins were exhausted in 1882, copper was waiting in the wings. Copper veins often passed into the silver veins, so mines in the area tended to extract whatever was at hand.

◆ Idaho, only a dry place to get through quickly during Oregon Trail days, suddenly became a destination in 1860 after gold was discovered. Rich strikes of gold and silver continued to be made, including discoveries of the richest deposits ever found in the United States. Leesburg, on the Salmon River, provided the richest placering grounds in mining history in 1866, with $40 million in coarse gold and nuggets extracted there.

Discovery of gold and silver lured so many thousands to Idaho, which was still part of Washington Territory, that in 1863 Congress created Idaho Territory, and in 1890, the state of Idaho. Idaho's boundaries were carefully drawn to include all mines.

◆ The most profitable Idaho strike was made in 1884 when silver, lead, and zinc were found in the Coeur d'Alene Mining District. That district, a 20-mile area between Kellogg and Mullan within the canyon of the South Fork of the Coeur d'Alene River, became one of the world's richest mining areas and the largest silver producer in terms of total historical production. More silver and lead were mined there from 1886 to 1888 than had ever before been mined in one place. Since 1884 the district has produced metals worth $2 billion, three-fourths of Idaho's total ore production. The district's Sunshine Mine, the nation's largest silver mine, has by itself outproduced Nevada's famed Comstock Lode.

◆ Despite the enormous value of the precious metals discovered in Idaho during the early gold and silver strikes, half of Idaho's total mineral wealth has been extracted since World War II. From 1860 to 1960, mineral production in Idaho totaled $2.5 billion, with $537 million of that amount earned by silver.

◆ Most mineral wealth in the Northwest is associated with masses of granite that intruded into sedimentary rocks from 190 to 50 million years ago. The hot gases and liquids of molten rock bear chemicals that form metallic ores, spreading out in dikes, sills, and larger intrusions. They concentrate in cracks and fractures of batholiths and the surrounding rock, sometimes extending for a mile or more. Most of Idaho's ore deposits contact its huge batholith, which reaches into the Bitterroot Mountains of western Montana, with smaller masses of that granite reaching out as far as southwestern Montana. The important Montana mining centers of Butte and Helena developed on either side of

Montana's largest batholith, the Boulder Batholith. (See Batholiths.)

GRAND COULEE Washington's Grand Coulee is one of the world's largest coulees (a coulee is a steep-sided gulch or water channel) and the most impressive example of glacial and flood drainage in the world. The coulee is actually two coulees at different levels—Upper Grand Coulee and Lower Grand Coulee—joined by Dry Falls. The entire chasm runs for about 50 miles. Upper Grand Coulee, with sheer walls for much of its 33-mile length, often measures 4 miles wide and 900 feet deep. (See Dry Falls.)

Grand Coulee, in eastern Washington, is one of the largest coulees in the world.

Some 10,000 years ago, the Okanogan Lobe of glacial ice buried northeastern Washington's Okanogan Highlands under thousands of feet of ice, freezing water that formerly flowed south as the Columbia River. Along the western edge of the plateau, the Columbia, diverted by the ice from its normal channel near Big Bend, must still have received glacier melt and drainage water from the east.

When the floodwaters poured west from Glacial Lake Missoula, they must have overwhelmed the river. It formed a temporary lake, Glacial Lake Columbia, which deposited over the years thick sediments of silt and sand that are still visible; the river continued rising until it spilled onto the lava plateau at the head of Grand Coulee. Flowing down the natural slope, the Columbia found a temporary channel in the Grand Coulee, both levels of which trend southwest. The silty, rock-bearing waters scoured out the walls and floor of fractured lava in Grand Coulee, deepening and widening the coulee each time the Spokane Floods recurred, perhaps as many as forty times. (See Glacial Lake Missoula and Spokane Floods.)

After the ice lobe retreated, and Glacial Lake Missoula passed into prehistory, the Columbia returned to its normal channel, leaving both coulees high and dry. After Grand Coulee Dam was built nearby, Upper Grand Coulee became Banks Lake, a reservoir for water that irrigates eastern Washington farms.

HELLS CANYON Hells Canyon, through which the Snake River runs along the border between Oregon and Idaho, ranks as the deepest, most rugged river gorge in North America. For some 40 miles the canyon depth averages 5,500 feet. The world's deepest gorge in low-relief territory, the canyon measures 7,900 feet to the highest peak of Seven Devils Mountains, a range that flanks it in Idaho. The Blue Mountains border it in Oregon.

Hells Canyon, the deepest river gorge in North America, spans several ecosystems from its rim to the canyon depths.

HELLS CANYON

Hells Canyon Recreation Area contains the last primitive part of the Snake River, with 67½ miles of it protected under the National Wild and Scenic Rivers Act. Rapids alternate with quiet stretches as the river often drops more than 11 feet a mile. Almost inaccessible, the canyon is part of 100-mile-long Snake River Canyon.

◆ The Snake River, which is 1,038 miles long and the major tributary of the Columbia River, cut the huge canyon through Snake River Plain after the last layers of basalt lava were laid down some 13 million years ago. Upper canyon walls reveal 4,000 feet of old lava flows, with prominent ledges and the columnar basalt that often forms in plateau lava. Lower walls reveal older, light-colored sedimentary rocks that were once a continental shelf extending into the Pacific, laid down 160 million years ago when the western border of North America lay just beyond Hells Canyon. (See Snake River Plain.)

Like the Columbia River, the Snake cut through a rising mountain range, the Blue Mountains, located at the time on Oregon's ancient coastline along with the Wallowa Mountains. Pushed east by the rising mountains, the river was forced to carve its canyon through very hard oceanic greenstone. Floodwaters from enormous, ancient Lake Bonneville overflowed and surged through Red Rock Pass south of Pocatello, increasing the river's flow. Later, the largest of the Spokane Floods poured into the Snake River and reversed the direction of its flow, backing it up into a temporary lake 600 feet deep near Lewiston, Idaho.

As the Snake River continues to carry eroded canyon rock into the Columbia, the load on the earth's crust lightens, causing the canyon rim and mountains above the canyon to rise. Basalt flows that cap Seven Devils Mountains high above the canyon— the highest Columbia Plateau basalt found anywhere—indicate major uplifting.

◆ Hells Canyon is so deep that several ecosystems exist within it. Mild winter temperatures on the horizontal basalt ledges that out-crop in the upper walls prompted native Americans—and later, settlers—to spend the cold months in pit dwellings or in caves gouged in the canyon walls by swift water. Petroglyphs, trails, and artifacts on the terraces document this use.

HIGH LAVA PLAINS Located on a high, cool plateau in Deschutes National Forest in southeastern Oregon, High Lava Plains shares with Idaho's Craters of the Moon a reputation for displaying some of the continent's more concentrated and varied recent volcanic landforms.

◆ A narrow road winds to the top of the symmetrical, extinct cinder cone, Lava Butte, in High Lava Plains, making it one of the most accessible of all Cascade cones. It ranks among the largest cinder cones in the world—500 feet high with a crater 150 feet deep. Blocky lava that covers 10 square miles of the High Lava Plains poured from the base of the steep-sided cinder cone, the northernmost of eight vents along the rift zone of Newberry Volcano. (See Newberry Crater.)

◆ Lava Cast Forest, several miles east of Lava Butte, is one of the world's largest lava cast forests—which form in basaltic lava flows that engulf living forests. Six thousand years ago Newberry Volcano, one of the world's largest calderas, erupted with a 9-mile-long river of lava that inundated a forest of pines. Some of the trees are now "stone trees"—hollow lava tubes rising 2 feet above the surface of the flow. Other trees, knocked down by the lava flow, form pipelike casts. Not all trees are preserved within a searing lava flow. Most trees burst into flames and burn when covered with hot lava, but sometimes lava cools so quickly upon contact with moist wood that a thin crust of lava hardens around the tree trunk before it burns, preserving even delicate details of bark.

◆ Also located in Oregon's High Lava Plains are the Lava River Caves. (See Lava Tube Caves.)

Striking volcanic landforms, including one of the world's largest cinder cones, are on display at Oregon's High Lava Plains.

HUMBUG SPIRES Weathered pinnacles of dark reddish granite rise in a pine grove south of Butte, Montana, providing a striking contrast with the evergreen trees. The towering spires, 300 to 600 feet high, the featured attraction of Humbug Spires Primitive Area, probably split off from a satellite batholith of Montana's nearby Boulder Batholith, 70 million years old, which forms the entire northern end of the Highland Range.

Dark granite pinnacles 70 million years old tower over a pine grove near Butte, Montana.

JOHN DAY FOSSIL BEDS NATIONAL MONUMENT

Oregon's John Day Fossil Beds National Monument is significant not only for the fossils it contains in volcanic ash sometimes 1,000 feet deep, but also for the lengthy geologic tale its varied formations in three widely separated units tell about the basin situated between the Blue Mountains and the Cascade volcanoes.

Layers of red soil, especially in the Clarno Unit, testify to the subtropical climate, animals, and lush vegetation that characterized this region 36 to 54 million years ago. Volcanic ash and rubble and mountainous mudflow deposits have weathered into brown pinnacles and ruined-castle palisades in that unit.

Between 20 and 36 million years ago, enormous eruptions of

Varied rock formations in Oregon's John Day Fossil Beds tell a geologic tale of subtropical climate, animals, lush vegetation, and volcanic eruptions.

volcanic ash, which later washed off hills into streams and ponds, created the John Day Formation, noted for its many fossil bones of exotic animals. The Painted Hills Unit, part of the John Day Formation, displays colorful layers of volcanic ash—bronze, gold, and green—that band the gentle hills formed during that era.

SHEEP ROCK

Basaltic lava that welled up from fissures 17 million years ago deposited layer after layer of Picture Gorge basalt over the ash. The John Day River cuts a narrow, steep-walled gorge through the region, slicing through mudstone, sand and gravel, colorful ash, and Picture Gorge basalt layers interbedded with red sub-tropical soil.

Today, remnants of that black lava cap the colorful ash layers of the massive promontory of Sheep Rock (the largest of the three units that make up the monument) and other high formations. The hard basalt protected soft rocks beneath them from erosion until the Ice Age increased river runoff, which began to cut through the basalt. Later aridity in the area preserved the formations and the fossils in them.

The region's conspicuous brick red ridges and ledges of welded tuff were formed 6 million years ago when glowing lava flows cooled and hardened.

LAKE CHELAN Fjordlike Lake Chelan in north-central Washington ranks as the state's largest, longest, and deepest natural lake. The lake is 55 miles long, ¼ to 2 miles wide, and 1,475 feet deep. The second-deepest natural freshwater lake in the Lower 48, Lake Chelan descends at its deepest point nearly 400 feet below sea level. The depth of the trough makes the Stehekin Valley one of the West's outstanding glacial canyons, some 8,500 feet from the bottom of the trough to the highest peak above it.

Fjordlike Lake Chelan, the second-deepest lake in the Lower 48, extends 55 miles up a narrow glacial canyon.

Chelan Glacier, originating near Cascade Pass in the North Cascades, gouged out the bed of the lake and the U-shaped glacial valley. By the time the Chelan Glacier had retreated several miles back toward the Cascades, the Okanogan Lobe of the continental glacier moved into the Chelan valley, its farthest southern advance. When the Okanogan ice finally receded, it left a moraine dam across the mouth of the deepened valley. Torrents of meltwater from the receding ice and water draining the hillsides formed the lake. Part of the Chelan Glacier, forced up against the northeast side of the valley by the continental glacier, carved hanging valleys from which waterfalls now plunge to the lake.

Fifty-nine streams and twenty-seven active glaciers of the

North Cascades now feed the lake. At the rugged upper end of the valley, sheer cliffs often rise directly from the water.

LAKES Lakes rarely form in lava tube caves, but Malheur Cave, a mile-long lava tube cave in Oregon not far from Malheur Lake, contains a lake that ranges up to 2,000 feet in length, 25 feet in width (the width of the lava tube), and 23 feet in depth. It is North America's largest permanent lake located within a lava tube cave. A thermal spring and regional groundwater feed the lake, which varies seasonally. Two crustacean species, a flatworm, and a pseudoscorpion live in its depths.

Borax once coated the shoreline of one Northwest lake; another lake is located deep within a cave.

◆ The highest lake in Oregon nestles in an almost perfectly round volcanic crater at the 10,358-foot summit of South Sister, the least eroded of the Three Sisters Peaks. The small crater lake is seasonal, at its deepest in spring and summer.

◆ A hot spring feeds Borax Lake, an unusual desert lake in Oregon's Alvord Valley. The spring deposits a salty white crust of borax, which once thickly covered the lake shore. From 1898 to 1907 Chinese laborers scraped up the crust and extracted borax from it in big boilers fired by sagebrush. The small-scale mining enterprise ended when deposits and sagebrush ran out about the same time.

◆ A great mass of Epsom salt once lay beneath eastern Washington's Poison Lake, having precipitated out of lake water heavily saturated with magnesium sulfate. Miners removed most of the mineral in the early 1900s. (See also major lakes listed by names.)

LAVA FLOWS Oregon boasts two of the most recent large lava flows in the Lower 48. Only 500 years ago, Jordan Craters Lava Flow covered an area 30 miles long and 4 miles wide. Lava flows sometimes 6 miles wide formed McKenzie Lavafields 1,500 years ago. The basalt flowed for 12 miles, moving into the canyon of the McKenzie River and altering the river's course so that it disappears into permeable volcanic sediments along the flow margins, runs underground, and then reappears at Tamolitch Falls.

Two of the most recent lava flows in the Lower 48 occurred in Oregon.

◆ Montana's ancient Purcell Lava Flow, really a series of flows, oozed thick layers of coarse-grained basalt between rock layers of the Siyeh Formation of Glacier National Park, forming a volcanic sill—a horizontal version of the lava-filled vertical dike. The black lava contrasts sharply with the white limestone layers over and under it, which the hot lava baked into marble. The sill is easily visible in road cuts along Logan Pass and in a dark layer of the cliffs along the entire length of Thunderbird Mountain. The lava flowed between rock layers 1,200 million years ago while they lay beneath a shallow sea in which blue-green algae proliferated.

LAVA TUBE CAVES The Northwest, although not prime limestone cave country, boasts many lava tube caves, found only in the west. Lava tube caves form when a fairly thin, gaseous basaltic lava flowing down a gentle slope begins to slow, cooling rapidly enough on the top and bottom to solidify, while molten lava continues to flow beneath the crust. That fiery flow may be 50 feet thick. In some caves, the lava empties out completely; in others, a solid fill of undrained lava remains at the end of the tube. Later flows may occupy the same channel, remelting and glazing the earlier surface, adding new formations. Most lava tube caves form only a single level, although later flows can superimpose several other partial levels. Many lava tube caves lie only a few feet under the crusted surface, so shallow that their roofs collapse. Then the cave becomes an open trench, often 30 to 40 feet deep. (See also Limestone and Marble Caves.)

The longest unbroken lava tube in the Western Hemisphere stretches along the southern flank of Mount St. Helens.

◆ Although Oregon and California boast more numerous lava tube caves than Washington, the Western Hemisphere's longest unbroken lava tube cave lies in Washington. Ape Cave stretches for 12,810 feet along the southern flank of Mount St. Helens. Located within a 1,900-year-old ropy lava flow, the cave is 700 feet deep. The 1980 eruption of Mount St. Helens, which blew out the north side of the mountain, did not damage the lava tube cave. Among the varied formations of Ape Cave is a unique large lava ball suspended between two walls about 10 feet above the floor. The cave also displays lava falls, floor ripples, and tubular and ribbon stalactites.

◆ A few miles from Ape Cave is Lake Cave, which is 3,775 feet long and displays a rare brick red lava.

◆ Other lava tube caves honeycomb an area of lava beds 9 miles long and up to 4 miles wide, formed from Mount Adams and Mount St. Helens lava flows. Within Mount Adams lava, Cheese Cave is 1,814 feet long and maintains a temperature of about 44°F. Pioneers stored potatoes in the vaulted cavern for many years before it was used for commercial production of Roquefort cheese.

◆ Ole's Cave is 5,800 feet long. It was created in the most recent ropy lava flow in the Lower 48 in which caves were formed, during either the 1842 or 1954 eruption of Mount St. Helens. The cave's numerous features include pipestem lava stalactites, a tube within a tube (formed by a later lava river entering the original tube), casts of tree parts, projecting cupolas, calcareous stalactite tubes, and a projection of lava from bedrock that resembles George Washington's profile.

◆ In Oregon's High Lava Plains, near Bend, lie the Lava River Caves. Thousands of years ago, long lava tube caves formed in a flow from Newberry Volcano. The roofs of many lava tubes in this area have collapsed, leaving steep-sided trenches, but Lava River Cave remains intact. The largest uncollapsed cave, it formed in lava 100 feet thick and extends for 6,700 feet. Some of its passages are 50 feet long, 35 feet wide, and 58 feet high. Inside, rare lava-cicles hang from the roof, formed by the dripping of molten lava. Wall-to-wall rock shelves form horizontal partitions, and "bathtub rings" on the side walls show previous levels of the draining lava.

◆ Ice can form in lava tubes where winters are severe. Cold moist air enters, sinking to the lowest part of a poorly ventilated cave. Some lava tube caves in Idaho's Craters of the Moon contain ice, even though the surface environment is arid desert. Caves in glacial ice, such as the once-spectacular Paradise Ice Caves at Mount Rainier, shrink as the glaciers retreat, becoming so unstable that they are dangerous to visit.

◆ Idaho's Crystal Falls Cave boasts perhaps the only subterranean glacier in the Lower 48. The frozen river that runs the length of the cave's main chamber actually flows.

◆ Crystal Ice Cave is a fissure cave 160 feet deep and 1,200 feet long in Idaho's Great Rift lava country. With a temperature of 32°F, the cave maintains a lake of ice and ice-covered walls and ceilings. Single ice crystals 12 inches in diameter have been found in Idaho ice caves.

◆ Ice Cave, in Gifford Pinchot National Forest near Mount Adams, supplied ice for Hood River and The Dalles, Oregon, in pioneer days. The cave has four sections separated by collapse sinks (pits formed when the cave roof collapsed), in which heavy, cold winter air is trapped, forming a seasonal floor of ice. It also contains large drip masses (ice masses formed from dripping water).

LIMESTONE AND MARBLE CAVES Limestone caves form while the soluble rock lies below the water table. Slightly acidic groundwater seeps through fractures and joints in limestone or marble (a crystallized, metamorphosed form of limestone), honeycombing and latticing them, and enlarging some parts into chambers.

Natural forces have carved subterranean layers of limestone into the nation's third-largest limestone cavern and the West Coast's largest marble cave— both located in the Northwest.

OREGON CAVES
MONUMENT

Later, the cave drains, often as a result of regional uplift or lowering of the water table. As soon as air enters, mineral deposits can begin to form. Water bearing calcium carbonate drips from ceilings, trickles from ledges, and splashes onto the floor, depositing thin layers that build up into interesting formations. (See also Lava Tube Caves.)

◆ Most of Idaho's caves are desert country lava tubes, but the highest limestone cave in the Northwest is located in the Wasatch Mountains of southeastern Idaho. The entrance to Minnetonka Cave lies at 7,700 feet above sea level. Still largely unexplored, the cave boasts few mineral formations but has large chambers, including one 300 feet wide and 90 feet high. Imbedded in its limestone are fossilized tropical marine plants. Deposited in the vast shallow seas that covered Idaho for long periods, these sedimentary deposits were later uplifted into mountains.

◆ Washington's Gardner Cave, which extends for 1,050 feet, contains what many cave explorers rank as one of the Northwest's most spectacular single cave formations made by mineral deposition. At the end of a passage stands a broad, tapering column about 9 feet tall, with a base diameter of around 4 feet.

Another of the cave's extraordinary features is the channel, some 200 feet long, that a former stream cut into the ceiling of one of the cave's narrow passages. Evidently flowing on top of compacted sediments that once almost completely filled the passage, the stream dissolved the limestone ceiling, softer than the fill below. A later stream removed the fill, leaving coarse deposits on the floor and revealing the channeled ceiling.

◆ Montana's Lewis and Clark Cavern ranks as the Northwest's largest limestone cavern, third largest of its type in the nation after Carlsbad and Mammoth caverns. Its entrance lies high on a sloping sandstone cliff, Cave Mountain, overlooking the Jefferson River near historic Three Forks Missouri Headwaters State Monument. The cavern, around which Montana's first state park was created in 1937, was dissolved within a block of limestone 1,400 feet thick.

Several levels of large vaulted chambers and intricate passages wind through the complex and beautiful cave system. Cathedral Room, 100 feet high, extends 450 by 600 feet. Multicolored stalactites and stalagmites stud floors and ceilings of other rooms, which are also decorated with cascades, flowstone draperies, and pools. The cavern is noted for its delicately beautiful helectites—calcite crystals spiraling out from stalactites—and for clusterites that resemble multicolored clusters of grapes.

A limestone prospector discovered the high cavern entrance in about 1900 when he saw an eagle hovering over and then entering a 4-foot hole high in the cliff. Now a narrow-gauge railway and a cliffside tramway lift visitors to the entrance.

♦ Isolated high in the Siskiyou Mountains near Grants Pass is Oregon Caves National Monument. A single cave, this is the largest cave on the West Coast formed completely in marble. Some 135 million years ago, when this area formed the western-most part of the Northwest coast, the North American continent collided with and overrode the East Pacific ocean plate. That collision folded, crumpled, and steeply tilted the limestone of the cave region. Heat from nearby igneous intrusions caused the limestone to crystallize and metamorphose into a bluish marble.

The cave, formed like all limestone and marble caves from the dissolving action of acidic groundwater, includes five levels with 3 miles of passages and an underground stream. The largest chamber, the Ghost Room, measures 50 feet wide, 250 feet long, and 40 feet high. The different kinds of formations in Oregon Caves, unusually varied for so small an area, include stalactites and stalagmites, and dripstone and flowstone resembling water-falls, chandeliers, draperies, soda straws, grape clusters, and popcorn.

MALHEUR LAKE Malheur Lake in southeast Oregon, one of the few natural marshes in the West, is the largest freshwater wet-lands system in the western United States. It is the centerpiece of Malheur National Wildlife Refuge, a major feeding stop on the Pacific flyway for thousands of geese, ducks, swans, and cranes.

Thousands of migrating waterfowl stop to feed at Oregon's Malheur Lake, the largest freshwater wetlands system in the western United States.

The lake is fed by a dozen small streams flowing down the gentle side of Steens Mountain and by the Silvies River of the Blue Mountains. The water level of Malheur Lake normally fluctuates. Harney Basin, in which the lake and two smaller lakes lie, has had no natural outlet since lava flows blocked an ancient river long ago.

Dry in 1930, Malheur had formed three large separate lakes by 1971. In the 1980s the lake reached an all-time high, covering 180,000 acres of land to become one of the largest inland bodies of water in the Northwest. Higher than normal precipitation during that decade caused the water to rise 8 to 10 feet, flooding 70,000 acres of public and private land.

MARIAS PASS Marias Pass in Montana crosses the continental divide at 5,280 feet, the lowest elevation of any other pass

Early explorers searched for thirty years before finding Marias Pass in Montana, one of the lowest passes across the continental divide.

north of Lordsburgh, New Mexico. Located near Montana's southern boundary where two broad valleys meet, the naturally concealed pass eluded discovery by early explorers for thirty years during the late nineteenth century.

John F. Stevens, a railway surveyor and engineer hired by the Great Northern Railway to find the long-rumored low pass through the Rockies, discovered Marias Pass in December 1889. He was the first to record accurately its location near the headwaters of the Marias River. Within less than two years, train tracks had been laid to the summit, and in 1893 trains began running regularly over Marias Pass between Seattle and St. Paul.

The Willamette Meteorite, discovered in Oregon in 1902, is the largest meteorite ever found in the United States.

METEORITES The largest meteorite ever found in the United States, the Willamette Meteorite, weighed 13½ tons even after scientists broke off several pieces. A woodcutter discovered it in Oregon in 1902. After digging out the cone-shaped, embedded meteorite, he winched it into a homemade wagon and spent three months hauling it ¾ mile by horse and wagon over steep hillsides and through a forested canyon to his own land. There he built a shed over it and charged the public twenty-five cents to see it.

Oregon Iron and Steel, owners of the land on which the meteorite was found, won a legal suit to recover it. Hayden Planetarium in New York City became its final home after it was exhibited at the 1905 Lewis and Clark Centennial Fair in Portland.

Long before the woodcutter's discovery, local Indians knew about the meteorite, which they called a "visitor from the moon." Before battles, warriors dipped arrowheads into rainwater that filled surface pits on the meteorite.

WILLAMETTE METEORITE

♦ Ants in Oregon sometimes gather particles of meteorites for their anthills, either accidentally or because they prefer the smooth bits. The heavier meteorite pieces are noticeable after wind winnows the anthills, blowing away lighter material.

♦ In 1856 Dr. John Evans, a geologist on a government survey, found a meteorite in the hills east of Port Orford, Oregon. He estimated that it was almost as large as the Willamette Meteorite, weighing perhaps 10 tons. Evans, who sent specimens to the Smithsonian Institute for identification, described the meteorite as projecting 5 or 6 feet from the ground in a treeless, rockless area, with Bald Mountain as a landmark. But the Port Orford Meteorite has never been seen again, even though hundreds have searched for it.

MIMA MOUNDS Few geological oddities in the Northwest have undergone such intensive study as Washington's Mima

Mounds and still remained a mystery. Geologists who have solved the complex mysteries of the Spokane Floods and the docking of two subcontinents with the North American continent near the Washington-Idaho border shake their heads in puzzlement at the thousands of circular mounds that dot a grassy prairie near Olympia. From 1 to 7 feet high, and up to 40 feet in diameter, the mounds consist of a random mix of silt, sand, and loam with gravel and small pebbles, resting on a base of coarse gravel deposited by the meltwater of the Puget Lobe of glacial ice.

The origin of thousands of circular mounds dotting a grassy plain in Washington remains a mystery despite years of study.

Similar mounds have been found elsewhere at the limits of glaciation, and have been explained as the result of repeated freezing and thawing; however, mounds also appear in frostless areas. Other theories center around differential erosion by wind or water, wind-borne deposits surrounding trees or bushes, and gravel piles left behind when Ice Age glaciers retreated.

Whimsical explanations of the mysterious mounds abound, and include buffalo wallows, anthills, shellfish feast remains, and nests made by prehistoric fish.

Once, nearly a million mounds cast their rounded shadows in the area, but plows, grazing cattle, and sand and gravel miners have taken their toll. The 445-acre Mima Mounds Natural Area protects about 4,000 of the best mounds.

MINERALS The yearly value of all Montana's minerals amounts to more than $1 billion. Coal ranks first in value, petroleum products a close second. In all, Montana recovers fifty-eight minerals from her earth.

Northwest mines are the nation's only source of palladium and a leading source of copper, talc, mercury, nickel, and phosphate.

♦ Montana boasts the nation's only mine of palladium, a rare, silver-white metal found in the Absaroka mountain range. Automobile catalytic converters and electronic components require this strategic mineral.

♦ Montana is one of only two states in the nation that produce antimony. This brittle, silvery metal is used in hardening lead alloys for storage batteries, in ceramic enamels, in fireproofing chemicals, and in medicines.

♦ Copper mining began in Montana in 1882 after the readily available gold and silver deposits were exhausted. By 1887 Anaconda Copper Mining Company was the largest copper producer in the world; in 1889 it produced 61 percent of the nation's copper and 23 percent of the world's copper.

The 5-square-mile Butte Hill area, "the richest hill on earth," has produced gold, silver, and copper in turn, along with zinc, manganese, lead, and minor amounts of other metals. Silver is now only a by-product of copper refining. Although Montana soil has yielded more than 18.5 billion pounds of copper, Butte Hill still holds an estimated 20 billion pounds of the metal, currently not heavily mined because of its low market price.

♦ Montana is first among all the states in the production of vermiculite, high-grade manganese, and talc. Talc is used in products such as talcum powder, filler for pills, chocolate candy, paints, and the manufacture of paper. Montana's talc—especially valued because it lacks asbestos, a common impurity in talc—comes from several large mines in Montana's Ruby and Gravelly ranges, which constitute the world's largest talc district.

♦ Members of a wagon train party in 1864 who noticed oil scum on a pool are credited with first discovering petroleum in Montana. Major oil discoveries occurred much later, during the late 1930s. Oil and natural gas are critical to Montana's economy.

♦ All four Northwest states, as a result of glaciation by continental ice sheets, contain large amounts of glacially deposited sand and gravel.

♦ Oregon's mercury mines include one of the largest in the nation, between Roseburg and Eugene. Oregon mines produced nearly 4.5 million pounds of mercury between 1900 and 1956.

♦ The only major nickel mine in the nation operates sporadically, west of Riddle in Oregon's Nickel Mountain. The nickel lies in a belt of heavily weathered serpentinite that has turned into red laterite soil. Even though Oregon has abundant serpentinite, no other profitable nickel deposits have been found. Unable to compete with low-cost African nickel, Oregon's nickel is seldom mined without subsidies.

♦ Idaho contains the world's largest reserve of phosphate, one-third of all the phosphate known in North America. An area of 268,000 acres of phosphate is mined near Montpelier and Soda Springs at 5,779 feet elevation near highly mineralized hot springs. Phosphate's most important uses are in sulfuric acid, fertilizers, and phosphoric acid.

♦ Oregon mines important deposits of diatomaceous earth near Lakeview and Klamath Lake; the lake turns green each summer with diatom "blooms" of the microscopic, one-celled algae. Diatomite deposits consist of uncountable numbers of the tiny skeletons of these algae. At the turn of the century, people mounted the skeletons on slides in order to admire their intricate beauty. Diatomaceous earth, which provides the abrasiveness in some toothpastes and silver polishes, also makes an ideal lightweight filtering material used in beer and wine making and in swimming pool filters.

Because volcanic rocks are rich in silica, lakes in Oregon's volcanic country are ideal homes for diatoms, which take up the dissolved silica into their flint-hard skeletons and divide every 12 to 24 hours, proliferating in numbers as unimaginable as the United States debt.

MOUNT ADAMS

Mount Adams, the oldest and most quiescent Cascade volcano, is Washington's second-highest peak at 12,307 feet. Even though most active volcanoes emit sulfurous gases, Mount Adams is the only large Cascade volcano that formed sulphur deposits, and the only volcano in the nation on which sulphur was once mined. On its 210-acre summit plateau, Mount Adams bears extensive areas of sulphur-laden rock. Hydrogen sulphide gas passing through the loose, porous rocks on the crater floor concentrated sulphur in the rocks. Mining of the sulphur proceeded on a small scale from 1932 to 1959, with mules bringing supplies and workers up, then carrying the sulphur back down the volcano's steep slopes. The venture proved unprofitable.

Sulphur was once mined on Washington's Mount Adams, the oldest and most quiescent Cascade volcano.

◆ Klickitat Glacier on the east side of Mount Adams is second in size only to Emmons Glacier on Mount Rainier in the Cascade Range. Glaciers have heavily furrowed the steep, mudslide-prone slopes of the mountain.

◆ Evidence of an Indian racetrack still remains on the broad southeast slope of Mount Adams. The hoofs of Indian ponies cut furrows 10 feet wide and nearly 2 feet deep during races held when native Americans met in the fall to pick blueberries and to play games.

MOUNT HOOD

Oregon is home to North America's most frequently climbed glaciated peak. Worldwide, only Japan's Fujiyama hosts more climbers.

Oregon's highest mountain, Mount Hood, is also North America's most frequently climbed glaciated peak.

◆ At 11,235 feet, Mount Hood ranks as Oregon's highest mountain, in past centuries cut down at least 1,000 feet by severe glaciation. In the Northwest only Washington's Mount Adams and Mount Rainier are higher and larger.

◆ During the Fraser Glaciation 25,000 years ago, an ice cap almost completely covered Mount Hood, extending down adjacent valleys. Glaciers sculpted all sides of the peak, forming the classic proportions, but scouring it so deeply that its original conduit was exposed. That volcanic neck—a column of solid lava—stands among cliffs and icefalls on the north face of the summit. Eleven high-altitude glaciers continue to carve away tons of the mountain.

MOUNT MAZAMA

The violent final eruption of Mount Mazama, once Oregon's highest mountain and now the site of Crater Lake, spewed more pumice than has any other known volcano.

MOUNT MAZAMA Mount Mazama may have been Oregon's highest volcano 6,700 years ago, almost 12,000 feet high before its summit collapsed. In some of the most violent eruptions of any recent Cascade volcano, Mount Mazama (which now contains Crater Lake within its caldera), ejected the largest amount of pumice of any volcano known.

After thousands of years of violent eruptions of pumice and ash, Mount Mazama's final chapter opened with an enormous eruption that piled up ash 70 feet thick at the volcano's base and filled canyons to the top with 250 feet of pumice and ash. Airborne ash blanketed thousands of square miles in Oregon, Washington, and Idaho, even reaching central Montana and Saskatchewan.

Glowing avalanches of pumice frothed out of the summit and raced down the mountain at 100 miles an hour. Some flows cooled at the volcano's base, forming hard welded tuff, but other flows raged across the countryside. One incandescent flood maintained enough momentum to hurtle across flat land for 40 miles along the Rogue River Valley, incinerating trees along its route. Another swept across Diamond Lake, leaving behind pumice piles 30 feet thick. The avalanches muscled 6-foot pumice boulders along for 20 miles before droppping them.

Pumice and volcanic ash from those final eruptions covered 350,000 square miles. In its final days Mount Mazama may have blown out 42 cubic miles of pyroclastic material, expanded from 16 cubic miles of liquid magma. Without the magma chamber to support the enormous weight of the top, the summit was undermined. Its collapse created one of the world's largest calderas, 6 miles wide, nearly 4,000 feet deep, with a high point on the rim of 8,156 feet. Crater Lake now occupies that caldera. (See Crater Lake.)

Scientists now use the distinctively colored Mazama ash, which is easily identifiable in sedimentary layers, to date other events in the Northwest's geologic history. A human skeleton buried by Mount Mazama ash has to be at least 6,700 years old.

MOUNT RAINIER

Mount Rainier in Washington is the nation's highest volcano outside Alaska and its fifth-highest peak.

MOUNT RAINIER At 14,411.1 feet, Mount Rainier, the Northwest's highest mountain, ranks as the highest volcano and the fifth highest peak in the Lower 48. This impressive volcano has the greatest mass of any Cascade volcano. No other U.S. mountain rises so far above its foothills.

Once nearly 16,000 feet high, Mount Rainier was lowered by several huge mudflows, including the world's largest, the Osceola Mudflow. The mudflow changed the summit crater into a caldera nearly 2 miles in diameter. Relatively recent lava flows bult a new cone on the old base, filling in most of the caldera and making the mountain more symmetrical. Still later, lava eruptions east of the older vent formed a larger crater, which is 1,300 feet across and 500 feet deep. Columbia Crest, the highest point of Mount Rainier, rises where the two craters overlap.

◆ Measured by satellites for Washington's centennial year of 1989, Mount Rainier was found to be 1.1 foot taller than when previously measured at 14,410 feet by less accurate methods.

MOUNT ST. HELENS On May 18, 1980, at 8:31 A.M., the largest volcanic eruption in the recorded history of the Lower 48 burst from Mount St. Helens, one of the youngest Cascade volcanoes. This first U.S. eruption since 1917 was one of the most powerful witnessed by humans, exploding with 500 times the force of the atomic blast over Hiroshima. The eruption reduced the mountain's symmetrical cone from 9,677 to 8,364 feet and dropped Mount St. Helens from fifth highest mountain in Washington to thirtieth.

In 1980 Mount St. Helens erupted with a force 500 times greater than the atomic explosion over Hiroshima.

On the morning of May 18 a powerful earthquake measuring 5.1 on the Richter scale shook Mount St. Helens. Fifteen seconds later, a bulge on the volcano's north flank, which pressurized magma had been pushing outward for more than a month, blew apart. The release of pressure triggered an explosion of superheated, highly pressurized steam and gases that hurled 3 billion cubic yards of rock debris through the breach with a shock wave heard 225 miles away in Vancouver, B.C. An avalanche of snow and ice roared down the mountain. A mudflow covered or destroyed miles of highway and buried or swept away several hundred homes. Pouring into the Cowlitz and Columbia rivers, the mudflow destroyed bridges and filled the Columbia's narrow shipping channel, stranding ships in several ports. The unexpected lateral blast increased the range of damage, destroying more than 150 square miles of forest, including 60,000 acres of 200-foot-high Douglas firs. At least fifty-seven people were dead or missing.

MOUNT ST. HELENS

◆ The huge ash cloud that erupted soon after the blast dumped 600,000 tons of ash on Yakima, 85 miles to the east, darkening the daytime sky so that automated streetlights turned on. The purplish clouds of ash poured from the summit for nine hours, eventually reaching an altitude of 63,000 feet and traveling around the earth.

◆ Spirit Lake, a favorite pre-eruption subject for photographers that reflected the symmetrical volcano in its calm, clear waters, was ravaged. Hot, rocky debris filled in the south end of the lake and covered the nearby ground. Three days after the eruption, pyroclastic flows near the lake registered 626°F at 10 feet below the surface. Thousands of uprooted and broken trees still choke the lake.

♦ More than a decade after the eruption, Mount St. Helens remains the most studied volcano in the world, with temperature probes in steam vents and seismic monitors on the crater dome and mountain. The still-restive volcano, with its shattered crater, looms over the 110,300-acre Mount St. Helens National Volcanic Monument. (See also Animals, Mount St. Helens Animal Life, and Plants, Mount St. Helens Plant Life.)

Oregon's two-tiered Multnomah Falls is the fourth-highest waterfall in the country.

MULTNOMAH FALLS Oregon's Multnomah Falls, 620 feet high, ranks as the Northwest's highest waterfall, and fourth highest among the nation's falls that do not diminish significantly or dry up seasonally. The main part of the two-tiered falls cascades 541 feet over a sheer cliff of basalt. Lower Multnomah Falls drops another 69 feet, with a 10-foot drop between them.

Multnomah Falls is at its most spectacular when it freezes almost solid with stalactitelike icicles. Such freezing can occur with a week of below-freezing temperatures and a strong wind chill factor.

Before its summit collapsed, Newberry was Oregon's highest shield volcano.

NEWBERRY CRATER Newberry Crater's low profile is misleading. It does not appear to have been a huge volcano, yet before its summit collapsed, Newberry ranked as Oregon's highest shield volcano, reaching 10,000 feet. Today Newberry is by volume the largest of all Northwest volcanoes; it is approximately 20 miles in diameter and encompasses 320,000 acres. Its highest point is Paulina Peak at 7,985 feet.

Its eruptions were more frequent and varied in lava type than those of Mount Mazama, but most of its flows consisted of very thin basalt, the type that forms broad shield volcanoes. The summit collapse probably resulted from great flows issuing from the more than 150 basalt cinder cones that stud the mountain's gentle outer slopes.

Within its caldera rest an enormous obsidian flow, an obsidian cataract, and two lakes. The lakes were formed during a late eruption, when a lava flow from one of the cinder cones within the caldera divided a single lake. Central Pumice Cone, largest of the cinder cones topping lava flows within the caldera, measures 1 mile wide and 700 feet high, with a crater 250 feet deep.

OBSIDIAN The caldera of Oregon's Newberry Crater contains some of the world's most extensive obsidian flows. The largest and most recent, Big Obsidian Flow, erupted 1,350 years ago from the south wall, covering a square mile and creating a dome over the vent from which it flowed. Its glossy, wrinkled surface ends in cliffs 100 feet high. Nearby, a frozen cataract of obsidian descends from a high vent.

A mountain composed entirely of obsidian rises from the desert floor of central Oregon.

◆ One of the most beautiful of Northwest obsidian formations is Oregon's Glass Buttes, 75 miles east of Bend. A mountain made entirely of obsidian rises from the desert floor, a single flow of several cubic miles of glassy lava so viscous it piled up several thousand feet thick around the vent.

Streaking the basic black obsidian are red, brown, green, gray, gold, silver, and blue caused by iron oxide, chrome, nickel, manganese, cobalt, and vanadium contained in the lava. Fault movements over the past few million years have fractured the obsidian into pieces of all sizes that spread out for 5 miles.

◆ Because the Northwest has little flint for tools and weapons, Northwest Indians traded obsidian and traveled long distances to obtain it. Obsidian fractures well, with curved surfaces and edges sharper than those of any other cutting tool known. Electron microscopes show an edge 500 times sharper than a razor blade's, and 2 to 3 times as fine as diamond-edged scalpels or surgical steel.

◆ Southeastern Idaho's Menan Buttes, two huge obsidian cones built of small particles of volcanic glass, rise abruptly above the plain. They may have formed when a lava flow chilled suddenly as it met cold surface water in the wet floodplain of the Snake River, exploding in a great steamy spray to form particles of volcanic glass. The fragments falling around the vents would have created the buttes.

OLYMPIC MOUNTAINS Washington's Olympic Mountains are among North America's most recently created mountains. The mountains' oldest rocks date from 30 to 40 million years ago. The youngest rocks, only 3 to 12 million years old, are some of the youngest rocks in the world contained in a major mountain range. Considered part of the West's coastal mountains, the isolated Olympics are separated from the Oregon Coast Range by the Chehalis River valley and Willapa Hills.

Washington's Olympic Mountains are among North America's youngest mountain ranges, containing rocks that date back only 3 to 12 million years.

◆ The Olympic Mountains present an outstanding example of the result of plate tectonics, the collision between ocean and continental plates. The mountains are composed primarily of river-deposited sand and silt that later were jumbled together in a deep ocean trench and metamorphosed by intense heat and pressure into sandstone and shale. The deformed rock was uplifted into a dome in at least two stages.

Glaciers, much larger than those of today, sculpted many Olympic Mountain peaks into knife ridges and matterhorns, and scooped out cirques at the mouths of high hanging valleys. Mount Olympus, the highest peak in the entire coastal belt, reaches 7,965 feet.

Streams originally eroded the domes and continue to do so. They feed major rivers that travel only 10 miles from headwaters to sea. Born in glacial cirques and fed by snowmelt and glacier melt all year long, the rivers have cut inner gorges 100 feet deep within their broad, glaciated valleys.

♦ The Olympics were once believed to have a granite core because so many massive granite boulders lie in Olympic Peninsula rivers and on mountain slopes as high as 3,000 feet, and because basalt almost completely surrounds the base of the mountain range. Outcroppings show such volcanic rocks as tuff, pillow basalt, and breccia. But the boulders are erratics rafted in by glacial ice from British Columbia mountains during several ice ages. Not one Olympic peak is volcanic. (See Erratics.)

OREGON COAST Oregon's scenic coast is known as one of the most unspoiled and least developed coastlines on the U.S. mainland, despite the nearness of large urban areas and a road that hugs the coast for most of its 362-mile length. Along much of the coast highway runs one of the Northwest's most popular bicycle trails and one of the best networks of state parks in the nation, with recreational areas and state parks roughly every 5 miles.

Because of the difficulty of carving roads around the lava headlands and Coast Range, many of Oregon's beaches were used in early days as roads. Governor Oswald West, maneuvering to protect the beaches, declared them public highways in 1913. Now Oregon law requires public access to beaches at least every 3 miles.

♦ The Oregon coast has the most varied geological formations of any coast of similar size: jutting lava headlands and capes that are often former volcanoes; vast expanses of wind-sculpted sand dunes; river mouths pouring fresh water into the sea; freshwater lakes trapped behind sand dams; driftwood-piled beaches; tide pools rich in marine organisms; sea caves and arches; huge offshore sea stacks often taken over by nesting seabirds; black sand beaches scattered with agates, garnet,

Public access is required by law every 3 miles along Oregon's scenic and largely unspoiled coastline.

SEA STACK

petrified wood, and jade pebbles; former beach terraces high above the present shore; and mountains rising directly from the sea. Any high-profile mountain in the Coast Range with pillow basalt on its slopes was once either submerged or was an off-shore island volcano.

OSCEOLA MUDFLOW
One of the nation's largest, most catastrophic mudflows occurred 5,700 years ago when the Osceola Mudflow streamed down the slopes of Mount Rainier, lowering the mountain by more than 1,500 feet.

Mount Rainier lost more than 1,500 feet in elevation when the Osceola Mudflow swept down its sides 5,700 years ago.

Violent steam explosions collapsed the summit and triggered the flow of more than half a cubic mile of mud and debris. Rain and groundwater seeping into the soil had chemically altered rock near the summit to form clay, which slides easily.

Starting at Steamboat Prow, one lobe of the mudflow raced down White River valley in a wall of rock and mud 500 feet high when it passed the present White River campground. Another lobe descended Winthrop Glacier into the West Fork of the White River. The two lobes joined, covering more than 100 square miles and burying the sites of today's Auburn, Kent, Enumclaw, Sumner, and Puyallup in up to 70 feet of mud. Mud poured into Tacoma's Commencement Bay.

The mountain shows evidence of more than fifty large mudflows down its slopes in the past 10,000 years. With steam jets in its craters and a ground temperature of 174°F near the vents, Mount Rainier remains vulnerable to mudflows.

PALOUSE SOIL
Wind-borne Palouse loess of the richly productive Palouse Hills in eastern Washington and Idaho rates among the most fertile of all Northwest soil. The soil, which covers an area 85 by 100 miles straddling the Idaho-Washington border, produces crops of wheat, peas, and lentils of greater quantity and of superior quality to those grown in most other regions of North America.

The productive farming soil of the Palouse Hills was carried in by the wind.

It derives not from weathered lava but from silt blowing for thousands of years on the prevailing northwesterly winds into the Palouse from the White Bluffs near Hanford and from glacial outwash deposits, old dunes, and ancient lake beds of the Pasco area. Deposits of loess are thickest and most continuous in Washington's rolling Palouse Hills, parts of which were just beyond reach of the Spokane Flood, thus escaping the devastation that occurred in the channeled scablands area. (See Spokane Floods.)

PEND OREILLE LAKE The largest of Idaho's Panhandle lakes, Pend Oreille Lake is 43 miles long and 6 miles wide. With a depth of 1,150 feet, it ranks among the nation's deepest lakes. Storms can raise waves 40 feet high on the lake. The lake, encircled by four mountain ranges, is noted for its scenic coves, sandy beaches, islands, and world-class trout fishing. Pend Oreille Lake still holds the world record for bull trout; a 32-pounder was caught there in 1948.

The largest of Idaho's Panhandle lakes holds the world record for bull trout.

POINT ROBERTS Point Roberts, Washington, is the only land in the contiguous United States that cannot be reached except by sea or by traveling across foreign land—Canada. Kaiser Wilhelm I was responsible. His 1872 arbitration of the boundaries of the San Juan Islands, disputed during the bloodless Pig War between the United States and Great Britain, resulted in U.S. ownership of this 5-square-mile tip of a Canadian peninsula through which the 49th Parallel slices.

To reach Point Roberts, Washington, from the United States, one must travel by sea or across foreign land.

Point Roberts connects by land with the rest of the United States only by way of 30 miles of Canadian roads and two customs stations. Most Point Roberts babies are born in Canadian hospitals and are citizens of both Canada and the United States. Prisoners are transported by boat to Bellingham, Washington, because U.S. police driving through Canada lose jurisdiction over their prisoners.

POMPEY'S PILLAR The only surviving physical evidence of Lewis and Clark's presence along the route of their expedition is Captain Clark's name and the date July 25, 1806, carved into the rock of Pompey's Pillar, an isolated, eroded sandstone tower that rises 200 feet on the south bank of the Yellowstone River northeast of Billings, Montana. The inscription, now protected by a glass plate, is joined by the names of hundreds of early trappers, soldiers, and settlers.

The only physical evidence of Lewis and Clark's presence along their expedition route is carved into a stone pillar in Montana.

Native Americans, who used to send smoke signals from the high rock, carved animals upon its surface. Clark named the rock after Sacajawea's son Baptiste, to whom he gave the nickname of Pompey, from the Shoshone word for chief.

PRIEST LAKE One of Idaho's three lovely, glacier-carved Panhandle lakes, which cluster within a few miles of each other, Priest Lake is, in reality, two lakes. It consists of a 19-mile-long lower lake and a 3-mile-long upper lake. They are joined by a spectacular 2-mile channel that resembles a leisurely river except during spring runoff. Only boats without motors are allowed on

Idaho's Priest Lake is really two lakes, joined by a 2-mile channel.

Upper Priest Lake. Smaller and more isolated than Pend Oreille Lake or Lake Coeur d'Alene, Priest Lake is also more protected. The state and federal governments own 80 percent of the lake's shoreline. A Mackinaw lake trout caught there in 1970 held the world record—57 pounds, 8 ounces—for nearly 20 years. Near the lake stand two impressive groves of ancient cedars almost 1,000 years old.

PUGET SOUND Puget Sound ranks as the largest glacier-carved basin in the West, a deep trough that was a depression in the lowlands even before the last Ice Age lobe enlarged it. The Puget Lowlands were probably formed by the buckling downward of underlying material and the uplifting of mountains both to the east and to the west.

Puget Sound is the largest glacier-carved basin in the West.

The deepest water in the main basin of Puget Sound, which is formed of a series of basins, lies at 920 feet, just south of the Kingston-Edmonds ferry route. The Sound might be deeper had the glacial ice melted rapidly enough for sea water to fill the trench quickly, before the land had rebounded from the great weight of ice.

◆ Sediments on the bottom of Puget Sound reach extraordinary depths. The top layer of 450 feet is boulder-filled debris from the foot of the Puget ice lobe. Under it, 600 feet of fine sediment accumulated when a large temporary lake, fed by glacier melt, formed in the Sound in front of the retreating ice. Another 600 feet of sediment was deposited after the glacial ice had receded and salt water was able to reenter Puget Sound. One last unexpected layer lies under the trench gouged during the last Ice Age—1,350 feet of sediment left by a previous glacier. The grand total is 3,000 feet of sediment.

QUICKSAND One of the few places in the Northwest where quicksand forms is the Oregon Dunes. Quicksand is ordinary sand that is saturated with water and acts as a liquid, losing its ability to support weight. Located at or near the water table in shallow, standing water with little or no surface flow, quicksand in the Oregon Dunes generally will pull a person in only up to the hips. It can, however, bury one of the recreation vehicles allowed in certain dune areas. Treacherous at any time, Oregon Dunes quicksand is most dangerous from November to May.

Quicksand, unusual in the Northwest, is found in portions of the Oregon Dunes Recreation Area.

ST. JOE RIVER The world's highest navigable river, Idaho's St. Joe River cuts across the Panhandle at an elevation of 2,100 feet. Born high in the Bitterroot Mountains, the river passes

Cutting across the Idaho Panhandle at an elevation of 2,100 feet, the St. Joe River is the world's highest navigable river.

through three lakes before emptying into the southern end of Lake Coeur d'Alene.

After a dam raised the level and increased the length of Lake Coeur d'Alene in the early 1900s, water backed up from the lake into the St. Joe, shortening the river by a few miles and permanently submerging some of its tree-lined shores. Most of the trees survived, and now mark the former shoreline of the river, which lies within the lake. This part of the river is called the "Shadowy St. Joe."

Once, stern-wheelers traveled on the slower parts of the St. Joe. Now, long log rafts move on it to sawmills on Lake Coeur d'Alene's shores.

SALMON RIVER Idaho's Salmon River, which Indians named the "River of No Return," is the longest major river in the Lower 48 lying wholly within a single state. The turbulent, 420-mile-long river, which rises in the Sawtooth Mountains, joins the Snake River 40 miles upstream from Lewiston, still within Idaho's borders. The gorge it has cut varies from a steep-walled slot to gently sloping hills and rounded bluffs.

In the Lower 48 the longest major river to be contained within one state is Idaho's Salmon River.

◆ The Salmon River is one of only a few large rivers in the nation that are completely undammed. Those who fought for the Hells Canyon Natural Area made sure that the Salmon River was protected from dams forever.

Each spring, the river becomes a torrent sweeping through the gorge, carrying large trees it has uprooted from the shore. High-water marks of stranded driftwood logs reach 40 feet above the Salmon's normal level. Studded with huge rocks, the river abounds with sharp bends, foaming rapids, and waterfalls plunging over steep cliffs.

SAN JUAN ISLANDS One of the most picturesque chains of islands in the world, Washington's San Juan Islands are the drowned foothills of the North Cascades. The same material built them both—seafloor lavas and sedimentary rock metamorphosed in oceanic trenches. Identical fossils of marine life appear in both the North Cascades and in the San Juans.

Washington's San Juan Islands, a cluster of more than 760 rocks, islands, and reefs exposed at low tide, are the drowned foothills of the North Cascades.

The islands dot Washington's inland sea in all sizes and shapes. Low tide exposes 768 rocks, reefs, and islands (175 of them named); high tide covers all but 475 of the largest. From Lummi near Bellingham and Guemes near Anacortes, they spread westward for 30 miles to the international boundary line in the center of Haro Strait. Located within the Olympic rain shadow, the islands receive only 15 to 29 inches of annual rainfall.

Buried deep under the ice lobe that extended from Canada down Puget Sound as far south as Olympia, the San Juans were sculpted by ice that carved out deep channels with steep sides. The underwater terrain of those deep channels now creates powerful currents in the salt water surrounding the islands.

♦ As in the North Cascades, sandstone and other sedimentary rocks abound in the islands. San Juan Island sandstone provided raw material for a profitable limestone quarry and kilns during the early nineteenth century. Wind and waves have carved sandstone bluffs along many island beaches, and the ocean has excavated small coastal sea caves in sandstone cliffs along the shore. English Camp Cave on San Juan Island displays beautiful limestone deposits.

Half the islands' permanent residents live on San Juan Island, second largest island in the group. It boasts the only sand dunes in the islands at Cattle Point.

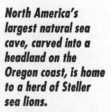

MOUNT CONSTITUTION
OBSERVATION TOWER

♦ Largest of the islands—by 1 square mile—Orcas is also the most mountainous. From the summit of the highest mountain peak of the islands, Mount Constitution (2,407 feet elevation), Orcas Island offers a dazzling 360-degree view of islands, lakes, forests, and snowy mainland peaks such as Mount Baker. During the final glacial period, ice one-half-mile thick covered the summit of Mount Constitution.

♦ Some eighty-six islands—comprising the San Juan Islands National Wildlife Refuge—are off-limits to the public.

♦ Orcas boasts the largest state park in the islands, donated by a millionaire shipbuilder. The 3,600 acres include 1,800 acres of saltwater shoreline—the only publicly owned shoreline on Orcas—5,000 acres of forest, five freshwater lakes, four waterfalls, and Mount Constitution.

SEA CAVES North America's largest natural sea cave, Sea Lion Caves, extends into a 300-foot-high basalt headland south of Heceta Head on the Oregon coast. The cave, along with its outside rocky ledges, forms the only known mainland breeding site of the large Steller sea lions. The sea-level cave was excavated by waves pounding against an almost perpendicular wall of volcanic basalt and agglomerate, exploiting faults and a soft sedimentary layer below the hard basalt of the headland. The sea washes constantly through a short natural entrance with enough force to carry sea lions into the vaulted main chamber, which is 125 feet high, with a floor area of 2 acres. (See Animals, Sea Lions.)

North America's largest natural sea cave, carved into a headland on the Oregon coast, is home to a herd of Steller sea lions.

A 2-million-year-old slab of serpentinite rock, originally formed below the ocean floor, stands nearly on edge in central Oregon.

SERPENTINITE ROCK The nation's most outstanding slab of exposed serpentinite rock stands nearly on edge in central Oregon's Canyon Mountain near the John Day Fossil Beds National Monument. The 2-million-year-old mountainous piece of ocean crust is notable for its highly polished surfaces.

Serpentinite, formed when the rock of the earth's mantle absorbs sea weater, normally belongs below the basalt ocean floor. But during mountain-building collisions between ocean and continent plates 150 million years ago, serpentinite slabs were sometimes folded into the newly built mountains. Green when freshly broken, the rock also is called soapstone because of its greasy feel. The soft rock is easily cut with a knife.

The high metal content of serpentinite causes oxidation, and the rock weathers to a rusty brown. Parts of southwestern Oregon are banded with serpentinite rock, including one severely weathered concentration with scattered grains of chromite, the only source of chromium, and enough nickel to mine. Attractively colored and sculptured examples of the rock are visible outside the town of Gold Beach.

♦ "Serpentine barrens," where little vegetation grows, cause greenish and rusty red peaks south of Washington's Mount Stuart in the Wenatchee Mountains. The calcium-poor and nickel-rich soil proves toxic to many plants, yet nourishes some odd subspecies that grow nowhere else.

♦ Washington's Twin Sisters Peaks in the North Cascades consist of a 3-mile by 10-mile mass of dunite. It rates as the largest single mass of dunite and the largest unaltered piece of exposed mantle in the Western Hemisphere. Dunite is thought to be a recrystallized form of serpentinite.

The Northwest's largest waterfall is 1,000-foot-wide Shoshone Falls in Idaho.

SHOSHONE FALLS The Northwest's largest waterfall and Idaho's pride, Shoshone Falls, flaunts its beauty at full flow in spring and early summer, before being diverted for power production. The 1,000-foot-wide cataract on the Snake River east of Twin Falls thunders down 212 feet over horseshoe-shaped lava ledges, tumultuously rejoining the river below.

The country's second-largest accumulation of basalt lava forms Idaho's Snake River Plain.

SNAKE RIVER PLAIN Idaho's Snake River Plain—the eastern extension of the Columbia Plateau—boasts the nation's second-largest accumulation of basalt lava. (The Columbia Plateau basalt is the largest.) The plain runs from the city of Weiser to the Wyoming border and is 100 miles wide and 400 miles long.

The Lewis and Clark journals described it as "the most

Barren Sterril region we have yet passed . . . covered with broken
Cynders much resembling Junks of pot mettal & Now & then a
cliff of Black burned rock which looks like Distruction
brooding over despair."

The plain is a jumble of basaltic flows, interbedded gravels,
sand, and silts. Underlying later flows is Columbia Plateau basalt,
which spread into west-central Idaho from eastern Washington,
ponding against Idaho highlands. Next came lava that originated
from mile-long fissures fed by the Great Rift. After those flows
came the Idavada Volcanics and the Snake River Group, which
cover most of the plain.

♦ On the Columbia Plateau, all the lava flows came from long
fissures and the same flow spread for many miles; in Idaho, however, many flows issued from vents that built up cones or broad
shield volcanoes. One of the reasons the Snake meanders is that
new cones often formed in the river's channel, filling it with lava
and forcing the river to go around them.

SPOKANE FLOODS The world's most catastrophic and
largest known floods, the Spokane Floods created much of the
distinctive topography of eastern Washington.

A lobe of ice from the Purcell Trench ice sheet caused the
floods some 16,000 years ago. The 20-mile-wide ice lobe acted
as a dam 2,000 feet high at the beginning of a series of nearly
forty dammings of the Clark Fork River at the mouth of its
canyon. It backed the river into a number of western Montana
valleys, to a maximum height of 4,350 feet far upstream. Glacial
scratches on the walls of the canyon are found only at its mouth,
proving that the ice did not move very far into the canyon.

The impounded water formed Glacial Lake Missoula, one of
the largest bodies of water ever to collect in the world. When the
ice dam was at its thickest, it held back five hundred cubic miles
of water. As the ice sheet receded, the lobe grew thinner, so that
successive dams were lower and the lake smaller. Lakeshore
benches at varying heights testify to the cycle of filling and emptying that recurred over a period of 1,000 years. (See Glacial Lake
Missoula.)

Whenever the dam was breached, floodwaters rushed out in a
towering wall, sweeping across Idaho's narrow Panhandle into
eastern Washington, carrying tons of gravel and silt, and rafting
huge chunks of rock-studded ice from the breached dam.

At the site of Grand Coulee dam, the wall of water was 2,000
feet high, higher than the present-day dam. Even 200 to
300 miles from the ice dam, the waters were still at least

*The world's largest
and most catastrophic
floods swept across
eastern Washington
16,000 years ago,
shaping the
present-day landscape.*

700 feet high.

As the floodwaters raced along, they swept the plateau clean of thick layers of wind-borne soil right down to basalt bedrock, creating the channeled scablands that are found only in eastern Washington. Evidence that the Spokane Floods created the scablands is ample: high-water benches on loess hills and islands, water-worn gravel, sedimentary beds in temporary lakes, potholes in the scoured-out bedrock, and huge river bars.

Neither the Columbia nor its tributaries could handle so much water. They backed up, forming temporary lakes in which the suddenly slowed floodwaters deposited thick layers of sediment. Further evidence of the surging floodwaters lies in enormous ripple marks visible in silt, sand, and gravel in broader flood channels in eastern Washington and on Montana's Camas Prairie. Some of the ripples are more than 30 feet high and 300 feet from crest to crest.

All flood channels led the torrents of water eventually to the Pasco Basin, where water was backed up again, forming the largest temporary lake of all behind narrow, steep-sided Wallula Gap. There the Columbia finally cut a gap through the Cascades, probably spilling water over the edge of the basalt and gradually wearing it away. The violent rush of water spilled out of that bottleneck into the gorge at 40 cubic miles a day, scrubbing the walls clean below 1,000 feet.

SPRINGS Montana's Giant Springs rank as one of the largest freshwater springs in the world. Located on the south bank of the Missouri River near the eastern edge of the city of Great Falls, the springs flow at a rate of 388,800,000 gallons of water a day, with a constant temperature of 52°F. The water forms a pool that cascades over a low stone wall, creating a 201-foot-long "river" into the Missouri. That short passage, named the Roe River, contends with Oregon's coastal D River for champion status as the world's shortest named river.

One of the largest freshwater springs in the world is Montana's Giant Springs, which spills more than 388 million gallons of water a day into the Missouri.

♦ More than 100 steaming mineral springs issue from Idaho's Portneuf River at Lava Hot Springs, 20 miles south of Pocatello. The springs offered a diverting stopping place for Oregon Trail travelers, who often mentioned them in their diaries.

The temperature of the springs ranges from 110°F to 184°F and is believed to have maintained this same range for 50 million years. Each day the springs pour out 6,711,000 gallons of geothermally heated water. The water at Lava Hot Springs reportedly contains the most highly mineralized water of any spa in North America, with an average mineral content of 962 parts per million. Each spring contains a different mix of minerals.

◆ Each summer after irrigation water is withdrawn from Oregon's Deschutes River, which flows in an arid region with only 8 inches of rain a year, the river often dries up near Prineville. But farther on, warm springs issuing from the canyon floor and walls refill the river. One of those springs, Opal Springs, washes opals to the surface; however, none are of gem quality. Common opals, dull in color, full of impurities, and comprising as much as 20 percent water, are often found around hot springs.

STEINS PILLAR One of Oregon's many unusual volcanic formations, an enormous chunk of welded tuff called Steins Pillar, resembles a mushroom stem 400 feet high and 120 feet in diameter, thrusting up through a pine forest. After the area west of Prineville in Ochoco National Forest was buried by ash and lava 30 million years ago, differential erosion attacked the softer rock, leaving a number of pillars formed of harder rock. Steins is the largest.

A volcanic plug shaped like a chunky mushroom stem rises above a pine forest in Oregon.

STEPTOE BUTTE Rising 1,200 feet above the surrounding wheat fields one hour's drive south of Spokane, Steptoe Butte is the best known of a group of buttes in the area. Formed of ancient Precambrian rock not found in other parts of Washington, the butte may have been a 9,000-foot-high peak of the Selkirk Mountains. Flows of Columbia Plateau basalt filled some of the valleys of the northern Rockies, but the highest peaks either were not completely covered or were buried and later exposed by erosion. Such outposts of the northern Rockies rising above the plateau between Spokane and Clarkston mark the western edge of the old North American continent.

A group of buttes in eastern Washington, rising 1,200 feet above surrounding wheat fields, marks the edge of the old North American continent.

THREE FORKS The headwaters of the Missouri, one of North America's longest rivers, rise in Montana near Three Forks. Here the Jefferson, Madison, and Gallatin rivers, discovered and named by Lewis and Clark, merge in southwestern Montana and form the Missouri. Beaverhead County, Montana, rates as the most distant source of the Mississippi-Missouri River System.

The headwaters of the Missouri River rise in Montana.

TRIPLE DIVIDE Montana is the only state in the nation that has within its borders parts of three major drainage systems. At Triple Divide in Montana's Glacier National Park, water flows from three rivers in separate directions, eventually draining into three different oceans—the Arctic, the Pacific, and the Atlantic.

Some sections of the park and Teton County lie on the

From Triple Divide in Montana, water drains into three different oceans.

northern side of the continental divide; waters from this side flow to Hudson Bay and the Arctic Ocean via Belly and St. Mary's rivers, which flow into the Saskatchewan River. The Clark Fork gathers waters of the Blackfoot, Bitterroot, and Flathead rivers, among others, and they flow to the Pacific by way of the Snake and Columbia rivers. The Missouri River, which makes a huge, irregular northern arc from its beginning in southwestern Montana, flows east to the Gulf of Mexico, which joins the Atlantic.

VOLCANOES Portland contains the largest number of volcanoes in or near its city limits of any city in the nation and may be the only major U.S. city that contains within its limits cinder cones that are not extinct. Dozens of small volcanoes cluster around Portland; at least thirty-two centers of past volcanic activity lie within 13 miles of each other. On the western flank of the Portland hills runs a small chain of volcanoes 3 to 5 million years old. Many of the city's volcanoes are well known, including Rocky Butte, Powell Butte, and Mount Tabor, which forms a natural amphitheater used in summer for musical events. (See also major volcanoes, listed by name.)

Portland may be the only major U.S. city to contain cinder cones that are not extinct.

WASHINGTON COAST Along the Pacific Ocean boundary of Washington runs the longest roadless seacoast in the Lower 48, the most undeveloped and primitive Pacific Ocean shore, and its last undisturbed coastal ecosystem. From Cape Flattery south to Kalaloch, the narrow 60-mile-long roadless shore belongs either to the Quinault tribe or to Olympic National Park, the only national park in the nation that offers high mountains, coniferous, temperate-zone rain forests, and wilderness seashore in one park.

The longest roadless expanse of seacoast in the Lower 48 stretches along Washington's coastline.

Washington's seacoast totals 157 miles, varying sharply from north to south. The rocky, inaccessible northern two-thirds contrasts with the flat, sandy, and accessible southern beaches. Washington's many inlets, coves, islands, bays, and inland seas give it one of the nation's longest saltwater shorelines: 3,026 undulating miles.

The northern seacoast is battered by some of the most powerful wave action in the world, especially in winter. Waves race across open ocean and crash against Washington's headlands and offshore islands with the force of two tons for each square inch.

♦ One of the most beautiful of all Washington's northern beaches is Point of Arches on the Olympic Peninsula, which is accessible only by a challenging trail. Point of Arches displays the full spectrum of sea rock sculpted by waves in great and picturesque abundance: windows and arches cut into rock; towering sea stacks, including flattops that once formed part of a wave-cut bench and were later uplifted; and islets, wave-eroded sea cliffs, and offshore rocks 300 feet high.

WATERFALLS   More than 700 waterfalls have been mapped in the Northwest, and hundreds more may yet be discovered in rugged wilderness country. The Northwest is rich waterfall country, partly because of abundant water, but also because of ideal locations—basalt cliffs, cirques, and steep canyon walls.

Over 700 waterfalls have been mapped in the four Northwest states.

♦ The most extensive group of large and accessible waterfalls in North America plunge over basalt cliffs along Oregon's Columbia Gorge Scenic Highway. In all, seventy waterfalls tumble down the south side of the gorge, most of them within 20 miles of one another. The Road of Falling Waters passes nine major falls in 10 miles, including two-tiered Multnomah Falls, fourth highest in the nation at 620 feet.

♦ Oregon boasts an extensive area of waterfalls plunging over steep canyon walls in Silver Falls State Park, on the eastern edge of the Willamette Valley. A 7-mile trail winding through the park passes ten major waterfalls, five of them exceeding 100 feet in height. The trail zigzags down into Silver Creek Canyon and through grottoes carved from lava to pass behind South Falls, highest of the park's falls at 177 feet, and 136-foot-high North Falls.

♦ Within or near Mount Rainier National Park, 122 waterfalls plunge, mist, and cascade over rocky ledges. Two of the largest are Clear Creek and Sluiskin falls, each 300 feet high. Comet Falls—like many of Mount Rainier's waterfalls, a result of glaciation—plunges 320 feet from a hanging valley.

MULTNOMAH FALLS

♦ Palouse Falls in southeastern Washington near Washtucna plunges 185 feet over the basaltic rim of the Columbia Plateau. Like Dry Falls, this waterfall was swollen by the Spokane Floods and carved a canyon (in this case, 7½ miles long) as it receded, the edge of the falls continually crumbling under the silty torrent. The floodwater changed the course of the Palouse River, which once flowed directly into the Columbia; after the floods, it emptied into the Snake, as it does today.

WEATHER   Montana holds the record for the coldest temperature ever recorded in the Lower 48 states, minus 69.7°F in 1954 at Rogers Pass (5,470 feet elevation) northwest of Helena. Idaho

Montana holds the record for the lowest temperature recorded in the Lower 48; Idaho comes in second.

rates second with a shivery minus 60°F in 1943 at Island Park Dam (6,285 feet elevation).

♦ Montana holds the weather record for the biggest one-day range of temperature in the nation. On a single winter day in 1916, temperatures in Browning ranged from minus 44°F to 56°F, a 100° change. Chinook winds are responsible for the wide range; these hot, dry winds can melt snow within a few hours. While the winds can be beneficial, exposing grass for hungry cattle, for example, the resulting sudden temperature changes can also cause avalanches in the mountains.

♦ The most snow ever recorded in one spot in one year—93 feet—piled up from February 19, 1971, to February 18, 1972, at Paradise Ranger Station on Mount Rainier. That area, at 5,450 feet elevation on Mount Rainier's southern slope, also holds a world record for the greatest depth of snow in a single month— 25 feet, 5 inches in April 1972. Snowfall (which is heavier farther up the mountain where no recording station exists) tapers off at about 10,000 feet because very cold air holds less moisture, and the mountain top rears up above many of the storms. Cold weather on Mount Rainier's upper slopes can rival that of Mount Everest, with temperatures hitting minus 55°F and winds gusting at 80 to 100 miles an hour.

♦ Montana suffered one of the most devastating statewide droughts in the nation's history, beginning in 1917 and continuing to the mid-1930s. The state also was plagued by some of the nation's worst dust storms and a serious grasshopper infestation in 1934.

♦ The winter of 1861-62 was so cold that the steamer *Multnomah* was frozen in ice along the Columbia River shore near Cathlamet.

♦ The most rain recorded in one year in the Lower 48 reached a soggy 184.56 inches in 1933. It drenched the community of Wynooche-Oxbow, located in a rain forest on the southwest flank of the Olympic Mountains. Although the nearby Quinault Rain Forest, called by locals the "Quinault Rain Barrel," averages 134 inches a year, the 1968 rainfall totaled 175.45 inches.

♦ Two climatic zones divide the Olympic Peninsula. Clouds sweeping in from the Pacific become chilled in rising to clear high Olympic peaks. Less able to hold moisture when cold, the clouds dump rain on windward Olympic slopes, resulting in the heaviest average precipitation in the Lower 48—140 inches of rain on the coast and 20 feet of snow on Mount Olympus and other high peaks. Having already dumped their precipitation, these clouds have little moisture left as they pass over the

Olympic rain shadow side of the mountains. Sequim, for example, is one of the driest coastal regions north of San Diego, receiving only 16 to 17 inches of rain a year.

◆ Despite its reputation as a rainy city, Seattle, with an average rainfall of 38 inches, receives less rainfall than any major city on the East Coast. Because it drizzles instead of pours, however, that precipitation spreads over an average 158 days a year.

◆ On February 1, 1916, 21.5 inches of snow buried Seattle, an all-time record for a 24-hour period in Seattle. It piled on top of 7 inches already on the ground from the day before. The total snowfall in Seattle in 1916 was 60.9 inches, still a city record.

◆ The most savage storm in recorded West Coast history hit the Northwest on Columbus Day 1962, courtesy of Typhoon Frieda sweeping in from the Pacific. In Washington's Pacific County, winds reached 160 miles an hour at Naselle Radar Site. The storm blew off roofs, smashed windows, jerked power poles out of the ground, and separated log booms. Trees totaling 1.5 billion board feet of lumber blew down, a ten-car ferry sank at Lummi Island, and an ocean liner was ripped loose from its moorings in Seattle. Thirty-five people died in Oregon and Washington.

◆ Perhaps the most memorable comment ever made about Puget Sound weather was uttered by Mark Twain in 1895: "The pleasantest winter I ever spent was a summer on Puget Sound."

WHIDBEY ISLAND The longest island in the Lower 48 surrounded by salt water and the largest island in Puget Sound, Whidbey Island is more than 45 miles long and 10 miles across at its widest. From some points on the narrow-waisted island, both of its flanking bodies of water can be viewed at the same time—Saratoga Passage to the east and the Strait of Juan de Fuca to the west. The island boasts 200 miles of shoreline, eight lakes, and four state parks.

Washington's Whidbey Island is both the largest island in Puget Sound and the longest island in the Lower 48 surrounded by salt water.

◆ Whidbey Island's varied geology includes headlands and beaches on which some of Puget Sound's largest sand dunes rise. The northern half of the island, which lies in the lee of the Olympic rain shadow, is so dry that cactus grow naturally there. The climate at the south end matches that of Seattle.

◆ Joseph Whidbey, Captain Vancouver's sailing master, discovered in 1792 that what Vancouver had thought was a bay indenting a peninsula was actually a passageway around an island. Captain Vancouver promptly named it Deception Pass. The 500-foot-wide pass at the north end of Whidbey Island has gained notoriety for the 8-knot tidal current that boils through the passage at the turn of the tide.

WILDERNESS   Ten percent of Washington's land has been set

Outside of Alaska,
Washington has more
land set aside as
federally mandated
wilderness than any
other state.

aside in federally mandated wilderness, the largest amount of any state except Alaska. Its thirty federal wilderness areas total 4,252,344 acres.

◆ Idaho has the second-largest amount of mandated wilderness in the Lower 48, with 4,001,535 acres in six units. Idaho also boasts the largest wilderness preserve in the Lower 48, the River of No Return Wilderness, created in 1980 and consisting of 2,362,487 acres.

◆ Montana's Bob Marshall Wilderness, created in 1964 in north-central Montana, ranks as the Lower 48's third-largest wilderness area, with 1,009,356 acres. One of its outstanding features, the 1,000-foot-long Chinese Wall of limestone, runs for 15 miles. The towering white wall is formed from Montana's conspicuous Madison Limestone Formation.

◆ Montana contains the greatest expanses of roadless and wild country left in the United States outside Alaska—9 million acres.

SUGGESTED READING

Alt, David D., and Donald W. Hyndman. *Roadside Geology of Oregon.* 2d ed. Missoula: Mountain Press Publishing Co., 1981.

————. *Roadside Geology of Washington.* Missoula: Mountain Press Publishing Co., 1984.

————. *Roadside Geology of Montana.* Missoula: Mountain Press Publishing Co., 1990.

Angell, Tony, and Kenneth C. Balcomb III. *Marine Birds and Mammals of Puget Sound.* Seattle: Puget Sound Books, Washington Sea Grant, University of Washington Press, 1982.

Armstrong, Robert H. *Guide to the Birds of Alaska.* 3rd ed. Seattle: Alaska Northwest Books, 1990.

Arno, Stephen F. *Northwest Trees.* Seattle: The Mountaineers, 1977.

Carson, Rob. *Mount St. Helens: The Eruption and the Recovery of a Volcano.* Seattle: Sasquatch Books, 1990.

Chronic, Halka. *Pages of Stone: Geology of Western National Parks and Monuments* series: Vol. 1 *Rocky Mountains & Western Great Plains* and Vol. 2 *Pacific Coast.* Seattle: The Mountaineers, 1986.

Dicken, Samuel, and Emily Dicken. *The Making of Oregon.* Portland: Oregon Historical Society Press, 1979.

Ekman, Leonard. *Scenic Geology of the Pacific Northwest.* Portland: Binfords & Mort, 1970.

Ervin, Keith. *Fragile Majesty: The Battle for America's Last Great Forest.* Seattle: The Mountaineers, 1989.

Fries, Mary A. *Wildflowers of Mount Rainier and the Cascades.* Seattle: The Mountaineers, 1970.

Halliday, William R. *Caves of Washington.* Olympia: Washington Department of Conservation, Division of Mines and Geology, 1963.

Harris, Stephen L. *Fire Mountains of the West: The Cascade and Mono Lake Volcanoes.* Missoula: Mountain Press Publishing Co., 1988.

Jolley, Russ. *Wildflowers of the Columbia Gorge.* Portland: Oregon Historical Society Press, 1988.

Kelly, David (author), and Gary Braasch (photographer). *Secrets *of the Old Growth Forest.* Layton, UT: Peregrine Smith Books, 1988.

Kirk, Ruth, and Carmela Alexander. *Exploring Washington's Past: A Road Guide to History.* Seattle: University of Washington Press, 1990.

Kozloff, Eugene N. *Plants and Animals of the Pacific Northwest.* Seattle: University of Washington Press, 1976.

Lewis, Mark G., and Fred A. Sharpe. *Birding in the San Juan Islands.* Seattle: The Mountaineers, 1987.

Mathews, Daniel. *Cascade Olympic Natural History: A Trailside Reference.* Portland: Raven Editions, 1988.

McKee, Bates. *Cascadia: The Geologic Evolution of the Pacific Northwest.* New York: McGraw-Hill Book Co., 1972.

McKenny, Margaret, and Daniel E. Stuntz. *The New Savory Wild Mushroom.* Rev. by Joseph F. Ammirati. Seattle: University of Washington Press, 1987.

McNulty, Tim (author), and Pat O'Hara (photographer). *Washington's Wild Rivers: The Unfinished Work.* Seattle: The Mountaineers, 1990.

Plumb, Gregory A. *A Waterfall Lover's Guide to the Pacific Northwest.* 2d ed. Seattle: The Mountaineers, 1989.

Ricketts, Edward F., and Jack Calvin. *Between Pacific Tides* 4th ed. Rev. by Joel W. Hedgpeth. Palo Alto: Stanford University Press, 1968.

Schofield, Janice J. *Discovering Wild Plants: Alaska, Western Canada, the Northwest.* Seattle: Alaska Northwest Books, 1989.

Slack, Adrian. *Carnivorous Plants.* Cambridge: MIT Press, 1980.

Smith, Lynwood S. *Living Shores of the Pacific Northwest.* Seattle: Pacific Search Press, 1976.

Steelquist, Robert U. *Ferryboat Field Guide to Puget Sound.* Helena, MT: American Geographic Publishing, 1989.

Van Gelder, Richard. *Mammals of the National Parks.* Baltimore and London: Johns Hopkins University Press, 1982.

Yates, Steve. *Marine Wildlife of Puget Sound, the San Juans and the Strait of Georgia.* Chester, CT: The Globe Pequot Press, 1988.

Alaska Northwest Books™ proudly recommends several of its outstanding books on nature and the environment.

Wild Echoes: Encounters with the Most Endangered Animals in North America, by Charles Bergman
"In the company of wolves in Alaska, right whales in the Atlantic, and the endangered Florida panther, Bergman closely examines his own and society's relationship to these 'shadow creatures' . . ." —*The Seattle Times.* Author Charles Bergman explores the question of what is lost when a species dies forever.
17 b/w photographs, 344 pages, softbound, $12.95 ($15.95 Canadian), ISBN 0-88240-404-0

Living by Water: Essays on Life, Land, and Spirit,
by Brenda Peterson
In the tradition of Henry Thoreau's reflections on Walden Pond to Annie Dillard's journal of life at Tinker Creek, novelist and environmentalist Brenda Peterson writes from her Puget Sound home about the ways in which water can shape a life and a philosophy.
144 pages, softbound, $9.95 ($12.95 Canadian), ISBN 0-88240-400-8

Grizzly Cub: Five Years in the Life of a Bear,
by Rick McIntyre
Grizzly Cub is the true story of a young bear's first five summers of life, as recorded in words and color photographs by Denali National Park ranger Rick McIntyre.
56 color photographs, 104 pages, softbound, $14.95 ($18.95 Canadian), ISBN 0-88240-373-7

Discovering Wild Plants: Alaska, Western Canada, the Northwest,
by Janice J. Schofield, illustrations by Richard W. Tyler
This beautiful book profiles 147 wild plants, with definitive information on botanical identification, history, harvest and habitat, as well as recipes. Each plant illustrated with color photos and elegant line drawings.
190 color photographs, 144 drawings, 354 pages, softbound, $24.95 ($29.95 Canadian), ISBN 0-88240-369-9

Ask for these books at your favorite bookstore, or contact Alaska Northwest Books™ for a catalog of our entire list.

Alaska Northwest Books™
A division of GTE Discovery Publications, Inc.
P.O. Box 3007
Bothell, WA 98041-3007
1-800-343-4567